AMERICA

(THE BOOK)

★ ★ ★

AMERICA

(THE BOOK)

★ ★ ★

A Citizen's Guide to Democracy Inaction

With a Foreword by Thomas Jefferson

Written and Edited by

Jon Stewart

Ben Karlin

David Javerbaum

Writers

Rich Blomquist, Steve Bodow, Tim Carvell, Eric Drysdale, J.R. Havlan,
Scott Jacobson, Tom Johnson, Rob Kutner, Chris Regan, Jason Reich, Jason Ross

Additional Material

Samantha Bee, Stephen Colbert, Rob Corddry, Brendan Hay, Ed Helms

Designed by Pentagram

Special Thanks

Dave Blog, Adam Chodikoff, Jen Flanz, Christopher Martin,
Matt Moses, Nan North, Karen Perrine, Robin Sanders

WARNER BOOKS

NEW YORK   BOSTON

Warner Books

Time Warner Book Group
1271 Avenue of the
Americas, New York, NY
10020
Visit our Web site at
www.twbookmark.com.

Printed in the United
States of America

First Printing:
September 2004
10 9 8 7 6 5 4 3 2 1

ISBN: 0-446-53268-1
LCCN: 2004109358

To the huddled masses,
Keep yearnin'!

Table of Contents

AMERICA
(THE BOOK)
Study Guide

Chapter 1

Democracy Before America

In this chapter you will:
- Witness thousands of years of history casually dismissed in a few pages
- Learn the difference between a totalitarian regime and a post-Communist kleptocracy
- Read a cuneiform public opinion poll

- Realize that no matter how horrible your life is, it's not as bad as a feudal serf's ————
- Make your own flag (spangles not included)
- Have a hard time keeping the book open on a table while you read it

Chapter 2

The Founding of America

In this chapter you will:
- See graphic, full-color photos of America's birth
- Learn about the Founding Mothers and find out which ones were FMILFs ————

FMILF?

- Not fire until you see the whites of their eyes
- Become increasingly skeptical of the authors' scholarship
- Get sick of always hearing about how great Ben Franklin was
- Circle every fifth letter until you find the clue that leads you to the treasure!

Chapter 3

The President: King of Democracy

In this chapter you will:
- Learn that *not* everyone can be President and why people should really stop spreading that rumor
- Discover that most of what you've seen on *The West Wing* is total fucking bullshit
- Find out where *you* fall in the line of succession

- Be surprised to read who our gayest president was
- Take a virtual ride in Stagecoach One ————

- Lose your virginity (maybe, if you play your cards right)

Chapter 4

Congress: Quagmire of Freedom

In this chapter you will:
- Gain new appreciation for rotundas
- Compare and contrast the soulless gray-faced bureaucrats of the Senate with the soulless gray-faced bureaucrats of the House

- Embark on an exotic journey of the senses as you are ———— exposed as a leftist and homosexual by this man

- Meet and immediately dislike lobbyists
- Gerrymander
- Learn how to hide your purchase of this book in a much larger book appropriations bill

Chapter 5 — The Judicial Branch: It Rules

In this chapter you will:
- Desegregate a school
- Take this book all the way to the Supreme Court
- Learn how to operate a gavel responsibly and safely – even a stretch gavel

- See all nine Supreme Court justices naked (see pp. 98-99)
- Discover how to know pornography when you see it (see pp. 98-99)
- Notice that twelve pages are missing from the middle of the chapter. Our bad.

Chapter 6 — Campaigns and Elections: America Changes the Sheets

In this chapter you will:
- Marvel at colonial-era button-making technology
- Go negative
- Learn why your vote counts, but not nearly as much as your money

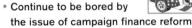

- Take a ride on a state-of-the-art campaign bus
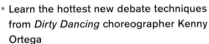
- Continue to be bored by the issue of campaign finance reform
- Learn the hottest new debate techniques from *Dirty Dancing* choreographer Kenny Ortega

Chapter 7 — The Media: Democracy's Valiant Vulgarians

In this chapter you will:
- Learn how to identify political bias in today's liberal, bleeding-heart, Jew and gay-run media
- Become an unnamed source
- Be given important interview facial expression tips by Stephen Colbert

- Create your own "no-spin zone"
- Discover which media conglomerate now owns you
- Not have your opinion of Geraldo Rivera particularly improved upon

Chapter 8 — The Future of Democracy: Four Score and Seven Years from Now

In this chapter you will:
- Experience democracy in pill form
- Learn how America's growing ethnic diversity will enhance your take-out options
- Take a look at the Washington of the future, and the crumbums of the future who occupy it

- Angrily say aloud, "*Future* of democracy? How 'bout some democracy right friggin' *now*?" *(Michael Moore only)*
- Blow it up! Damn you. God damn you all to Hell!
- Be so close to finishing the book you can taste it

Chapter 9 — The Rest of the World: International House of Horrors

In this chapter you will:
- Meet the rest of the world in 22 pages
- See most common stereotypes reinforced
- Learn nothing whatsoever about St. Kitts
- Do an exciting Middle East Jumble

- Discover that denial ain't just a psychological coping mechanism
- Find out in which countries you definitely don't want to get arrested
- 日本人友情

Foreword

When *America (The Book)* first approached me about penning the foreword to their tome, I was surprised. Firstly the foreword is not my bailiwick, but rather the Declaration. Forgive my conceit, but if one is looking to introduce a grand composition with a pithy and clear pronouncement, my declaratives are second to none. "Life, Liberty and the pursuit of Happiness…" Google it if ye doubt the claim! Also of some concern, I have been dead for…oh lord, has it really been 178 years? My goodness, time certainly flies when you are no longer consigned to your earthly vessel.

Notwithstanding, Irv over at Warner Books sent me some galleys, and I have to say…funny. Not John Winthrop's *A Comparative Treatise on the Most Unusual of Distinctions 'Twixt the Fairer of Species and Her Masculine Counterpart* funny…but funny. Of course, Sally was less enthused. "You are the author of the Declaration of Independence. A scholar. A statesman. This is beneath you. It's not even network." But truth be told, I was itching to get back to the quill and paper, and declaration work is not as steady as it used to be. Sally may not like it, but as we used to say in the back parlours of 18th-century Paris, "tough titties."

I was also looking forward to this opportunity to dispel some of the mythology surrounding myself and my fellow Founders—particularly the myth of our infallibility. You moderns have a tendency to worship at the altar of the Fathers. "The First Amendment is sacrosanct!" "We will die to protect the Second Amendment!" So dramatic. Do you know why we called them amendments? Because they **amend!** They fix mistakes or correct omissions and they themselves can be changed. If we had meant for the Constitution to be written in stone we would have written it in stone. Most things were written in stone back then, you know. I'm not trying to be difficult but it's bothersome when you blame your own inflexibility and extremism on us.

Not that we weren't awesome. We wrote the Constitution in the time it takes you nimrods to figure out which is the aye button and which is the nay. But we weren't gods. We were men. We had flaws. Adams was an unbearable prick and squealed girlishly whenever he saw a bug. And Ben Franklin? If crack existed in our day, that boozed-up snuff machine would weigh 80 pounds and live outside the Port Authority. And I had slaves. Damn, I can't believe I had slaves!

Yes, we were very accomplished. We discovered electricity, invented stoves, bifocals, the lazy susan, efficient printing presses, and the swivel chair. But in the 18th century it was nearly impossible not to invent something. "What if we put this refuse in a receptacle?" "Oh my God you just invented a sanitation system!" We lived in primitive times. Hell, I shit in a bucket and I was the president.

But I digress. My point is composing the Declaration of Independence and the Constitution was hard work. God didn't dictate it for us to transcribe from some sort of dictation-transcribing machine. Hey, did I just invent something? Do you have anything like that? You do? Hmm. Well, our purpose was to create a living document based on principles that transcended the times we lived in, and I think we did that. We created a blueprint for a system that would endure, which means your lazy asses shouldn't be coasting on our accomplishments. We were imperfect. It was imperfect. And we expect our descendents to work as hard as we did on keeping what we think is a profoundly excellent form of government supple, evolving and relevant. After reading this book, you should be better prepared to do just that.

As Always,

Th "J.J." Jefferson

P.S. Oh, and is it true Halle Berry is once again single? If so, I'd be forever in your debt if you would put in a good word for T.J. Oh how I loves the mochachina.

"It is true that
we are called a
democracy, for the
administration
is in the hands of
the many and not
the few."

— *Pericles*

"Yes, Pericles,
but have you
gotten a load of
the many?"

— *Socrates*

Thucydides, *History of the
Peloponnesian War*

Chapter 1

Democracy Before America

It is often said that America "invented" democracy. This view is, of course, an understatement; America invented not only democracy, but freedom, justice, liberty, and "time-sharing." But representative democracy is unquestionably our proudest achievement, the creation most uniquely our own, even if the rest of the Western world would have come up with the idea themselves by the 1820s. So why, then, has participation in this most wondrous system withered (Fig. 1.1)?

As heirs to a legacy more than two centuries old, it is understandable why present-day Americans would take their own democracy for granted. A president freely chosen from a wide-open field of two men every four years; a Congress with a 99% incumbency rate; a Supreme Court comprised of nine politically appointed judges whose only oversight is the icy scythe of Death — all these reveal a system fully capable of maintaining itself. But our perfect democracy, which neither needs nor particularly wants voters, is a rarity. It is important to remember there still exist many other forms of government in the world today (see chart on pages 8-9), and that dozens of foreign countries still long for a democracy such as ours to be imposed on them.

To regain our sense of perspective and wonder, we must take a broader historical view, looking beyond America's relatively recent success story to examine our predecessors and their adorable failures. In this chapter, we will briefly explore the evolution of an idea, following the *H.M.S. Democracy* on her dangerous voyage through the mists of time, past the Straits of Monarchy, surviving Hurricane Theocracy, then navigating around the Cape of Good Feudal System to arrive, battered but safe, at her destined port-of-call: Americatown.

Reasons for Decline in Participation in Democracy

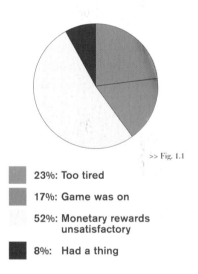

>> Fig. 1.1

23%: Too tired

17%: Game was on

52%: Monetary rewards unsatisfactory

8%: Had a thing

Early Man: More Animal Than Political

>> Fig. 1.2

Caveman *posited a prehistoric quasi-autocratic polity headed by Tonda (John Matuszak).*

The human race is by nature brutal, amoral, unreasonable and self-centered, but for the first few hundred thousand years of our existence as a species, we were way too obvious about it. Primitive culture centered on survival of the individual and, occasionally, survival of someone the individual might want to reproduce with (see 1981's harrowing documentary *Caveman* [Fig. 1.2]). Civic institutions were non-existent, as was debate, which would appear later after the invention of the frontal lobe. For prehistoric man the rule of law, such as it was, could best be summed up by the seminal case *Marbury's Head v. Madison's Rock.*

Early man lived this tenuous Darwinian nightmare for an age or two, until a peculiar thing happened: The unfittest decided they wouldn't mind surviving either. The feeble and weak realized that without a good plan they weren't going to make it out of the Stone Age to see the wonder that was clay. Alone, they were mammoth meat. Together, they would become a force with a chance to see the day when their children's children would be only 75% covered in hair. From these noble impulses, the groundwork for the first civilizations was laid.

>> Fig. 1.3

Neanderthals had to get their political news from only three networks.

"The feeble and weak realized that without a good plan they weren't going to make it out of the Stone Age to see the wonder that was clay."

Athens: Our Big Fat Greek Forerunners

Ancient Greece is widely credited with creating the world's first democracy. It would be a worthy endeavor to travel back in time to the feta-strewn shores of fifth-century B.C. Athens and ask Plato to define democracy, and not only to make money gambling on Olympics results that we, being from the future, would already know. Plato would tell us, in that affectionate but non-sexual way of his, that "democracy" is a Greek word combining the roots for "people" ("*demos-*") and "rule" ("*-kratia*"). In Greek democracy, political power was concentrated not in the hands of one person, or even a small group of people, but rather evenly and fairly distributed among all the people,[1] meaning every John Q. Publikopolous could play a role in Athenian government. The main legislative body, the Assembly, was comprised of no less than the first 6,000 citizens to arrive at its meetings — and bear in mind, no saving seats. Jury duty was considered an honor to be vied for. Membership in most other civic institutions, including the Supreme Court, was chosen…by lot! Imagine a system in which anyone could wind up serving on the Supreme Court. *Anyone*. Think about your own family. Friends. The guys you knew in college who would eat dog feces for ten dollars (Fig. 1.4). Now picture one of them as your randomly chosen Chief Justice, and you'll appreciate just how fucked-up this system was.

>> Fig. 1.4

The guys you knew in college who would eat dog feces for ten dollars.

Compared with American democracy, the Athenian version seems simplistic, naïve, and gay. Transcripts of early Athenian policy debates reveal a populace moved more by eloquence and rationality than demagogues and fear-mongering. Thankfully, this type of humane governance wasn't allowed to take root. Athens's great experiment ended after less than two centuries, when, in 338 B.C., Philip of Macedon's forces invaded the city, inflicting on its inhabitants the eternal fate of the noble and enlightened: to be brutally crushed by the armed and dumb.

Rome: The First Republicans

The fall of Athens was followed by the emergence, overnight, of **Rome**. At first glance its people[2] appear to have enjoyed a system of representative government similar to ours. True, behind its façade of allegedly "represen-

(Continue on page 6)

---

[1] For purposes of Greece, "people" means "free adult males."

[2] For purposes of Rome, "people" means "free adult males with property."

Timeline of Democracy

Work begins on Stonehenge. First known use of unionized labor force. Construction time: 1,500 years.

3100 B.C.

Code of Hammurabi radically redefines social contract from "I will kill you" to "I will kill you if you do one of the following 282 things."

1775 B.C.

God gives Ten Commandments to Israelites, making them His Chosen People and granting them eternal protection under Divine Law. Nothing bad ever happens to Jews again.

1300 B.C.

After heated debate, Athenian Assembly passes Pythagorean Theorem Act, requiring all right triangles conform to "$a^2 + b^2 = c^2$" standard.

431 B.C.

Taxpayer revolt halts construction on Great Square of China, only 25% complete.

215 B.C.

Prehistory

Hunters, Gatherers form two-party systems across the globe.

1352 B.C.

Egyptian pharoah Akhenaten conceives principle of "one man, one vote." However, both "one man" and "one vote" refer only to him.

776 B.C.

Greek city-states hold first Olympic Games to show individual achievement can transcend petty nationalism.

772 B.C.

Second Olympic Games. Corinth boycotts to piss off Sparta.

May 3, 325 B.C.

Rome built.

Gutenberg Bible, first book printed with movable type. Begins world trend toward dumbing down literacy.

1455

Death penalty debate heats up after controversial execution of alleged "Son of God."

30 A.D.

In milestone for orderly succession of power, Attila names brother Bleda "Vice-Hun."

440

First printed newspaper appears in China; contains only obituaries, "Funky Winkerbean."

748

Chinese develop gunpowder, banking, newspapers, advanced medicine, paper money. Not Western; doesn't count.

8th - 9th century

Magna Carta (see p.10).

1215

America discovers white people.

1492

Using calculus, Newton estimates that 1 man = 1.00423 votes. History proves him startlingly accurate.

1687

284-305

Emperor Diocletian orders feeding of Christians to lions, violating principle of separation of heads and bodies.

613

Muhammad begins publicly preaching Islam. Can democracy be far behind?

1066

The British Invasion. Norman-mania takes England "by storm." Thousands killed.

1480s

Spanish Inquisition pioneers use of target demographics as focus groups.

1347

Black Death kills 1 in 3 Europeans. Leech lobby touts 67% success rate.

1732

George Washington fathered in his country.

27 B.C.-476 A.D.

"Pax Romana," period of comparative tranquility in Western world engineered by global superpower. Like the 1950s, but *way* more fuckin'.

1000

Althing, world's first Parliament, formed in Iceland. Mainly for warmth.

1620

Pilgrims land at Plymouth Rock.

1621

Rock gets too crowded. Pilgrims leave.

(Continued from page 3)

>> Fig. 1.5

tative" officials lurked a *de facto* oligarchy ruled by entrenched plutocrats. But the similarities don't end there. In fact, the Founding Fathers borrowed many of their ideas from the Roman model, including its bicameral legislature, its emphasis on republicanism and civic virtue, and its Freudian fascination with big white columns.

>> Fig. 1.6

However, there was very little real democracy in Rome. While the Senate theoretically represented the people, in reality its wealthy members covertly pursued pro-business legislation on behalf of such military-industrial giants as JavelinCorp (Fig. 1.5), United Crucifix (Fig. 1.6), and a cartel of resource-exploiting companies known as Big Aqueduct. They even monopolized the most notorious aspect of Roman life, instituting an orgy policy that can literally be described as "trickle-down."

Vomitoriums aside, Rome's biggest contribution to American government was probably its legal system, which codified key concepts like equal protection, "innocent until proven guilty," and the right to confront one's accusers. These very same issues would later form the basis of both the Bill of Rights and a mind-numbing quantity of *Law and Order* scripts. But by the time of Rome's huge millennium celebration marking the beginning of 0 A.D., the faint light of Roman democracy was all but extinguished. The Republic had given way to Empire. The only voting to speak of took place in the Colosseum and was generally limited to a handful of disembowelment-related issues. In time, the Empire itself fell, as history teaches us all empires inevitably must.[3] Its most enduring legacy: a numerical system that allowed future generations to more easily keep track of Super Bowls.

(Continue on page 10)

[3] Except America.

Were You Aware?

Plato did not originally want to call the Athenian form of citizen-government "Democracy," but rather, "Plato 'n' Friends."

"Rome's most enduring legacy? A numerical system that allowed future generations to easily keep track of Super Bowls."

Philosophical Roots of American Democracy

Plato
427-347 B.C.
(Greek)

John Locke
1632-1704 A.D.
(English)

Niccolo Machiavelli
1469-1527 A.D.
(Italian)

Jesus Christ
0-33 A.Himself
(Judean)

Political Philosophy:

In *The Republic*, Plato said that a government fulfilling the highest ideals of human society can be achieved, but only if the right people are put in charge. Plato generally made this point while clearing his throat and yelling, "Helloooo?!? Author of *The Republic* here?!?"

Notable Quote:

"The perfect society will occur only when kings become philosophers or philosophers are made kings."

Less Notable Quote:

"You want it *when*?!?"

Fun Fact:

In spite of his reputation as a thinker for the ages, during his lifetime Plato's only best-seller was a mass-market scroll entitled *Reason Yourself Thin!*

Political Philosophy:

In his *Second Treatise on Government*, Locke argued government is a voluntary creation by people who give up complete freedom in order to better safeguard their inalienable rights to life, liberty, and property. Locke conceded, however, that "the right to party" was alienable, and had to be fought for.

Fun Fact:

Locke's *Second Treatise* was roundly panned by critics, who saw it as a flimsy pretext to bring back the characters from the *First Treatise*.

Political Philosophy:

Machiavelli's best-known political doctrines were: 1) it is better for leaders to appear virtuous than to actually be virtuous; and 2) for a politician, the ends justify the means.

Impact on American Democracy:

None.

Machiavelli on Leadership:

"A leader ought to inspire fear in such a way that, if he does not win love, he avoids hatred."

Machiavelli on Himself:

"Call me a dreamer, but one day, my name will become an adjective for everything cynical and untrustworthy in human nature."

Political Philosophy:

In The New Testament, Jesus says, "Render therefore unto Caesar the things which are Caesar's; and unto God the things that are God's"—an early call for the separation of church and state. Jesus goes on to say, "But when it cometh to things neither Caesar's nor God's, feeleth free to write them off; for yea, they be deductible."

Jesus Irony #639:

Jesus was a steadfast pacifist whose teachings advocated turning the other cheek for the purpose of universal brotherhood. Funnily enough, more people have died "in his name" than any other human in recorded history. (Even Hitler!)

Fun Fact:

Jesus lived to be 33, one fewer than the number of home runs Boog Powell hit in 1966!

What type of government best suits you?

	Democracy	Totalitarian Regime	Theocracy	Socialist State
Your typical day	Counting your money and deciding which fast food to eat	Marching, marching, marching	Avoiding the opposite sex while waiting quietly for death at the hands of American soldiers	Standing in line for tickets to the Toilet Paper Line
Your favorite kind of war	A glorious battle for liberty, preferably fought by proxy army	Seizing territory necessary for new and bigger monuments to the Beloved Despot	One loosely resembling prophesy in religious texts	Let's check in with local Revolutionary Council
Your standard breakfast	Crispix	Tree-bark frittata	Blood of first-born son	Vodka
How are you most likely to die?	Ski-Doo accident	Pick one: Killed by enemy soldiers, killed by own soldiers	Bunker-buster	Combination boredom/industrial mishap
Why are you being jailed?	Possession of marijuana with intent to sell	Poor dancing at Dear Leader's birthday extravaganza	Apostasy	First-degree yard sale
Your pet peeves	Voting	Figuring out what to do with your life	Having to leave the courthouse to talk to a priest	Money
What's your take on genital mutilation	Foreskin is gross/hilarious. Off with it	Only for Olympic athletes	Why stop at the genitals?	I support mutilating people's genitals if it helps the people
You hate America because...	Sales tax	Propaganda doesn't lie	The Great Satan exports misery and irresistible dance music	They're capitalist pigs... and they won't trade with us
Favorite punk-rock band	Circle Jerks	Dead Kennedys	Early Black Flag	Ramones

As wonderful as democracy is, it is only one of the many exciting options available to the discriminating "government hunter." The following chart offers a helpful comparison among some of today's most popular options—along with a sneak peek at what may very well be the government of the future!

Third-World Resort Island	Post-Communist Kleptocracy	Military Junta	Constitutional Sultanate	Occupied Territory	Constitutional Robocracy
Earning $5 a day moving chairs around a pool for white kids who ask if you can get them pot	Managing Ukrainian prostitutes by day, planning your coup by night	Polishing the Colonel's boots	Lounging around His Excellency's disco, awaiting fondling	So many rocks, so little time	Obeying the robots
Any war where you get to kill whitey	Civil war between the power company and the phone company	Favorite *kind*?	Pillow fight	Anything in front of the cameras	Disobeying the robots
Table scraps from last night's All-Inclusive Caribbonanza	Crispix	Chilequiles	Belgian waffle w/fruit, pecans, birth-control pill	Gravel sausage	RAM
Hit by Ski-Doo	Stabbed in own basement casino	Jungle rot	Forgot S&M "safe word"	Sneezing at checkpoint	Body energy over-siphoned by the robots... the horrible, horrible robots
Arrived late for dishwashing shift	You were late mailing your bribe	Your grandfather's brother backed the wrong side	You won't wear the sheer pants	Rock you threw actually hit soldier (who knew?)	Laughter/weeping
They had to call it "Paradise Island"?	Having to leave the courthouse to buy heroin	Where's a checkpoint when you need one?	Choosing your own mate	Shade	Being carbon-based
I'd like to mutilate the genitals of the guy in the Piña Colada Suite	Is there money in it?	Sounds more fun than it really is	Only way to make a eunuch	As long as it doesn't hinder my rock-throwing	Anything to feel again
Wild On... crew stiffed you for tip	Anti-piracy DVD technology	They only sent you 50 fighter planes this year	The carpeting of their whorish blondes fails to match the drapes	Shrapnel in your bedroom reads "Lockheed Martin"	America?!?
Sex Pistols	The Clash	Does Pavement count?	Rage Against the Machine	Social Distortion	Devo

> "The Magna Carta continues to shape twenty-first-century views on topics as diverse as escheat, socage, burage, novel disseisin, and the bailiwicks of Gerard of Athee."

Were You Aware?

The Roman Republic lasted 558 years, or approximately 557 years longer than any elected Italian government since.

The Magna Carta: Power to the Extremely Wealthy People

And then, darkness. For more than 1,000 years democracy disappeared from the European scene. The period instead saw the blossoming of an exciting array of alternate forms of government, such as monarchy, absolute monarchy, kingship, queenhood, and three different types of oppression (religious/ethnic/"for shits and giggles"). As for individual liberty, "innocent until proven guilty" was rapidly supplanted by a more aggressive law-and-order approach better characterized as "guilty until proven flammable."

>>Fig. 1.7

The original Magna Carta, now sadly ravaged by Carta Weevils.

Democracy had disappeared. The people needed a champion, and as is usually the case, the obscenely rich rode to the rescue. In 1215, England's wealthy barons refused to give King John the money he needed to wage war unless he signed the **Magna Carta** (Fig. 1.7). The document codified that no man was above the law. Unfortunately for the peasant class, it did little to address how many were below it (Fig. 1.8). Startlingly ahead of its time, this extraordinary document had a profound effect on people[4] and continues to shape twenty-first-century views on topics as diverse as escheat, socage, burage, novel disseisin, and the bailiwicks of Gerard of Athee. But even more importantly, the Magna Carta set a powerful precedent for our own Founding Fathers: There was no more powerful means of safeguarding individual liberty than a vaguely worded manifesto inked in inscrutable cursive on dilapidated parchment.

>>Fig. 1.8

A feudal serf, unaware a wonderful new document is protecting his master's rights.

The Magna Carta served as a wake-up call that Europe would be forced to answer … in about five hundred years. For Lady Democracy, having lain

---

[4] For purposes of the Magna Carta, "people" means "free adult males with property who signed the Magna Carta."

dormant for more than a millennium, had risen from its slumber only to stretch its arms, reach for the clock, and groggily set the snooze bar for "The Enlightenment."

The 17th and 18th Centuries: Enlightening Strikes

Though a promising development for democracy, the Magna Carta was mostly ignored as the world plunged into what would be known as the Dark Ages. It was an apt title for an era when amoebic dysentery was considered the *good* kind of dysentery. Oppression and high mortality rates seemed ready to swallow what remained of mankind, when through the darkness emerged the light that would be its salvation: Reason. It began slowly. "Hey, what if we stop storing the corpses in the drinking water and see if that makes any difference to our health?" From there, it gathered momentum. Soon, all conventional wisdom, from the shape of the Earth to whether the ruling class could have your hut burned and your organs removed because they thought you caused an eclipse, was up for grabs. This last question proved especially pertinent for the future of democracy and ushered in an era known as **the Enlightenment**.

The Enlightenment, with its emphasis on reason, would finally provide democracy with its philosophical underpinnings. The 17th and 18th centuries produced a wave of prominent thinkers espousing political systems based on what they called "the social contract." Government, they theorized, was a sort of legal agreement between the rulers and the ruled, the terms of which were binding on both parties. It was a groundbreaking theory. All they needed now was some country dumb enough to try it before the King found out and had them all drawn and quartered.

Democracy needed a fresh start — hearty and idealistic champions who would strike out for a new world, willing to risk everything for the principles of equality, liberty, justice … and slaves. We'd need some slaves and guns. But we're getting ahead of ourselves. A new world awaited. ◉

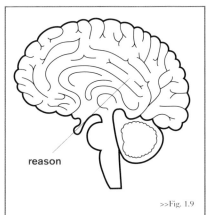

>>Fig. 1.9

The Enlightenment's focus on reason raised the profile of the brain, which became the organ considered most important to human character, overtaking the spleen.

"Hey, what if we stop storing the corpses in the drinking water and see if that makes any difference to our health?"

The Ages of Democracy: A Guide

Like snowflakes or Sting albums, no two democracies are exactly alike, but they all tend to follow the same basic pattern. This guide will help steer you through the turning points of your democracy's life.

1. Infancy

Congratulations! You've ended your religious/economic/ethnic repression and thrown off the yoke of your despot/king/ayatollah through a bloody/bloodless war/coup/voluntary exile. Now it's time to choose your first leader. He/she (OK, "he") may have commanded your war effort, but could also be a prominent exile returning home from his villa on the Côte d'Azur. First step: Draft a new constitution. (Use pencil.) Next, hold your first election. Is it fraudulent? Don't worry—everybody's proud of you just for trying!

(Tip: Naming a new national capital? Why not call it "[Your Country] City!")

6. Old Age

Your legislative sessions now deal almost exclusively with health-care and social security. The dependent nations you've created no longer want anything to do with you. But worst of all, your mind is going. The best and brightest of your nation shun public service, and the resulting brain drain wracks your bureaucracies, rendering you unable to perform even the most basic tasks, like balancing a budget or conducting a legitimate election. Your body politic is clogged with incumbents, and worst of all, your Vice President once played someone named "The Geech" on a UPN sitcom. By the end, you can't even recognize your own ideals. Your few remaining friends may be tempted to end your misery and bomb you out of love. But at least they can take some small comfort in the saying, "Old democracies never die, they just get overthrown by military juntas/peasant insurrectionists/rural militias."

5. Middle Age

One day, your democracy will look in the mirror and behold a scary sight: Voter turn-out is thinning, your welfare system is bloated, you're completely dominated by corporate interests, and you haven't had a proper election in years. When this happens, a nation may go through a mid-life crisis, seeking solace in superficial "toys," like satellite-based lasers to shoot down missiles or action stars turned politicians. Don't be surprised if old allies decide to leave you and start referring to you as a "once-great" nation. Ultimately, you will have to decide whether to quietly make peace with your declining power, or to go out in a blaze of glory, taking Mideast peace/world fish stocks/the ozone layer with you.

(Tip: Many middle-aged democracies find themselves turning to religion for strength, so don't be too "embarrassed" to erode church-state separation provisos.)

2. Childhood

Your democracy is up and running. You're ready to organize political parties—one ideally, two if necessary. During these formative years they'll prove invaluable in furnishing your citizens with opinions. Plenty of exciting discoveries await, but remember, youthful exuberance can sometimes lead to violent "acting out." Control yourself: Hire a police force, preferably led by some of the people you overthrew. Other milestones to look for: First war; writing national anthem about that war; and collecting taxes all by yourself, like a big country.

(Tip: This is also a good time to free any Nobel Peace Prize winners you may have had incarcerated.)

2.

Childhood democracies should not be allowed to play with these.

3. Adolescence

A democracy's most turbulent time. It usually starts with an assassination/waves of revenge killings/*Les Misérables*, and ends with a civil war ("population adjustment"). In between, you'll undergo a rapid growth spurt, possibly involving the annexation of Texas. Your relationship with your Founders will change; you'll find yourself questioning whether they had it all wrong when it came to, for instance, slavery. Physically, your private sector will mature, your mineral deposits will start surfacing, and you will experience the first stirrings of interest in women, specifically in letting them vote.

(Tip: You may also notice dissidents where you formerly had none. Don't worry; this is normal, and they can always be arrested.)

4. Adulthood

The prime of your life. By now you know who you are and which UN committee you chair. Your natural resources are at the peak of their exportability. It's time to think about building a future, settling down with the right alliances, maybe even raising little colonies of your own. But with success comes new responsibility. Other nations are now counting on you for aid and peacekeeping troops. You may find yourself compromising your youthful ideals, supporting regimes you know are violating human rights. Don't beat yourself up about it—you have to trade with someone.

(Tip: With a free press firmly in place, you may see the first appearance of political satire. Ignore it. It can do no harm.)

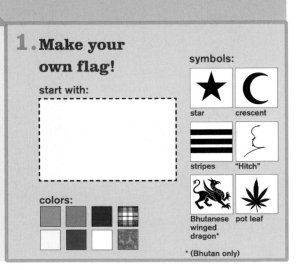

1. Make your own flag!

start with:

colors:

symbols:

star   crescent

stripes   "Hitch"

Bhutanese   pot leaf
winged
dragon*

* (Bhutan only)

Take the Mascot Quiz!

Great countries embody great ideals. But ideals are meaningless...without beloved national symbols to represent them, that is. Can you match the mascots below with the nations they represent?

1.

Uncle Sam

A.

Greece

2.

John Bull

B.

Russia

3.

The Great Bear

C.

Germany

4.

Nutsy

D.

The United States

5.

Epididymis, the Wan Boy-Child

E.

Great Britain

Answer Key:

1-D: Uncle Sam. A commanding mascot with extraordinary versatility, capable of leading men to both feats of valor on the battlefield and to car dealerships for insanely low APR financing. Also famously nimble on stilts.

2-E: John Bull is like Uncle Sam, only shorter and fatter, clearly playing to the British infatuation with stoutness.

3-B: Russia. The Great Bear is a symbol of power and mystery who can be frightened away if you attach a bell to your backpack.

4-C: Nutsy represented Adolf Hitler's brief flirtation with a "warmer, fuzzier" approach to Nazism. Nutsy died in Bergen-Belsen in 1943.

5-A: A discreet 11-to-12-year-old boy, Epididymis represented the ancient Athenians' love of discreet 11-to-12-year-old boys.

Discussion Questions

1. If you lived in a monarchy, would you rather be the king or a slave? Why or why not?

2. What is the central ideological difference between democracy and cannibalism?

3. You're a fifth-century Greek city-state growing increasingly concerned over repeated Persian incursions into the central Peloponnesian peninsula. How many hoplites can you dispatch to Thermopylae without jeopardizing the triremes commanded by Themistocles for the naval engagement at Artemisium? Show your work.

4. Does the expression "When in Rome, do as the Romans do" apply to all cities, or just Rome?

5. The notion that each individual has worth in society found political expression in the invention of democracy. What's bullshit about this?

6. Is direct democracy practical today? In a nation as big as ours, is it really possible to simultaneously gather the opinions of 300,000,000 people? (Log on to www.americathebook.com and vote in our poll!)

Classroom Activities

1. Have your students draw a topographical map of ancient Greece. For every elevation they get wrong, punch one in the arm.

2. Give your students a taste of Athenian life before democracy by implementing a "Draconian" measure, like forcing them to wear togas to class every day for a month. Then celebrate democracy by being named the principal defendant in a class-action lawsuit against the school.

3. Have the class perform a real-time, period-accurate reenactment of the Protestant Reformation. That should buy you plenty of time to step outside for a smoke.

Were You Aware?

One cup of green tea contains more vitamin C than an orange.

>>Fig. 1.10

Voltaire (1694-1778) was an important Enlightenment thinker. There must be a book about him somewhere. Read it.

"Jefferson, you're on the
two. Hamilton? You get
the ten. I'm calling dibs on
the one. That's all me,
baby. What's that, Adams?
You wanted the one? All
right, that's it: You don't
get to be on anything.
That's right, I'm taking
back the quarter. Anyone
else want to complain?
I didn't think so."

— George Washington, 1789

Chapter 2

The Founding of America

It had been hundreds of thousands of years since man first made his presence felt on planet Earth,[1] but had it been time well spent? Our species' progress had been steady but slow. Man had survived, but with precious little to show for his time, a frustration summed up in the famous cave drawing entitled "Enough Already with the Hunting and the Gathering" (Fig. 2.1). Of course, there had been great accomplishments along the way. Fire was a winner. Walking upright went a long way towards easing back pain. Even the wheel, the boat and language would prove quite useful, especially on the heels of the less successful parallelogram, rock, and grunting. All wonderful innovations that would, in their own tiny way, advance the cause of man.

>>Fig. 2.1

Discovered in the caves of Lascaux, France, "Enough Already with the Hunting and the Gathering" (c. 13,000 B.C.) is man's first known representation of ennui.

But nothing yet accomplished would rival in importance the discovery, colonization and eventual democratization of the New World. Yes, America would become what de Tocqueville described as the "total package."[2] America's journey from undiscovered frontier to independent nation to transcendently perfect beacon of freedom was long, complex, and fascinating. But to fully understand this journey you only have to memorize three dates.

---

[1] Or six thousand years, if you prefer to ignore all aspects of rational scientific discovery.
[2] Loosely translated from the French "Le Package Totale."

1492

In fourteen hundred ninety-two
Columbus sailed the ocean blue...

>>Fig. 2.2

America's path to democracy was cleared by the colonists' generous giveaways, like the much sought-after "Smallpox Blankets."

...and discovered America. Now, some have argued Columbus actually discovered the West Indies, or that Norsemen had discovered America centuries earlier, or that you really can't get credit for discovering a land already populated by indigenous people with a developed civilization. Those people are communists. Columbus discovered America.

1620

In sixteen hundred and two zero
The Pilgrims landed dressed real queero

Were You Aware?

The Pilgrims were searching for freedom to practice the most stultifyingly oppressive brand of Christianity ever known to man.

Pilgrim hat, with lesser-known Pilgrim mittens.

The next great date in the history of American democracy marked the **Pilgrims**' establishment of the first successful New World colony. Now, some have argued the first established colony was actually the ill-fated Roanoke colony or the slightly better fated Jamestown colony. Those people are mentally ill. Roanoke and Jamestown do not count because both settlements lacked the key ingredient necessary for the successful colonization of America: **religious fanaticism**. Plymouth succeeded because its inhabitants did not come to the New World searching for glory, adventure, or hot man-on-Indian action. Rather, the Pilgrims had come to escape religious persecution, to create a society where they could worship as they pleased and one day, God willing, even do some persecuting of their own. Said John Winthrop, the first elected leader of the Plymouth colony, "In England, we are looked upon crossly for what they deem our most unusual form of Puritan Orthodoxy. Well, I say unto those whose gaze be deemed disapproving...You call that persecution? Dirty

>>Fig. 2.3

Plymouth Rock. Later, it landed on Malcolm X, seriously injuring him.

looks?!? Watch as I have this young girl burned alive for having hiccups!" (Interestingly, almost four hundred years after the foundation of the Puritans' Plymouth colony, the state of Massachusetts became the first to guarantee the constitutionality of gay marriage. This act was misconstrued as a bold move forward in the cause of equality, but in reality was just a hilarious "fuck you" to the Pilgrims.)

In seventeen hundred and seventy-six
The Declaration of Independence was signed-ix

1776

Finally, the date of destiny. **July 4, 1776**. The day America officially broke with England. The day brave patriots signed a document stating, "We hold these truths to be self-evident, that all men are created equal."[3] The day most historians refer to as "Democracy's Money Shot." But was our journey to independence inexorable, or had it been, as some have claimed, exorable? Consider this remarkable fact: The United States of America, the greatest country in the history of the world, would not exist had England simply been less stingy with the chamomile.

Prelude to Revolution: You Can't Spell Tyranny without Tea[4]

Through most of colonial history, inhabitants of the 13 colonies were loyal subjects of the British crown — resourceful, dedicated, and as the Third Duchess of Kent (Fig 2.4) was fond of saying, "Some tea-drinkin' motherfuckahs." In fact, whenever the subject of the New World was mentioned within earshot, the Duchess could always be counted on for a wistful headshake and a hearty "Motherfuckahs love that motherfuckin' tea."

Yes, tea was not just a hot beverage in late eighteenth-century America, it was *the* hot beverage. So it came as quite a shock to the colonists when, in

>>Fig. 2.4

The Third Duchess of Kent's boorish manners and vulgar language made the Fifth Earl of Norwich look like the Ninth Viscount of Shropshire.

(Continue on page 22)

---

[3] Here, "all men" refers to those who had brought a pen.

[4] You can.

Your Unelectable Founders

The Founding Fathers: Young, Gifted, and White

Who were these renegades, these upstarts who dared challenge the might and majesty of Great Britain? The Founders represented a cross-section of colonial society and a broad range of political beliefs. We think of them as one unified body, but in reality their relations were fraught with tension, as evidenced by the heated December 1775 exchange at Carpenters' Hall when Patrick Henry referred to John Hancock as "fucknuts."

But as deliberations over independence wore on, leaders emerged. Libraries' worth of books have been penned about each of these men of genius, whose extraordinary achievements and revolutionary ideas are virtually impossible to encapsulate. We do so on these two pages.

Benjamin Franklin
(1706-1790)

Thomas Jefferson
(1743-1826)

Achievements

Tenth of seventeen children; had classic "tenth child" personality.

Wrote *The Autobiography of Benjamin Franklin*, the book he was born to write.

Proved lightning was electricity by flying a kite, vindicating 20 years of meaningless kite-flying.

Wrote immortal maxims like "$2,145.34 saved is $2,145.34 earned." (Figures adjusted for inflation.)

Invented Franklin stove, glass harmonica, bifocals, and essentially Philadelphia.

World-famous. Universally beloved.

Loved a good fart joke.

Reason why unelectable

Loved the ladies. Loved 'em old, young, fat, thin, whatever. Couldn't get enough. Just loved 'em.

Also, once wrote, "As to Jesus...I have some doubts as to his divinity." Kiss red states goodbye.

Achievements

Wrote Declaration of Independence, still highly regarded in some circles.

America's first Secretary of State, second Vice President— thus completing unprecedented governmental "Triple Crown."

Masterminded Louisiana Purchase; doubled size of the United States, while simultaneously halving quality.

Tinkered with architecture. Futzed around in mechanical engineering. Botany hobbyist. Animal husbandry buff. Enjoyed recreational paleontology.

Personal book collection became Library of Congress, so probably read a bit. Dabbled in French, Spanish, Italian, Latin, Greek, Anglo-Saxon.

Not averse to the occasional state-university founding. Expert on viticulture, whatever the hell that is.

Reason why unelectable

"Ms. Hemings? Connie Chung on line one."

For their times, the Founding Fathers boasted relatively impressive credentials. But would their so-called "genius" hold up against the more rigorous standards which we demand of today's office-seekers?

George Washington
(1732-1799)

Achievements

First and arguably greatest President.

First and arguably greatest Commander-in-Chief.

First in war, first in peace, first in the hearts of his countrymen.

First prize, 1764 Williamsburg Bake-Off, "Profiteroles à la George."

All-time record holder, Most Places Slept.

Carried himself in a manner that was, well, almost Reaganesque.

In his will, ordered Martha to free their slaves after her death. A nice gesture. Unfortunately, Martha lived to be 197 years old.

Reason why unelectable

Bad teeth and syphilis.

John Adams
(1735-1826)

Achievements

Most influential figure in Continental Congress due to primo alphabetical position.

Drafted Massachusetts Constitution in 1780, though delegates from his state refused to ratify the letter "R."

First Vice President; set the standard by doing nothing for eight years. Then made it through own presidency in half the time.

Forebear of long line of distinguished public servants, including son John Quincy (6th President), great-grandson Henry (historian), cousin Sam (brewer, patriot), and great-great-grandnephew Grizzly (bearded outdoorsman).

Claimed he was willing to make principled, unpopular decisions.

Reason why unelectable

Actually made principled, unpopular decisions.

Alexander Hamilton
(1755-1804)

Achievements

Author of majority of *Federalist Papers*, including the least boring ones.

Frequent foe of Jefferson. Put own face on $10, Jefferson's on $2. Smart move.

French-bashed before it was cool.

Huge fan of democracy, if "the people are turbulent and changing; they seldom judge or determine right" is any indication.

Founded *New York Post* in 1801; dubbed young Andrew Jackson "Wacko Jacko."

Reason why unelectable

Born in West Indies, so constitutionally impossible.

Had unfortunate tendency to duel…and lose.

James Madison
(1751-1836)

Achievements

Father of Constitution.

Co-author of *Federalist Papers*.

Sponsor of Bill of Rights.

Guarantor of church-state separation.

Creator of checks-and-balances system.

Consistently popular two-term President.

Chief negotiator for Louisiana Purchase.

Lived blameless life.

Died with no enemies.

Still less beloved than his wife.

Reason why unelectable

5' 4", and would weigh 108 pounds even *after* the camera added ten pounds.

High turnout at the Boston Tea Party forced many protestors to come up with alternative costume arrangements.

>>Fig. 2.5

>>Fig. 2.6

(Continued from page 19)

1773, the British government outsourced all American tea jobs to the East India Company, an offshore British multinational. In addition, the Crown passed the **Tea Act**, raising the tariff on tea one eighth-pence per dram, the modern equivalent of $5,000,000 per teabag.[5]

But the English-American relationship had been deteriorating for some time. In 1765, King George III imposed the Stamp Act, which in conjunction with the equally harsh Coin Act and Action Figure Act decimated colonial America's burgeoning nerd community. Their anger was soon given a voice by Pennsylvanian John Dickinson, who eloquently argued for greater colonial self-government in his classic *Letters from a Pennsylvania Farmer* and its less-popular sequel, *The Pennsylvania Farmer and the Goblet of Fire*. The first major act of violence occurred in 1770, when British troops fired into an angry mob and killed five citizens in what came to be called **The Boston Massacre**. (Yes, it was a happier, simpler time, when five deaths were seen as a "massacre," not the natural consequence of, say, a Detroit Pistons championship celebration.)

But it was the 1773 Tea Act that proved the tipping point in America's struggle for independence. The colonists gathered to debate their next move. Inspiration came in the form of Jebediah Sondheim, a New York-based wheelwright and lyricist whose catchy slogan "No taxation without representation!" galvanized the populace and marked the birth of a great American political tradition: the reductionist rhyming chant. But the Tea Act required immediate action. There would be no out-of-town previews. There were only two weeks until opening night, people ... two weeks.

And so, on a cold December night, a party of Bostonians dressed as Mohawk Indians boarded ships anchored in the harbor and dumped thousands of pounds of tea into the Atlantic, though due

(Continue on page 24)

[5] Give or take.

The Founding ... *Mothers?!?*

When the editors of this book asked me to contribute an essay or two, I only had one question: *"Quanto dinero por mi?"* Having resolved that issue, I was presented with the challenge of writing on a subject I admittedly knew little – okay, nothing – about: The Founding Mothers, or, as I have cleverly punctuated it in the title above, "The Founding ... *Mothers?!?*" Here's what I found on the Internet:

By Rob Corddry

Betsy Ross

Everybody knows Betsy Ross was the one who "got it all sewed up" in the theme song for that show *Maude*. But what you may not have known is the thing she "sewed up" was the American flag! I'm talking about Old Glory! The Ol' Red, White and Blue! Ol' Ironsides! Cap'n Jack! I did some research and it turns out if Betsy Ross was alive and sewing American flags today, she'd be a 13-year-old Laotian boy.

Abigail Adams

Abigail Adams was the wife of President John Adams and was widely considered his intellectual equal. (He must have been pretty stupid!) In fact, she once wrote to her husband, "Remember the Ladies, and be more generous and favorable to them than your ancestors," making her one of the country's first feminists. My guess? She was a dyke.

Mary Hays, a/k/a "Molly Pitcher"

This is actually a pretty cool story. During the Revolutionary War, soldiers would often get very thirsty while fighting. That's where Mary Hays came in, bravely carrying pitchers of water to the soldiers, running unarmed across the battlefield as bullets and shells whizzed by her. Once during Pledge Week, the brothers made us carry thimbles full of our own urine across the Quad while screaming "Faggots!" in our faces, so I know what she went through.

Sybil Ludington

Finally, there's Sybil Ludington, who at 16 years old rode 40 miles around the town of Fredericksburg, New York, to alert local militia the British were coming. She's often called "The Female Paul Revere." Although really, she rode twice as far as Paul Revere, so maybe he should be called "The Male Sybil Ludington!" Just kidding, that would be gay. I found this story by accident during my routine Google search for "16-year-olds + horses."

So as it turns out, alongside the dozens of Founding Fathers whose words and deeds continue to reverberate throughout American society, there were, what, four or five women of note? Yeah, that sounds about right. I'm outta here.

> **"The pen is mightier than the sword, if it has been sharpened to a fine point, dipped in deadly poison and is thrown from ten feet away. But really, you're better off with a sword."**
>
> — *Benjamin Franklin*, Poor Richard's Almanack *(first draft)*

>>Fig. 2.7

The Declaration of Independence, restored to its original color, "Fireball Fuchsia."

(Continued from page 22)

to better-than-expected turnout, not everyone got to dress up as an Indian (see Fig 2.5). British authorities immediately closed the harbor and clamped down on the Massachusetts government, a move brewer/patriot Samuel Adams called "wicked retahded" in *Ye Boston Globe*. Months later, the Battles of Lexington and Concord would make reconciliation impossible. England and her colony America would be forever separate.

How had it come to pass? Perhaps no one summed it up more eloquently than the Third Duchess of Kent: "Fuck with a motherfuckah's tea and the shit be on."

The Declaration of Independence: Brittle Parchment of Liberty

If you are going to sever ties to your Commonwealth through bloody struggle, it is considered polite to write down why. Nobody wants to get three years into a revolution only to realize the whole thing was a *Three's Company*-esque misunderstanding. **The Declaration of Independence** (Fig. 2.7) was the laundry list of grievances stating America's case for freedom. Its accusations against the King ranged from the egregious ("He has plundered our seas, burnt our towns and ravaged the lives of our people") to the trifling ("Sometimes when he sees us at a party he acts like he doesn't know us"). But proud men would not take up arms against the Crown solely because the King had "erected a multitude of new offices." The authors of the Declaration knew they would also have to appeal to man's higher nature, to stir men's souls. They needed something with some zazz. Enter a young hotshot tobacco executive from Virginia, **Thomas Jefferson**.

Jefferson had had great success marketing tobacco.[6] His task now would be to synthesize the unique

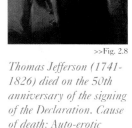

>>Fig. 2.8

Thomas Jefferson (1741-1826) died on the 50th anniversary of the signing of the Declaration. Cause of death: Auto-erotic asphyxiation.

---

[6] He is widely credited with inventing the cigarette slogans "All the cool kids are doing it!" and "You need something to do after fucking a slave."

brand message of America down to something that would captivate the hard to reach "12-28 ragtag militia" demographic, all the while not offending traditional "Butterchurn Moms." His first attempt at a Preamble was:

> *"AMERICA. A is for All the tea they taxed, M is for the Minutemen they shellaxed..."*

It tested poorly. But his rewrite would be a win-win:

> *"We hold these truths to be self-evident, that all men are created equal, that they are endowed by their Creator with certain unalienable Rights, that among these are Life, Liberty and the pursuit of Happiness."*

(Continue on page 27)

Would You Mind If I Told You How We Do It In Canada?

By Samantha Bee

The story of America's independence from England is very well known, but did you know Canada was also once part of the British Empire? It's true! We Canadians threw off the same British yoke as you, only we took a more leisurely route to liberation. In fact, you might say, we've been "declaring" our "independence" for more than 200 years! Kind of!

Our style of revolution centered less on bloodshed and guerrilla warfare and more on the time-tested strategy of "not making a fuss." For example, at the same time you were declaring war on the English monarchy, *we* were enjoying privileges granted to us by King George in the Treaty of Versailles, which gave us fishing rights off the coast of Newfoundland, provided we not dry or cure fish on land. (And by the way, we later got the right to cure and dry fish on land, thank you very much!)

All I'm saying is there is more than one way to skin a cat. Not that I am in any way saying I would like to harm a cat. Quite the contrary. I like cats. Unless America wants Canada to skin a cat, in which case we will gladly do it.

The point is we took our time, waiting for The Canadian Moment to arrive, rather than forcing it upon the world. We waited, in the cold, watching the U.S., most of Central and South America, Africa and Asia throw off their colonial oppressors. I think it was us and Belize that held out.

And our patience ultimately paid off, for in the glorious year of 1982, we took the bold step of getting permission from England to amend our constitution so we could amend our constitution—without getting permission from England. Let freedom ring!

Now the only remnants of the tyrannical rule of Queen Elizabeth II are an appointed "Governor General" who represents her in Canadian governmental affairs. And the Queen is still officially our head of state. Plus she's on all our money. And when we take a government job, we have to swear a loyalty pledge to her. All in all, a small price to pay for an independence achieved without bloodshed, violence, glory or independence.

I'm sorry if this in any way seems like I'm bragging.

Founding Father Fact and Fiction

In the horrific and unimaginable days before television, Americans learned about their public figures from stories passed along from person to person. Often these "stories" became "myths," which then grew into "legends," before reaching their final and most exalted status, "outright lies." Let's take a look at some of these tales and separate fact from fiction.

The Legend:

The young George Washington chops down a cherry tree, then famously confesses, "I cannot tell a lie. I did it."

What really happened:

Believe it or not, this myth is actually true. Washington was famously honest, even to the point of rudeness, as evidenced by his remark to Betsy Ross when she presented her first, more "avant-garde" design for the American flag: "I cannot tell a lie, Betsy: Is that a flag or did your sewing kit throw up?"

Someone, possibly George Washington, after cutting down a cherry tree.

The Legend:

Paul Revere rides through the streets of Boston shouting, "The British are coming! The British are coming!"

What really happened:

Historians say Revere probably would not have been yelling, "The British are coming," since at the time most colonists still thought of themselves as British. His actual cry was, "I say, representatives of the King's army will be arriving on our shores to do most grievous harm to us, their fellow subjects under the crown…so be mindful and watchful on this night!" Over the course of his 12-mile gallop he managed to complete the phrase three times.

Paul Revere's famous ride was delayed two weeks when he stopped to pose for this painting.

The Legend:

Alexander Hamilton was shot and killed in a duel with Aaron Burr.

What really happened:

Hamilton and Burr were actually best friends. One day they were rooting around in Burr's dad's house after school and found a pistol behind a stack of old girlie pamphlets. Believing the pistol empty, Burr suggested they use it to play Constables and Rogues. Minutes later, the architect of American capitalism was mortally wounded.

Our Founders lived in a simpler, more innocent time, when ceremonial murder was legal.

The Legend:

John Hancock signed the Declaration of Independence extra-large because he wanted "to be sure King George could read it!"

What really happened:

John Hancock was 23 feet tall and merely signed in his normal fashion.

Hancock (center) with other Declaration signers.

The Legend:

Before his execution at the hands of British authorities, patriot Nathan Hale said, "I regret that I have but one life to give for my country."

What really happened:

Continued Hale, "But what I really regret is that I'm giving it now." And then began the begging.

Nathan Hale was a coward.

(Continued from page 25)

In a scant 35 words, Jefferson had given the nation the kind of positive brand identity that rendered moot the issue of whether or not we had to live up to its ideals. Still, knowing the inherent contradiction between their noble words and the reality of a slave-owning nation, Jefferson and the Founders wisely decided to strike from the Declaration of Independence the phrase "or your money back."

The Declaration of Independence was signed and announced on July 4, 1776. A new nation was born. The Founding Fathers could now retire back to their respective states, knowing that all that was left to achieve was for their untrained militias to engage and defeat the most powerful empire the world had ever seen.

The Constitution:
Let's Get This Party Started Right

> *"The Revolution is over. America has triumphed.*
> *Let us continue to solve any and all disputes*
> *by using violence."*
> — *American General Anthony Wayne at the Battle of Yorktown (1781)*

The Founders realized a country forged in war would need a powerful legal blueprint to preserve its hard-won peace. **The Articles of Confederation**, drafted between 1776 and 1777, and ratified in 1781, was not that document. A series of confusing provisions (such as "Article IV: See Article XII," "Article XLIII: This is not an Article," and "Article XII: See Article IV"), the Articles vested the majority of power in the states' hands, a poor idea given South Carolina's immaturity and how angry New Hampshire got when it was drunk.

Why did the Articles fail so completely? Most historians believe the Founding Fathers spent a great deal of their first constitutional convention drafting the Declaration of Independence and only realized on July Third that the Articles were also due. By 1787 the inadequacy of this poorly conceived document was apparent to even the dimmest of framers.[7] That sum-

Were You Aware?

Despite working long hours in grueling conditions, most slaves received absolutely no college credit for their unpaid labor.

Were You Aware?

Due to an early typo, America very nearly became a "Democrasy."

mer, 55 of the country's greatest minds, led by Alexander Hamilton and James Madison, once again convened in Philadelphia. This time, their mission would not be dissolving bonds but forging them, and in so doing giving birth to a new, permanent, glorious law forever linking the diverse components of a young nation destined to spread across the continent.

They would name it "The Constitution," after Hamilton's mother.[8]

If the Declaration was our nation's sales pitch, the **Constitution** would be its owner's manual, and as the Founding Fathers knew all too well, no one ever reads the owner's manual. The Constitution would have to effectively vest power in the hands of the people (republicanism) without undermining the importance of central authority (federalism). It would thus need to be an all-encompassing document. The first few drafts even included recipes (see Fig. 2.9).

To achieve these ends, the Founders ultimately conceived the **three branches of government**, a notion insuring the separation of powers through a series of **checks and balances**.[9] It was a system reflecting the Founders' belief that

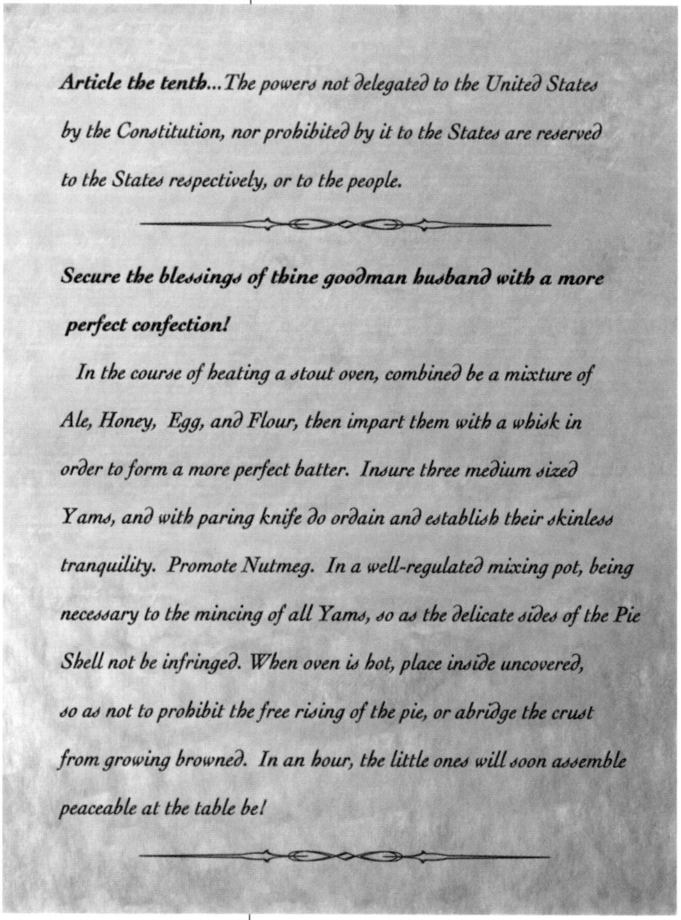

Article the tenth...The powers not delegated to the United States by the Constitution, nor prohibited by it to the States are reserved to the States respectively, or to the people.

───────◆◆◆───────

Secure the blessings of thine goodman husband with a more perfect confection!

In the course of heating a stout oven, combined be a mixture of Ale, Honey, Egg, and Flour, then impart them with a whisk in order to form a more perfect batter. Insure three medium sized Yams, and with paring knife do ordain and establish their skinless tranquility. Promote Nutmeg. In a well-regulated mixing pot, being necessary to the mincing of all Yams, so as the delicate sides of the Pie Shell not be infringed. When oven is hot, place inside uncovered, so as not to prohibit the free rising of the pie, or abridge the crust from growing browned. In an hour, the little ones will soon assemble peaceable at the table be!

───────◆◆◆───────

>>Fig. 2.9

---

7 Specifically, New Jersey's Francis "Little Bus" Witherspoon.

8 A comprehensive discussion of all specifics of this great document is beyond the scope of this book. Perhaps you could read it yourself? A perusal copy is available at the National Archives in Washington, D.C. (10am-6pm, Tues.-Sun.; appointment only.) Or are the authors to assume responsibility for everything?!? The authors are very disappointed in you.

9 Federal law dictates these phrases always appear in boldface...or else.

children should memorize not just dates, but also phrases. But on what basis should the three branches be divided? It came down to two dueling ideas: Madison's proposal of an executive, judicial and legislative branch, and Georgia's Joseph Morton's proposal to dole out power according to "The presence, forbearance, rectitude and largeosity of one's 'Plums and Carrot'."

(Continue on page 30)

"Give me liberty
or give me death . . .
but preferably liberty."

— Patrick Henry, 1775

The Federalist and Anti-Federalist Papers

The debate over The Constitution prompted the two most influential series of essays in American history, *The Federalist Papers* and *The Anti-Federalist Papers*, two exhaustive and thoughtful meditations on the merits and failings of the nation's new blueprint.

You can read these hundreds of pages of dense, turgid prose, or you could skim these blurbs taken from reviews of The Constitution.

"*The Constitution* grabs you right from the Preamble and doesn't let go until the last Article...the must-ratify document of the summer!"
-Alexander Hamilton, *New York Post*

"A pathetic excuse of a social contract that makes John Locke's *Two Treatises of Government* look like Baron Montesquieu's *The Spirit of Laws.*"
-Richard Henry Lee, *Richmond Chronicle-Courant*

"If you base your new nation on only one fundamental set of governmental principles this year, make it this one!"
-James Madison, *Hartford Gazette-Chronicle*

"The 'Foundering' Fathers are at it again...who told these guys they could Found?!?"
-Samuel Bryan, *Boston Courant-Gazette*

"... this follow-up to 'The Articles of Confederation' is the rare sequel that's more bicameral than the original! Gallop, don't trot, to your town square to pick up a copy!"
- John Jay, *Wilmington Gazette-Courant-Chronicle*

"Belongs to the so-bad-it's-good genre of political charters... destined to become the kind of camp classic revered by some of our more, shall we say, 'unmarried' friends."
- Melancton Smith, *"Melancton's Musings" (syndicated column)*

"Checkſ, balanceſ, executive, legiſlative, judiciary - thiſ babyſ got it all!"
- George Waſhington, *Mount Vernon Bee-Diſpatch*

"Reads more like a Con-*shit*-ution."
-Patrick Henry, *Inside Politics*

Were You Aware?

Delaware's status as the first state to ratify the Constitution is still, 217 years later, the only thing it has going for it.

⊛ THE FIRST STATE ⊛
484355
DELAWARE

⊛ FUCKING BORING ⊛
484355
DELAWARE

"The First State" replaced Delaware's previous license-plate motto.

(Continued from page 29)

After much deliberation, it was decided Madison's proposal would be accepted, Morton relenting only after the Constitutional Convention agreed to proclaim him "impressive." The three branches would in essence police each other with an elaborate system of safeguards and precautions that would prevent power from being concentrated in too few hands. Quipped a jubilant Hamilton, "The only way it could fail is if one party gained control of not just the Executive, but also the Senate and House chambers, and upon doing so, proceeded to bring in like-minded judges!!!!" And then the Framers all laughed and laughed and laughed.

Ultimately, the Constitution provided our fledgling democracy America with a bulwark against tyranny. A foundation based upon the rule of law, equality and a respect for the individual and property the world had not yet seen. They even graciously included a manner to amend the document as circumstances dictated for future generations.[10] The Founders prayed only that this Constitution be ratified, respected and upheld…and that nobody would tell the black people about it. ◐

---

[10] For example, if there was a sudden increase in gayness.

A Guide to World Revolutions

The American Revolution, while undoubtedly the best revolution, is far from the only one the world has seen. Below is a sampling of other history-changing revolutions you may or may not be familiar with.

	American	French	Russian	Cuban	Iranian	Digital
Year	1776	1789	1917	1959	1978	1993
Winners	U.S.A.! U.S.A.! U.S.A.! U.S.A.!	Le people	Lenin, Stalin, Joe McCarthy (R-WI)	Fidel Castro, muralists, Cuba's makeshift-raft-building industry	Ayatollah Khomeini, Jerry Bruckheimer, Allah	Dorks, nerds, dweebs, venture capitalists
Losers	U.K.! U.K.! U.K.! U.K.!	Opulent palace dwellers	Czars, tsars, tzars, csars	Bugsy Siegel, Legs Diamond, Gambly Goldberg, Muscles Shapiro	The Shah, non-flame-retardant American flags, Jimmy Carter, Billy Carter (loser for unrelated reasons)	Telegram industry, music industry, industry
Causes	God's Divine Will, taxation without representation	Having been let eat cake	Beet shortage	Failed Baltimore Orioles tryout	Too much "Shah," not enough "Na Na"	Inability to forward jokes to casual acquaintances
Weapons	God's Divine Will, muskets	Buttery puff pastries	Misery, snow, remaining beets	Tightly rolled Montecristo grenades	Allah's Divine Will, 56 U.S. embassy employees	000111100 011111100 010101010 001001001 000100010
Catch-phrase	"Don't shoot 'til you see the whites of their eyes."	"CLOUSEAU!"	"I am now and will always be a card-carrying member of the Communist Party."	"You broke my heart, Fredo. You broke my heart."	"Ayatollah Ass-a-hollah."	"e-(any word here)"
Lasting Effects	Only the greatest country the world ever has or will see!	Too tired to resist Nazis	Breakaway republic of Kookoostan now proud owner of 500 nuclear warheads	The Buena Vista Fucking Social Club. (Christ, we get it, they're good musicians!)	Middle East enters un-precedented era of peace and prosperity; virgins for everybody!	Carpal Tunnel Syndrome, vitamin E defi-ciency, spam (inedible)
Salad Dressing	No	Yes	Yes	No	Salad dressing is the milk of the infidel	No

Discussion Questions

1. Why do you think the Framers made the Constitution so soul-crushingly boring?

2. Have you ever founded anything? If so, is it something that went on to become a global superpower? If not, why not?

3. When, in the course of human events, is it necessary for one people to dissolve the political bands that connect it to another? Phrase your answer in the form of a Declaration.

4. Look in the Constitution for an example of each of the following:
   a)   A check or balance.
   b)   A reference to black people as being worth exactly three-fifths of white people.
   c)   The word "erection."
   d)   The part that keeps Arnold Schwarzenegger from becoming President.

5. Look in the Bill of Rights for the Amendment that makes specific reference to each of the following:
   a)   Affirmative action.
   b)   Partial-birth abortions.
   c)   Yelling "Fire!" in a crowded theater.
   d)   The homosexual agenda.
   e)   Arnold Schwarzenegger can now run for President.

6. Females and African Americans were excluded from the new government. Why didn't the Womyn's Center and the Multicultural Center organize a teach-in?

7. Thirteen colonies? That's bad luck. Who was the colony wizard who came up with that one?

Extra Credit:

Put the following amendments in order:
   5th Amendment
   2nd Amendment
   9th Amendment
   6th Amendment
   1st Amendment
   3rd Amendment
   7th Amendment
   10th Amendment
   4th Amendment
   8th Amendment

Classroom Activities

1. Found a country.

2. Make your own three-cornered hat out of whalebone, fine English felt, delicate imported lace, and a solution of mercury or other stiffening chemicals.

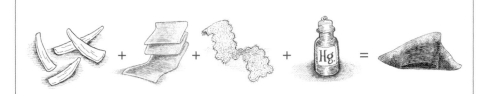

3. John Adams once said in reference to Thomas Paine, "Without the pen of Paine, the sword of Washington would have been wielded in vain." Make a diorama of John Adams saying this!

4. Tell your students about the Liberty Bell and its significance as a symbol of our independence. Then give each student a hammer and have them smash a bell. Make sure they really wail on it – the more broken the bell, the more the student loves freedom.

5. Independence Hall is steaming hot! Help constitutional delegate Charles Cotesworth Pinckney open a window, but watch out for trouble!

"[expletive deleted]"

— *Richard M. Nixon*

Chapter 3

The President: King of Democracy

The lights dim. The voice of God is heard over the loudspeaker. "Ladies and Gentlemen…The President of the United States of America." The crowd leaps to its feet as the tall, handsome, slightly graying-at-the-temples Ivy League graduate strides confidently to the dais, urged on by thunderous applause and the giddy strains of "Hail to the Chief." Born the humble son of salt-of-the-earth, quadriplegic immigrants, he has just been elected the most powerful man in the world. Yet in just four to eight years, you will be able to book him to speak in front of your Rotary Club or at a library opening. He will cost less than J. Lo. This is the magic of the presidency. Anyone can grow up to be president…but no one can stay.

The President of the United States is the most powerful, most recognizable, and best person on earth. As **Commander-in-Chief** of the world's only remaining superpower,[1] he wields enormous influence over global affairs. Indeed, if America is "the world's policeman," the president is the gruff-but-lovable police chief in charge of enforcing the law from his comfortable perch above it. Domestically, the president's agenda provides the nation with its economic, social, and moral compass (Fig. 3.1). Add to this a bewildering array of duties ranging from "giv[ing] to the Congress information of the State of the Union" to "feign[ing] enthusiasm for the visiting NCAA Women's Basketball champions," and you will still only begin to get a sense of the constitutionally mandated clusterfuck that is the modern presidency.

>>Fig. 3.2

Each incoming president has the above seal branded on his upper right shoulder upon taking office. It is said that those who cry during the branding are fated to be one-termers.

>>Fig. 3.1

Before the invention of the moral compass in 1907, Presidents had to rely on the crude and unreliable "moral sextant."

---

[1] Unless you count the Chinese, but at this point, *nobody* can count the Chinese.

"Every day brings the president that much closer to the time he will turn on the TV to see someone else's face burned in effigy outside a foreign embassy."

The man who holds this most exalted office does so not by birthright, but by merit. This notion has inspired children throughout the nation to dream that one day, if they worked hard enough, they too could become President of the United States. And even though all but 43 of those children would see that dream die and thus be forced to find satisfaction in some bullshit, low-level sales job a monkey could do...that's beside the point. We can all agree, dreaming is fun.

Once in office, the president becomes acutely aware he is temporary steward of a permanent position. The 22nd Amendment – passed in the wake of the Depression-ending, World War II-winning nightmare that was the Roosevelt Administration (Fig 3.3) – means the president has no more than eight years, and possibly as little as one month,[2] to put his stamp on the office. Every day brings the president that much closer to the time he will turn on the TV to see someone else's face burned in effigy outside a foreign embassy.

>>Fig. 3.3

We let a cripple be President? A cripple?!?

The moment, as you can imagine, is bittersweet.

Inventing the Presidency: Who's the Boss?

As outlined by the Founders in Article II of the Constitution, the office of the presidency is a masterwork of political compromise. It was devised as a leadership position incorporating the benefits of a strong central authority figure (i.e., accountability and protection) while avoiding the pitfalls (i.e., "I now proclaim myself Supreme Leader of The United States of Myselfia. Commence with the killing of the redheads"). The president would be the nation's chief administrator, a powerful executive with com-

(Continue on page 40)

[2] Assuming the jackass plans on delivering an hour-and-forty-minute inaugural address outside in a blinding snowstorm, then succumbing to pneumonia. (See Boorstin, Daniel, *William Henry Harrison: Idiot of Tippecanoe*, Viking Press, 1973.)

The Vice President:
A Heartbeat Away from Relevance

One of the White House's most enduring traditions is the Vice-Presidential Welcome Letter, left in the Vice President's desk by each administration's outgoing second-in-command. Its purpose: to explain to the new Vice President exactly what it is he or she will be doing over the next four to eight years. It is published for the first time ever here.

Hello Vice President _____,

If you are reading this letter you've just been elected Vice President. That means your most vital job is already done, namely, "balancing the ticket." Congratulations on being from a region geographically disparate from that of the President. Well done!

Now begins your term of duty. The hard work is about to begin. Are you sitting down? Good. That's it. Is there a clock nearby? Look at it. You will come to know it well, for its glacially turning second hand marks the excruciating march to the end of your meaningless days in this office.

Don't get too comfortable. Constitutionally speaking you are the President of the Senate and may therefore be called upon to cast a tie-breaking Senate vote. Don't worry though. It probably won't happen and if they need you, they'll call.

So that's about it. The liquor cabinet is usually fully stocked. Go ahead, fix yourself a stiff one. There's no reason why you shouldn't spend the better part of your days in a drunken stupor. Just remember, shave for the State of the Union. You have to sit behind the President for that one.

Sincerely,

P.S.. One other thing: You must be prepared to take over at a moment's notice if the Commander-in-Chief should be unable to serve. Just a heads up there.

Ranking the Presidents

One of the most time-honored hobbies amongst presidential historians is ordering the presidents based on various criteria. They do this because they are physically weak and can pass it off as "sport." Below, a sampling of just a few of the most well-known presidential rankings.

Presidents Who Lost the Popular Vote

John Quincy Adams
Rutherford B. Hayes
Benjamin Harrison
George W. Bush

(Interestingly, the phrase "Sore Loserman" originated with the Hayes election, in which Hayes lost the popular vote to Samuel Loserman Tilden.)

Our Gayest President

Grover Cleveland (2nd term)

When Cleveland returned to the White House at the height of the "Gay Nineties," it was after defeating Benjamin Harrison in a debate with shrieks of "Oh, listen to her!"

Our Whitest Presidents

1. George H.W. Bush *
2. Dwight D. Eisenhower #
3. George W. Bush †
4. John Q. Adams ††
5. John Adams ß

** tied with Washington, Jefferson, Monroe, Madison, Jackson, Van Buren;*
 # tied with W.H. Harrison, Tyler, Polk, Fillmore, Taylor, Pierce;
† tied with Buchanan, A. Johnson, Lincoln, Grant, Hayes, Garfield, Arthur, Cleveland (2nd term);
†† tied with Cleveland (1st term), B. Harrison, McKinley, F.D. Roosevelt, T. Roosevelt, Taft;
ß tied with Wilson, Harding, Coolidge, Hoover, Truman, Kennedy, L.B. Johnson, Nixon, Ford, Carter, Reagan, Clinton

Our Fattest Presidents

1. Harry S. Truman ‡
2. William H. Taft
3. Grover Cleveland
4. Chester Arthur
5. Zachary Taylor

‡ Though appearing fit in most photographs, President Truman tipped the scales at 360 pounds. He disguised his girth by always standing next to his wife Bess, who weighed in at more than 400.

Most Alphabetical Presidents

1. John Adams
2. John Quincy Adams
3. Chester Arthur
4. James Buchanan
5. George H.W. Bush
6. George W. Bush

As this list clearly shows, some fathers like to cruelly saddle their sons with middle names that appear later in the alphabet than their own.

Our Most Kennedyesque Presidents

1. William Clinton
2. Theodore Roosevelt
3. John F. Kennedy
4. Franklin Pierce
5. Thomas Jefferson

Fun fact: John F. Kennedy actually got to meet the young Bill Clinton when Kennedy was just 44 years old.

Though Ronald Reagan (1980-1989) was not considered Kennedyesque, many historians believe he was among our most Reaganesque commanders-in-chief.

Most Celebrated Facial Hair

1. Chester Arthur
2. Martin Van Buren
3. Abraham Lincoln
4. Rutherford B. Hayes
5. Jimmy Carter

1.
2.
3.
4.
5.

Only President Murdered by the CIA

~~has name blacked out~~

Warren G. Harding: Our Worst President

By Stephen Colbert

Historians debate feverishly over who is the best president in American history. However, there is little disagreement over who was the worst. His name was Warren G. Harding (1921-1923), and he sucked.

The reasons why he sucked are many and, to be truthful, have been widely catalogued in the annals of presidential history. So, with your indulgence, I'd like to focus instead on the intensity of his sucking.

Warren G. Harding was a worthless piece of shit. Fuck him. His presidency was a taint, not just in the sense of a "stain on the office," but literally a taint – the anatomical area between the anus and the testicles.

I hate Warren G. Harding.

Stephen Colbert is the Arthur Schlesinger Professor of American Studies at Harvard University.

(Continued from page 36)

>>Fig. 3.4

19th-century presidents traveled in a customized hansom carriage known as Stagecoach One.

Were You Aware?

William McKinley was our first African-American president. If this were true, it would have been an incredible achievement for all African-Americans.

"Why no women, blacks, or non-Christians have answered the Founders' challenge is a mystery, though most indications point to some inherent genetic flaw."

mand of the armed forces, bound by the rule of law to peacefully relinquish the job after his term. Room and board, a good salary and license to rape and pillage[4] were but a few perks of the office. Years later he would get his own plane.

By far the most revolutionary aspect of this new position would be who could hold it. The short answer: just about anyone. By placing no explicit race, gender, or religious requirement on the presidency, the Founders opened the door to true meritocracy. Why no women, blacks, or non-Christians have answered the Founders' challenge is a mystery, though most indications point to some inherent genetic flaw. (William Howard Taft came closest, having what most observers agreed were boobs.)

The Founders did see fit to place three small requirements on who could be president…technicalities, really.

1. *You must be a native citizen of the United States.* Very important. Imagine having fought for years to win your independence from England only to have King George get on the ballot and win. Very embarrassing.

2. *You must have been 14 years a resident within the United States.* Self-explanatory. Fifteen years is an inordinately long residence requirement to ask of candidates, and 13 years…please. Thirteen? Get fucking serious.

3. *You must be at least 35 years old.* Though one would think this was to ensure people seeking the office had the requisite experience and wisdom, in reality the clause again safeguarded against tyranny. The average life span in colonial times was 41.3, so with 35 as the minimum, even a brutal tyrant

---

[4] Later rescinded.

would have only five, seven years tops before gout, cholera, and/or syphilis re-democratized the nation.

The only other criterion considered was height. The debate over this proposal consisted mostly of Thomas Jefferson holding a stick over James Madison's head and shouting, "You must be this tall to be president." The vote on the motion was ultimately postponed due to "tears...tiny, tiny tears."

The Modern Presidency: The Oval Empire

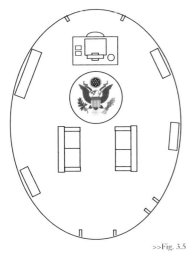
>>Fig. 3.5

The Oval Office. Because it has no corners, there is nowhere to make the president sit when he has shamed the nation.

Conceived as an executive with limited power who needs the approval of Congress to so much as take a shit, the office of the presidency has expanded over time.[5] While our first president, George Washington, summed up his initially modest expectations for the new job in a Farewell Address entitled *I Only Took the Job for the Poontang,*[6] the last two centuries have seen the president's role in government grow tremendously. Indeed, over the past 50 years, the office has frequently been accused of overstepping the boundaries set forth for it in the Constitution.[7] That's why many presidents think of the Constitution as, in the words of John Adams during 1798's signing of the Alien and Sedition Acts, "a decent jumping off point."

(Continue on page 44)

[5] This is equally true of the actual "office" of the presidency, which until 1894 was a walk-in closet at the back of the Library of Congress.
[6] Poontang, of course, was a colonial delicacy consisting of the fermented juice of the rare poonberry tree.
[7] For example, look in *The Encyclopedia Britannica* under "Nixon, Richard, entire presidency of."

Year One

The Game of the Presidency!

Take a break from reading this thoughtful, instructive tome and play this game. Use coins as pieces – they already have presidents on them. As for rules, like the presidency, make 'em up as you go! (Dice not included.)

Start presidency!

Upstaged at inauguration by high-profile celebrity. Lose 3 approval points.

Press honeymoon. Come in late, cut out early, and during the day? Minesweeper. Gain 10 approval points.

Post-Presidency

Third State of the Union Challenge! Deliver entire address without using words "brave," "jobs," "homeland," "growth," "God," "bless," or "America."

Optimistic press release on economy ineffective. Spin again.

"Happy Biiiiirthday, Mr. President!" Move ahead 1 space or fuck other player.

War dragging on a tad. Lose 5 approval points.

Revealed: Supreme Court nominee voted "White Power Man of the Year 1986." Lose 10 approval points.

Goodwill Tour Segment

"Jesus, how many 'Welcome Dances' does Burundi have?" Lose 1 turn for each dance endured.

Nod solemnly at site of centuries-old battle you've never heard of. Gain 5 approval points.

Mix up names of host countries. Move back 2 spaces.

Year Four

State dinner interrupted by loutish boor (played by Rodney Dangerfield). Go back 2 spaces.

Office of the president lampooned by mock "board game" in subversive publication. Gain 5 "meta" points.

Of *course* people will notice the president dyed his hair "Sandstorm Dusk." Submit to ridicule by other players.

Impeachment Alley

Write best-selling memoir.

Come to grips with shame of disappointing nation.

Self-imposed exile at country estate.

Cover Up

Pick another player as a fall guy. They lose 20 approval points.

Up all night shredding documents. Lose a turn.

Scandal

Tearful mea culpa airs after *Will & Grace.* Lose 5 approval points.

WEDGIEGATE: CNN cameras catch you in undersized jogging shorts. Lose 10 approval points.

Marvin Gardens. Rent $260.

War!

Add 40 approval points.

Daughter busted for DWI. Lose 3 approval points.

You are lampooned in *Doonesbury.* Nothing happens.

Second State of the Union. Deliver speech to other players blaming predecessor for nation's problems.

Shed tears at Martin Luther King Jr. remembrance. Gain 10 approval points.

Year Three

Private screening of latest Tom Clancy adaptation. Move ahead 1 space.

First 100 days in office. Other players criticize you for 15 minutes.

Gun lobby really wishes you'd reconsider signing that bill. Add 5 million to reelection fund.

Brother goes on 3-day meth binge. Distance self 3 spaces.

Grant frat buddy rights to build chemical plant next to Grand Canyon. Lose 5 approval points.

Harbor fantasy your policies affect stock market. Move ahead 1 space.

Post-Presidency

Golf!

"Election Day"

Flip a coin. Heads, you win! Start over, old and not much wiser. Tails, return to Lame Duck Lane.

"No new taxes" campaign pledge may have been a bit hasty. Lose 15 approval points.

First State of the Union. Have other players stand and applaud you 37 times.

At African Trade Summit, hang out with Bono. Move ahead 3 spaces. On second thought, move back 2.

Come in late, cut out early, and during the day? Minesweeper. Gain 10 approval points.

Misplaced decimal works out in your favor at $100,000 a plate fundraising dinner. Move ahead 1 space.

Make plans for presidential library: Microfilm or Microfiche? Lose 1 turn.

Remind speech-writers to remind everyone how great you are. Gain 10 approval points.

Lame Duck Lane

Just for kicks, hold press conference in fright wig. Gain 5 approval points.

Stock up on Wite-Out to update election year on old campaign signage.

"Summer of the Shark" coverage diverts attention from nature preserve oil-drilling measure. Move ahead 3 spaces.

Year Two

Re-election Plans

New mistress! Add 1 pink peg.

Big break! Whistle-blower commits "suicide." Move ahead 2 spaces.

Nice try! Exposed by the *NY Times.* Advance to Impeachment Alley.

State senators not returning phone calls. Lose 10 approval points.

Lose respect of the electorate. Advance to "Lame Duck Lane."

Mideast Peace Plan fails. Add 5 approval points for effort.

Wait, we're still at war? Bo-ring! Lose 20 approval points.

Fourth State of the Union: Take credit for delayed positive effects of predecessor's policies.

Natural disaster in Kansas. Lose a turn for perfunctory sympathy visit.

Oops! Child left behind. Go back 2 spaces.

Third-world coup you authorized was successful! Move ahead 2 spaces.

Assassination attempt!

Flip a coin. Heads you survive and gain 10 approval points; tails you die, with 100% approval rating.

Christmas Tree Lighting with Oak Ridge Boys. Quit game now.

Midterm elections! Lose control of both House and Senate. Move 3 spaces toward center.

Submit balanced budget to Congress that reduces deficit while funding both defense and health care. Just kidding. Roll again.

National Security

The president is commander-in-chief of the armed forces, a power vested in him whether he is a veteran of the military (Washington, Grant, Eisenhower, Kennedy, Bush Sr.) or a veteran of running away from the military (Clinton, Bush Jr.). Though many presidents have been humbled by this responsibility—Washington famously cautioned against its use in "foreign entanglements"—others viewed it as a muscle needing exercise to avoid atrophy. President Ronald Reagan invaded Grenada, a country with a drink bead-based economy.

"President Ronald Reagan invaded Grenada, a country with a drink bead-based economy."

>>Fig. 3.6

The president's most awesome responsibility is the power to press this button, which launches both the world's largest nuclear arsenal and a free play of Q-Bert.

Control of the armed forces is arguably the most important power entrusted to the president. The Constitution keeps him from abusing it by making him unable to declare war without the expressed written consent of Congress and, if possible, Major League Baseball. This provision was intended to prevent what the framers called "an impulse war."[8] It is a foolproof check on the president's power, as the only way to circumvent it would be citing "proof" of an "imminent threat" to convince Congress to grant him broader power through an ambiguously worded resolution.[9]

Or, if he called the war a "police action."[10]

Or if he didn't tell anybody.[11]

The president can also negotiate **treaties**, which is considered as vital a task as commanding the armed forces, but nowhere near as fun. Some presidents have proven abler negotiators than others; both Franklin and Theodore

---

[8] Remembering that the Hundred Years War began when Edward III claimed Philip VI of Valois had "cut him off" at Crécy.

[9] A laughable and unlikely scenario.

[10] Vietnam, Haiti, Kosovo, Grenada, Panama, and about 20 others.

[11] Nicaragua, Chile and Cana-…we've said too much.

Roosevelt showed themselves masters of the delicate art of diplomacy, while it was widely known Franklin Pierce couldn't treaty his way out of a paper bag.

Legislative Power

Though the president is very powerful, **he cannot make laws**.

The president can suggest laws. The president can call individual congressmen and threaten, beg and cajole them to make laws. The president can use the bully pulpit and appeal directly to the people to ask Congress to make laws. The president can promise that if these congressmen pass the laws the president likes he will make them a delicious sandwich. The president can hold his breath and pound his fists and threaten to run away. But the president cannot make laws.

>>Fig. 3.7

The president's signature is required for a bill to become law. In 1903, the Presidential Quill was replaced by the Presidential Fountain Pen, which in turn was replaced by the Presidential Fuzzy Troll Pen in 1966. President Nixon used this Fuzzy Troll to sign the SALT I Treaty in 1972.

The president can observe a vexing situation that seems to run counter to common sense, shake his head, and say aloud, "There oughta be a law," but the president cannot make that law. The president cannot even write up that law and submit it with his name on it. The president needs someone in Congress to submit it for him.

The president can only sit in his office and sign or not sign laws other people make. Sometimes this makes the president feel like a total pussy. Then the president realizes he is commander-in-chief of the armed forces and an island country is about to get a can of "police action" opened up on them. This makes the president feel better.

Were You Aware?

The office of president affords its holder many, many opportunities to have sex with women who would otherwise find him unremarkable.

(Continue on page 48)

The Cabinet: Yes-Men of Freedom

No president can execute his agenda alone, though James K. Polk tried and it nearly killed him after 13 days. Instead, the president assembles a crack team of racially and ethnically diverse experts to head up various departments within the federal bureaucracy. They are collectively known as the Cabinet, so naturally they sit around a giant conference table.

Secretary of Energy

Responsible for "getting this party started." Leads Cabinet in cheers, trust exercises, and rainy-day games. Never shows up without *Jock Jams Vol. 1* CD.

Director of Homeland Security

Came up with color-coded "terror" chart in 2002. Hasn't done jackshit since.

Secretary of State

Shakes hands with important people, then attempts to get those people to shake hands with each other. Applicants must supply their own American flag lapel pin. Must also learn phrase "Please, Your Excellency, the president didn't mean that" in 125 different languages.

Bowl of Jellybeans

Secretary of Defense

During diplomatic crises, initiates chant of "Fight! Fight! Fight!" Also, in charge of kicking sand in face of secretary of state.

Secretary of Treasury

Duties primarily concerned with, but not necessarily "all about," the Benjamins.

Attorney General

Nation's top law enforcement official; directly oversees bungled shootouts, standoffs gone amok. Also curious about what you've checked out of the library. (*Understanding Islam*...how interesting.)

Secretary of the Interior

In charge of nation's rich inner life. Divisions under his or her calm, watchful gaze include the Bureau of Contemplation and Federal Office of Feelings Management. Also, responsible for dismantling National Park System.

Secretary of Education

Charged with keeping our educational system among the world's best, using budgetary equivalent of one F-16 Tomahawk fighter jet. Often corrects other Cabinet members with the phrase, "You mean 'The president and *I*…'"

Tab Machine

Last remaining Tab Soda machine in Western Hemisphere.

Video Uplink

For receiving ransom demands from super villains.

Secretary of Agriculture

Monitors safety and quality of meat, eggs, and poultry. After that, it gets a little boring.

Bowl of Chex Mix

Secretary of Health and Human Services

Regulates Food and Drug Administration, which is responsible for second half of prescription drug commercials (the parts about nausea and diarrhea). Good place to plug in another minority.

Secretary of Transportation

Driven a car before? Seen an airplane? Hispanic? Good—put on this tie.

National Security Adviser

Advises president on national security. Pretty straightforward, really.

Sansevieria trifasciata

Sansevieria trifasciata—also known as common snake plant. Needs only occasional water, sunlight. Excellent secret-microphone camouflage.

Powers of Appointment

Yet another power the president enjoys is that of appointment. Ambassadors, judges, members of his Cabinet—you name 'em, he names 'em. Said President Martin Van Buren of this power: "Thanks, that completely makes up for not being able to make laws."

Typically, **Cabinet** appointments make up a new president's second order of business, right after calling up everyone he knows and passive-aggressively saying, "What's new with me? I don't know, not much...oh, I'M THE PRESIDENT OF THE UNITED STATES!" Then comes naming the Cabinet, which upon swearing-in assumes the day-to-day functions of government so the president can go have fun. (Presidents don't like to do very much work.) The president usually obtains speedy congressional approval of his Cabinet, unless he has a particularly contentious relationship with Congress. Then Cabinet nominees are picked off one by one for various offenses ranging from "tax law technicality" to rumored connections with white power/black power/gayness. It is a process called "vetting," and it keeps the Cabinet from becoming dangerously skilled. Most members of a president's Cabinet later admit the job was not worth the book deal (see diagram on pages 46-47).

The president's next power of appointment concerns **federal judgeships**. Most such appointments occur at levels of the judiciary with which the public is unfamiliar. But sometimes, if a president is truly fortunate, a Supreme Court justice retires or dies on his watch. This gives the president a chance to appoint to a lifetime term on the highest court in the land the craziest motherfucker he can sneak past Congress. Typically these appointees are jurists whose opinions run the ideological gamut from the right ("Jesus says retarded gays must be put to death") to the left ("Man-on-pumpkin sex is an inalienable right and should be taught to children"). Any Supreme Court nominee whose opinion falls in between is deemed ideologically unreliable and his nomination is killed in committee.

As for **ambassadors**, they are widely considered the least important of the presidential appointments. In the 228 years since the founding of the

>>Fig. 3.8

A good ambassador knows the little fork is for salad.

nation, no one has ever asked what they are doing. Often, the president will even write the names of potential ambassadors on scraps of paper and let his dog pick out where they are going, just to keep things fun.[12] Ambassadors tend to be donors and friends of the president who subsequently receive assignments in exotic locales with few, if any, sexual taboos. Run afoul of the chief executive, however, and you can also receive an ambassadorship. These posts are less desirable and often require vaccinations. A four-year stint as chargé d'affaires to Lower Asscrackylvania usually resolves any issue the president may have had with you.

Miscellaneous Duties/Perks

The office does entail a few other privileges and tasks worth noting:

- Every first Monday of the month the president must bring donuts to the Cabinet meeting.
- The president holds season tickets to all San Jose Sharks home games, including the playoffs.
- He can have gay sex "on the down-low" and still not be gay.
- When ordering Mexican, free guac.
- Whenever he wants, the president can go to the White House kitchen and eat all the chocolate out of the Neapolitan ice cream, leaving only vanilla and strawberry.
- He must begin every sentence with the words "My fellow Americans" or it doesn't count.

>>Fig. 3.9

The President of the United States of America knows this guy who can totally hook you up with San Jose Sharks tickets.

Quoting the President

On Honesty

"He who permits himself to tell a lie once, finds it much easier to do it a second and third time, till at length it becomes habitual."
— *Thomas Jefferson, August 19, 1785*

"Martha, when I tell you I was helping Ms. Hemings move her bed against the wall, I mean precisely that."
— *Thomas Jefferson, August 20, 1785*

---

[12] This seems as good a time as any to point out that the president, by law, must have a dog. The First Dog wields approximately the same power over other dogs as the president does over humans.

Quoting the President

On Illegal Drugs

"When I was in England I experimented with marijuana a time or two, and I didn't like it, and I didn't inhale, and I never tried it again."
— President William Jefferson Clinton, 1992, New York Democratic televised debate

"Put another brick in my hookah, Chow Ming, and fetch me fresh silks, I've soiled myself again."
— Franklin Pierce, April 6, 1856

"Today's president is loved and hated the world over. Even the world's stupidest schoolchildren can name him, while the nerdiest can name all of them in less than 30 seconds."

■ For his first year in office, he is required to drop and give 20 push-ups whenever any previous president demands it.

■ He has full access to the West Wing jacuzzi, but must turn his key at the same time as the chairman of the Joint Chiefs of Staff to activate the jets.

■ He can have his pick of up to, but no more than, seven of *People Magazine*'s "50 Most Beautiful People."

So There You Have It

The history of the presidency is a history of growth and expansion directly mirroring that of the United States itself. Even as visionary a group as the Founding Fathers could not have foreseen the office evolving from its modest goal of "national manager" to "Leader of the Free World." But that's just what the gig has become. Today's president is loved and hated the world over. Even the stupidest schoolchildren can name him, while the nerdiest can name all of them in less than 30 seconds.[13] Presidents have been assassinated, lionized, impeached, mocked, shaved, and fellated. Like it or not, more so than any other figure in our nation, the president embodies America. And one day, you could be him.

But not really. ⊘

---

[13] As for the world's "poorest" schoolchildren, they just wish he'd throw them a bone.

If I Were President

By Ed Helms

My fellow Americans: If I, Ed Helms, were president, I would serve the country I love by making things better, not worse.

For instance, health insurance. I believe every American should have health insurance, so I would write a law giving it to them - and then I'd sign it right away. I also don't think people should have to struggle to make ends meet, so I would fix the economy.

Now, it's no secret the Israeli-Palestinian crisis has been going on for months. I would get them together and let them talk. Why hasn't anyone done that yet? Sometimes, the simplest solution is the best one.

The president is also the nation's moral leader. I don't really know how I'd play this one.

If I were president, I would end the unfair taxation on tax the people already pay. It's called double taxation and it's totally unfair. Right now Uncle Sam collects 35 cents on every dollar I make. I'd change the law so I could write that off, and only pay tax on the remaining 65 cents. At a thirty-five-percent rate, that would leave me with 42 cents.

Wait, actually, that's less. I worked this out the other day...can I get back to you on the tax thing?

And what's the Department of Labor for? Here's a shocking fact I once heard: No one knows! If I were president, it would be gone. Unless there's something I'm not seeing here.

Also, I would order the immediate death of Roger Simpson. The one who lives at 1310 North Seventh Ave., Apt. 12A, Oroville, CA. He knows why.

Okay. That about does it. Oh, one more thing. In a Helms Administration, Air Force One would officially be renamed Air Force Fun.

I feel very strongly about this.

Ed Helms was the Prime Minister of New Zealand from 1994 to 1996.

Quoting the President

Last Words

"Good thing these tickets were free, Major Rathbone. This play su—"
— *Abraham Lincoln, April 14, 1865*

"Bury me next to my wife. But nothing too fancy."
— *Ulysses S. Grant, July 23, 1885*

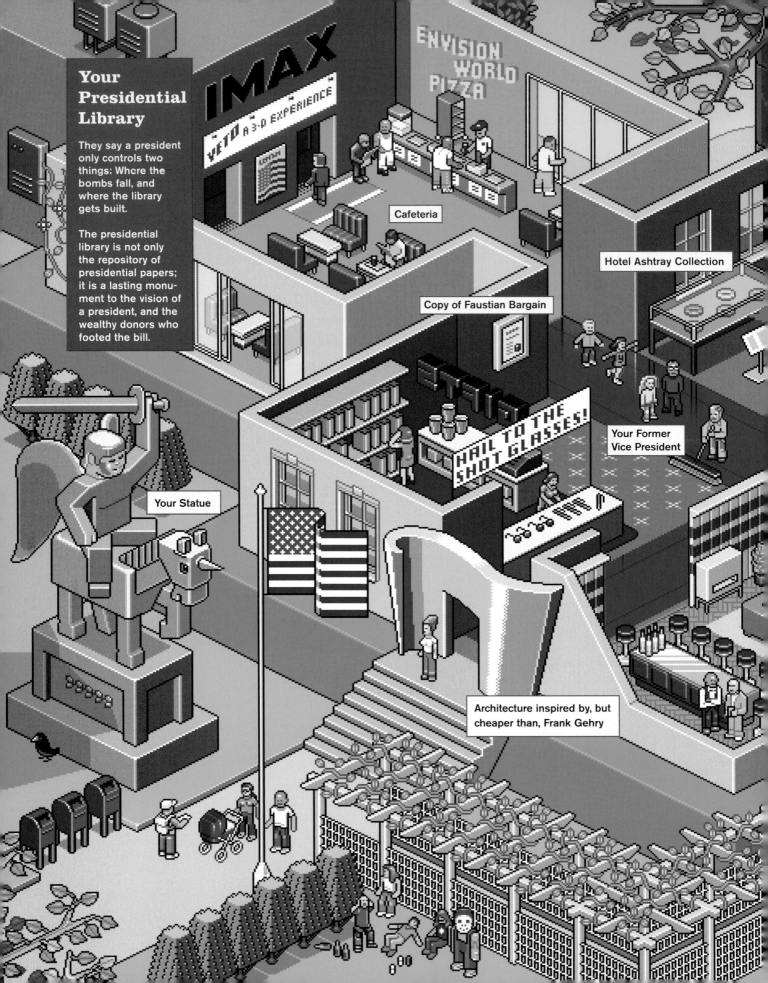

Your Presidential Library

They say a president only controls two things: Where the bombs fall, and where the library gets built.

The presidential library is not only the repository of presidential papers; it is a lasting monument to the vision of a president, and the wealthy donors who footed the bill.

IMAX

VETO A 3-D EXPERIENCE

ENVISION WORLD PIZZA

Cafeteria

Hotel Ashtray Collection

Copy of Faustian Bargain

HAIL TO THE SHOT GLASSES!

Your Former Vice President

Your Statue

Architecture inspired by, but cheaper than, Frank Gehry

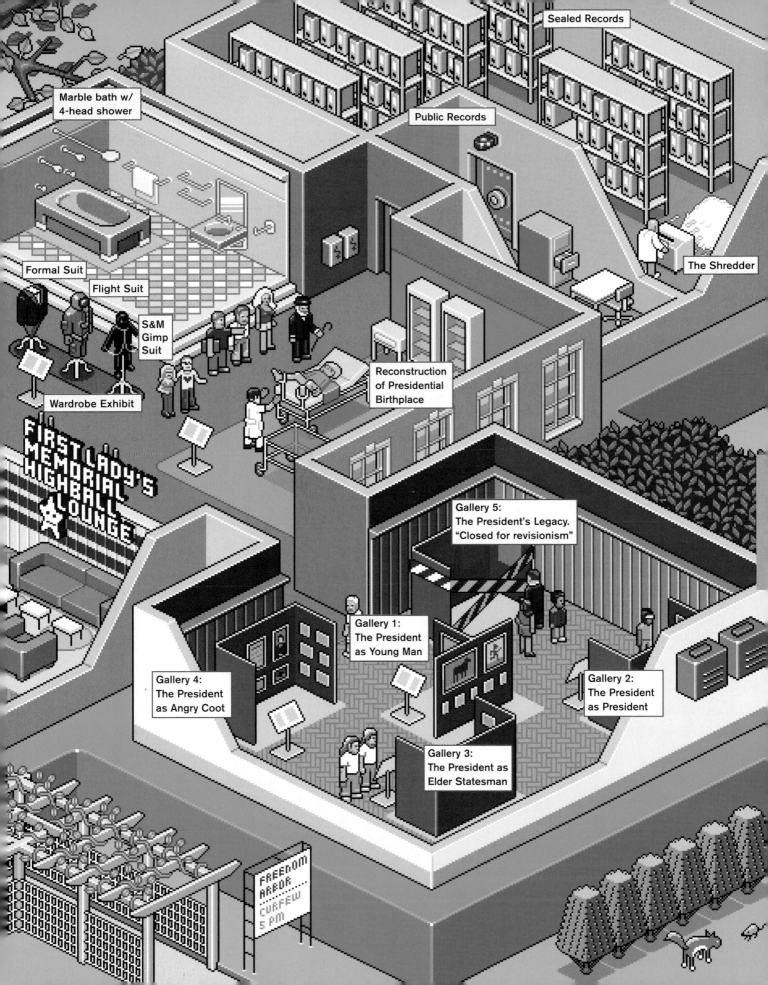

Presidential Nicknames

In light of their unlimited power, it's easy to forget that many presidents are human beings. So Americans like to bestow monikers on their Commanders-in-Chief to feel like they know them, even though in reality the president has a veritable army of people to keep regular "Americans" the hell away from him. But where do these familiar, or "nick," names come from?

"Mr. Norris"

Millard Fillmore

Fillmore, our 13th president, lived for eighteen years with a pair of magical talking cats, who for reasons known only to them insisted on calling their human master "Mr. Norris." Denise, the female of the pair, was also influential in the foreign policy of the Fillmore Administration, a period later dubbed by historians as "The Era of the President Who Was Batshit Insane."

Fillmore with Huey and Denise, twin architects of the Gadsden Purchase.

"Silent Cal"

Calvin Coolidge

Coolidge still ranks as the quietest president of all time. Famously, a woman once approached him, saying, "I bet my friend I could get you to say more than two words," to which Coolidge wittily replied, "Fuck you."

"The Great Emancipator"

Abraham Lincoln

Contrary to popular belief, Lincoln's nickname had nothing to do with the Emancipation Proclamation he signed in 1863. Rather, the name was given to him by high school classmates who took note of the gangly teen's penchant for getting stuck in, and then extricating himself from, difficult situations and spaces.

An 1854 lithograph depicts the young Lincoln before his "emancipation" from a bear trap.

"Tricky Dick"

Richard Nixon

Richard Nixon was regarded as an agile and "tricky" political opponent. Also, he was a dick.

"The Gipper"

Ronald Reagan

Though noted for his status as a conservative idealogue and effective communicator, Reagan was perhaps best known for his constant and exuberant gipping.

Discussion Questions

1. Who was your favorite American president? Why?

2. Surely somebody can name their favorite president.

3. OK, how about any president?

4. No?

5. Come on, people. We just did an entire unit on this.

6. No one in this class can name one single president?

7. Fuck it, man.

8. Does anybody have a light?

Come on, you don't know who this is? It's FDR! Jesus Christ!

Classroom Activities

1. Give each student a blue index card with the word "Veto" written on it. Explain that this may be redeemed to prevent any one classroom event (a quiz, a reading assignment) from happening. See how much shit gets done in the next month.

2. Determine a succession plan should you be assassinated.

3. Have the entire class write to the president in the style of letters to *Penthouse Forum.* Make sure each letter commences with the phrase, "I never thought this would happen to me, but…"

4. Make the Ford Administration come alive by making your very own WIN (Whip Inflation Now) buttons.

The first letter of each word combines to form a new word. What is it? (Hint: It's not what Gerald Ford did in 1976.)

Take the Presidential Pet Challenge!

You've already read about Millard Fillmore and the special relationship he had with his pet cats, Huey and Denise. (See p. 54.) But did you know nearly every president in U.S. history has had at least one pet? Match the president with his animal companion.

A. Richard Nixon
B. Theodore Roosevelt
C. Zachary Taylor
D. Martin Van Buren
E. Gerald Ford
F. Bill Clinton
G. Andrew Johnson

1. Old Fluff and Ready

2. Martin Van Goldfish

3. Kissinger

4. Buddy

5. The heads of many pets

6. Herpes Simplex 2

7. Owie, the inconveniently placed pipe

Answer Key: A–3, B–5, C–1, D–2, E–7, F–4, G–6

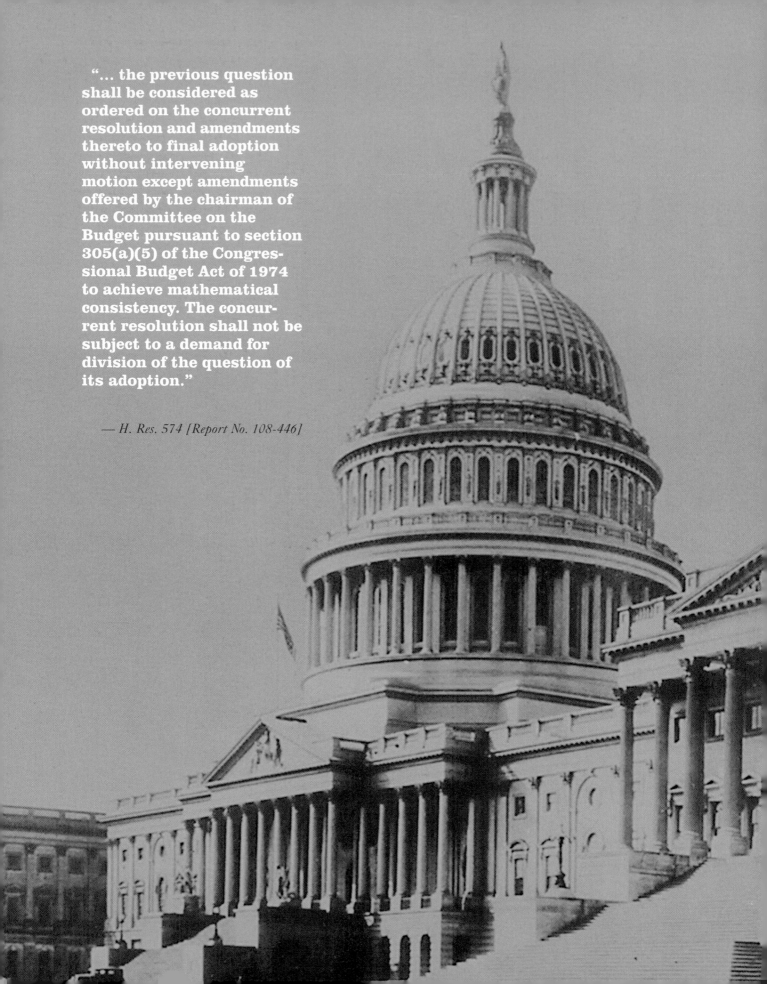

"... the previous question shall be considered as ordered on the concurrent resolution and amendments thereto to final adoption without intervening motion except amendments offered by the chairman of the Committee on the Budget pursuant to section 305(a)(5) of the Congressional Budget Act of 1974 to achieve mathematical consistency. The concurrent resolution shall not be subject to a demand for division of the question of its adoption."

— *H. Res. 574 [Report No. 108-446]*

Chapter 4

Congress: Quagmire of Freedom

If the president is the head of the American body politic, Congress is its gastrointestinal tract. Its vast and convoluted inner workings may be mysterious and unpleasant, but in the end they excrete a great deal of material whose successful passage is crucial to our nation's survival. This is Congress's duty.

To understand the need for a legislative branch in a democracy, we must first acknowledge two central truths:

1. Society needs laws. While anarchy can often turn a humdrum weekend into something unforgettable, eventually the mob must be kept from stealing the conch and killing Piggy. And while it would be nice if that "something" was simple human decency, anybody who has witnessed the "50% Off Wedding Dress Sale" at Filene's Basement knows we need a backup plan – preferably in writing. On the other hand, too many laws can result in outright tyranny, particularly if one of those laws is "Kneel before Zod." Somewhere between these two extremes lies the legislative sweet-spot that produces just the right amount of laws for a well-adjusted society – more than zero, less than fascism.

2. People are busy. *"Gee guys, I'd love to help you make some laws today, but the in-laws are coming this weekend and Jenny is gonna kill me if I don't clean my shit out of the guest bedroom...uh huh...look, I'm sorry. I know this is an important appropriations bill, but I'm telling you, she's still pissed at me for...well fine, don't set aside monies for municipal improvements in district 12, see if I give a fuck."* A dedicated legislative branch is comprised of representatives to do the people's work – giving citizens the freedom to pursue their own lives while still enjoying the benefits of a lawful society...even if they are too whipped to see it.

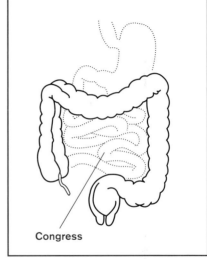

Congress

>>Fig. 4.1

But once empowered, what keeps the legislative body from becoming morbidly obese? Once again, our Constitution provides the healthy diet of checks and balances that keep our government from appearing on the local news, being removed from its bedroom by a crane. Unlike the president with his fancy-pants "electors," the Constitution requires Congressmen to be directly elected by regular-pantsed citizens. Thus, more than any other branch of government, Congress must heed the will of the people. The astute reader may rightly wonder, "But didn't you just say the people were busy?" Touché. This minor glitch in our representative government is rectified by the white knights of democracy—corporations. These altruistic entities hire **lobbyists** whose sole job is to insure, through persuasive argument and financial remuneration, that Congress never forgets the people's wishes. Especially the people's wishes for deregulation.

This model of direct elections by the people for representatives of a law-making body, to be overseen by corporate lobbyists with obscene amounts of cash, has proven so efficient that 96% of congressmen are re-elected.[1] Clearly the system is working. Why else would the same officials be elected over and over and over again? Voter apathy? Entrenchment born of a corrupt system designed to ensure those in power stay in power? Tell it to Castro, Paco! Congress and its remora, the lobbyists, allow Americans to enjoy the benefits of a lawful and functioning society while only having to think about it once every two to four years—if at all! Once again, the Founding Fathers are in line for a shout-out.

The Making of Congress: Hot Bicameral Action

When the Founders sat down to create this new civil order, they had two central truths in mind. One, representative democracy would be the most stable and lasting form of government. Two, when the Constitutional Convention wrapped up, they were all going to be out of work. The latter led to the formulation of what historians would come to know as the

(Continue on page 62)

[1] Or parlay the gig into a lucrative private-sector job with a shadowy Washington consulting firm. Six million of one, half a dozen-million of the other, really.

Would You Mind If I Told You How We Do It in Canada?

By Samantha Bee

Hi again! Sorry—I know you're probably really busy with the rest of the book and everything, but you know, in Canada, we have something *sort of* similar to Congress. Only with far more in the way of ceremonial weaponry.

We call it "Parliament," and it has two chambers, just like your Congress. But instead of electing both houses, we let a representative of the Queen appoint the Senate. We've been meaning to say something about that for the last 150 years, but the right moment hasn't come up.

On the other hand, the House of Commons is directly elected by the populace. Well, kind of. Actually, we have to vote for parties instead of individuals. Only instead of just *two* major parties, we have *four*. I guess you could say Canadians are "party animals!"

Sorry.

Politically speaking, having so many parties makes it harder for anyone to get a majority, and thus, to get anything done. But when we really need

to break a logjam, it's technically possible for a party to win control of Parliament without getting the most votes. Here, let me explain how! First, your party needs at least a plurality in sparsely populated "ridings," or... {*Note: Deleted due to extreme boringness – Ed.*}

One other neat thing about Canada: All governmental business is conducted in both French and English, because a small minority of Canadians, called "Québécois," never wanted to learn English, and we thought it was rude to ask them to. But the good news is, everyone in Canada has to learn French! Though actually, it's not really French, it's a regional patois that actual French people despise.

So there's that.

My point is, when you think about it, Congress and Parliament aren't that different at all. Or are they? I don't mean to be presumptuous.

Again, sorry to interrupt.

A Congressional Glossary

Gerrymander:

The process of reshaping an electoral district so as to maximize the electoral success of one's party.

Example:

*"The district was shrewdly **gerrymandered** so as to disenfranchise Hispanics."*

The Five ~~Most~~ Interesting Moments in Senate History

The Burning of the Capitol

During the War of 1812, British troops occupy Washington, D.C., setting numerous government buildings on fire, including the Capitol. The conflagration prompted a five-hour congressional debate over whether to evacuate the building or burn to death. Ultimately, the Senate voted 21-19 along strict party lines to run for their lives, but only after attaching a rider appropriating additional funds for fort construction in the Oregon Territory.

Since the Sumner Caning incident, the Senate has followed a strict "Wiffle Cane Only" policy.

Arrival of Senator Mr. Smith

Capitol Hill was turned on its ear by the arrival of Jefferson Smith, a wide-eyed, idealistic junior senator whose unerring moral compass inspired his colleagues to re-evaluate their attitudes towards democracy and the American spirit. Smith was later revealed to be not an actual senator, but rather actor Jimmy Stewart performing in the film *Mr. Smith Goes to Washington*. The resulting disillusionment triggered an onset of national cynicism from which America has never recovered. Years later, Eddie Murphy remade the film as *Here Come Mistah Smith*.

| August 24, 1814 | May 22, 1856 | October 17, 1939 |

The sight of the Capitol burning prompted Francis Scott Key to pen his immortal anthem, "The Heat, 'Tis On (On the Streets)."

The Caning of Senator Charles Sumner

In retribution for a speech insulting Southerners for their pro-slavery views, South Carolina Representative Preston Brooks beat Massachusetts Senator Charles Sumner with a metal-topped cane in the Senate chamber. Though rendered unconscious, Sumner miraculously arose and retaliated with his trademark "Sumner Triple Suplex," thereby retaining the Senate Wrestling Federation championship belt.

Despite a soft opening, Frank Capra's noble call to restore dignity to the political process rode good word-of-mouth and strong foreign box-office to better-than-expected DVD sales in the era before back-end participation and points against first-dollar B.O.

The name of Senator Joseph McCarthy (R-WI) became synony-mous with an era, not unlike his colleague, Representative William Pleistocene (D-MN).

April 22, 1954

Army-McCarthy Hearings Begin

The "Red Scare" reached a climax during Senator Joseph McCarthy's tel-evised subcommittee hearings, when Army lawyer Joseph Welch famously asked McCarthy, "Have you no sense of decency, sir?" McCarthy less famously responded, "Indeed I do, sir, only I seem to have left it on your mother's nightstand." And then they broke out the Wiffle Canes.

Strom Thurmond Filibuster

Senator Strom Thurmond (R-SC) set the record for longest filibuster with this 24-hour, 18-minute speech railing against a civil-rights bill. The marathon speaking session left Thurmond so drained, he could barely have sex with the underaged black woman in his family's employ. Thurmond's oration obliterated the previ-ous filibuster record, a 13-hour description by Daniel Webster of the massive dump he just took.

August 28, 1957

The leading segregationist of his day, Thurmond's racist rhetoric so appalled the state of South Carolina it re-elected him to the Senate seven times.

(Continued from page 58)

Madison Hypothesis. "What if," opined the diminutive Virginian, "we created a national legislature copious enough in membership, and curious enough in structure, as to provide the whole of us with a gig for life?" Added Gouverneur Morris (PA), "Verily, should not the designers of this government also be the stewards?" "We deserve a taste," said Barzini, a legitimate craftsman from Rhode Island. "In sooth, we should be able to dip our beaks, know what I'm sayin'?" Barzini then moved that New Jersey's John Witherspoon be kissed on the lips, signalling Witherspoon was now dead to him. That motion died in committee. But the larger point was agreed upon.

With the Founders' employment now secured, it was time to address specifics. What formula would determine the makeup of this legislature? Should the criterion be population with every person[2] equally represented? Or should every state be equally represented? Should black people still count as 3/5ths? Isn't even 5/16ths pushing it? Is it wise to found a new country using fractions at all? And is Franklin serious when he says "No Fat Chicks"?

If representation was calculated by person, states like Rhode Island or Delaware would be routinely voted down by the more populous New York and Virginia. That would be unfair. But if each state had the same number of representatives, states like Rhode Island and Delaware would have the exact same say as New York and Virginia. That would be unfair as well. And speaking of unfair, are those Indians going to be staring at us the whole time we're figuring this out?

The solution: determining representation by a complex equation involving total weight of the populace divided by virgins per square mile. Or so it might have been, had not a last-minute solution of Solomonic wisdom emerged. The baby legislature would be cut in half, creating a unique **bicameral** structure,[3] consisting of two distinct chambers: the Senate, or "Upper House," and House of Representatives, or "Lower House" (Fig. 4.2). One late night session led the Founders to consider the addi-

---

[2] For purposes of this chapter, "person" still means "white males" up until 1870, then "males" until 1920, then "all people but really still just white people" until 1964.

Were You Aware?

The Capitol Rotunda was made famous by the Stephen Baldwin/ Pauly Shore vehicle Bio-Rotunda.

A Congressional Glossary

Whip:
The senator or congressman of either party in charge of promoting party unity and rounding up votes. So named for the instrument used to this day to achieve that end.

Example:
*"Ow! Ow! Ow! The **whip** is whipping me!"*

Senate

House

>>Fig. 4.2

Congress has two chambers.

tion of a third chamber or "Waffle House," though by morning most agreed the idea, seemingly so brilliant at 3 A.M., now seemed stupid.

The **House of Representatives** would be the larger chamber and would directly reflect the nation's diversity. A state's number of representatives would be based on its population and its members would face re-election every two years. These rules established the House as Congress's rough-and-tumble populist forum—though a case could be made it merely created a haven for ideological wackjobs with job security issues. By contrast, the more deliberative **Senate** would be comprised of two men from each state, regardless of size or population. Its members would be richer, better groomed, smarter...their wives hotter. Passing senators would be greeted with respectful salutes and pleasantries such as "'ello, guvn'r!" and "Quite a day for a stroll, no?"—worlds away from the accepted House greetings of "Shoo!" and "Are there congressmen about, or is someone eating a shit sandwich?" Senators would also only face re-election every six years, as it was widely acknowledged they were three times better than congressmen.

The two chambers would be run, respectively, by the **Speaker of the House** and the Senate president *pro tem*.[4] Each chamber would have its own officers, majority and minority leaders, whips, and a sergeant-at-arms. The House would select one member each month as "Employee of the Month." The Senate would hold an annual canned-food drive. The senator who brought the most cans would receive a 10-speed. There would be interchamber dances and "spirit" rallies. Wednesdays, ladies would drink

(Continue on page 66)

---

[3] "Bicameral" literally means "with two cameras," thus cleverly foreshadowing the crappy production values that would one day be seen on C-SPAN.

[4] A Latin phrase meaning "for the tem."

A Congressional Glossary

Caucus

From an Algonquin Indian word meaning "to meet together," an informal congressional organization to discuss issues of concern to a particular group.

Example:

"The plan to drive the Algonquin Indians off their ancestral lands was hammered out in a congressional caucus."

Were You Aware?

Congressman Henry Hyde (R-IL) is our jowliest congressman.

Congressional Rotisserie League Update

Hey there, team captains! Well, there's been a lot of exciting legislative action already in Congress 108, but if past election seasons are any indication, the best bill-writing and vote-casting is still to come. Here's a look at how the teams are doing:

Heading into the homestretch, league leaders Robert's Rulers have both been putting up great numbers thanks to their deep-bench tax-cutting talent. The Rulers' early-year signing **Amo Houghton** (R-NY 31st) is paying off – Amo co-sponsored 42 successful tax reductions this session. And Lonesome Riders' Senate rookie **Saxby Chambliss** (R-GA) looks like a real comer, ballooning-deficit-wise.

The Arch Capitolists have dropped to 3rd, led by **Rep. Tommy DeLay** (R, 22nd District). Everyone knows he's one of the 108th's most powerful hitters. But he's swinging for the fences so much lately that he's striking out more than ever, going just 6 for 25 in recent votes. Ouch! More fundamentals, less funda-mentalism, Tommy. Take a lesson from statemate **Sen. Kay Bailey Hutchinson** (R-TX)– she may not swing as hard, but she gets bills passed and she still got

a nearly perfect 93 ACU (American Conservatives Union) rating.

Lennie's Legislators are having a turn-around Congress, but they have made some adept trades lately– they just picked up **Steve Horn** (R-CA 38th), an experienced, moderate Republican who can hit from either side of an issue. Put him up against a tough social policy issue and he looks just like a Dem. Great to have going into a general election.

And down in the cellar, the Ranking Members are scrambling for more power from the left side. The SM's have been getting competent outings from **Pete DeFazio** (D-OR), but his age is showing, and staff slugger **David Bonior** (D-MI), with 27 years in the House, is running on ideological fumes. What to do? Guys, you've got a state house honey in **Gov. Jennifer Granholm** (D-MI); can anyone say "gerrymander"?

On the Trading Block

Porter Goss (R-FL)– newly available; just got dropped by the PhillieBusters. Goss votes for power, votes for popu-larity, is strong on defense...Not cheap

to sign, but if you've got the cash, he'll give your roster a quick kick...**Tim Ryan** (D-OH)–31-year-old first-termer from Jim Traficant's old district won't do you any good for a couple terms yet, but a solid pick if you are building for the future...**Jennifer Dunn** (R-WA)– was recently rotated off the Select Revenue subcommittee at Ways & Means. Power potential, but only if you've got space to fill.

Notables

Rep. Sonny Callahan (R-AL) raised $50,000 with just three phone calls last week, a career best...**Rep. Ed Pastor** (D-AZ) finagled $14 million more for road improvement over lunch at La Brasserie on Monday. In September, **Sen. John McCain** (R-AZ) was on Larry King for a record 18th time in a calendar month...The Christian Coalition added 2 points to its rating of Honolulu **Rep. Neil Abercrombie** (D-HI), bringing his total to 6 out of a possible 100...**Sen. Zell Miller** (D-GA) extended his streak of giving the same speech at every public event to 29 occasions, raising his on-message percentage (OM%) to a league-leading .890.

Rotisserie 108th Congress
Fantasy delegation league

The Mean Machine (344 - 14 - 1)
(Bills Passed – $BB Pork Appropriated – Indictments)

Position *Committee*	Runs	Votes	Bills Spnsr'd	Amends	Bills Passed	Power %	Pork ($MM)	Media appearances	Georgetown parties	War Chest ($MM)
House	R	V	BS	A	BP	PW	PK	MA	GP	WC
Republican										
Tom DeLay (TX) *Majority Leader*	FR	FR	88	23	43	0.940	62.0	131	3	2.5
Chris Shays (CT) *Gov. Reform*	C	C	45	12	20	0.551	37.9	12	6	0.6
Ray LaHood (IL) *Appropriations*	CR	C	50	21	34	0.408	90.5	4	0	1.2
Billy Tauzin (LA) *Commerce*	C	R	103	80	60	0.775	58.8	45	18	4.5
Democrat										
Maxine Waters (CA) *Judiciary*	FL	FL	20	22	11	0.345	12.8	31	12	0.7
Barney Frank (MA) *Banking*	L	L	33	12	12	0.450	8.7	43	35	1.2
Senate										
Patti Murray (D-WA) *Finance*	CL	L	28	188	16	0.664	104.2	10	7	4.5
Trent Lott (R-MS) *Rules*	R*	FR	37	106	11	0.312	216.0	254	1	9.8

*ran C in early '03, reverted mid-year

Key: C = center, FR = far right, CR = center right,
CL = center left, etc.

PW = (BP+PK+GP)*(MA/100)/(Ethics
violations)

2003/4 Team Stats

		Rank in League
Bills Passed	207	2
Pork	$513.9BB	5
Media	450	1
Total Incumbency	85 yrs	3
Overall Standing		2nd

C-SPAN Drinking Game

C-SPAN was launched in 1979 in response to the massive public demand for more shows featuring agricultural subcommittee hearings, visits to presidential gravesites, and interviews with obscure professors at small liberal-arts colleges. But it has proven unexpectedly popular amongst college students, whose passion for government is exceeded only by their passion for consuming alcohol with a frequency many experts call the crisis of our time. Below are just a few of the drinking games C-SPAN's most dedicated watchers have devised.

Asshole

The partisan rancor in Washington is at an all-time high. While the collegial nature of Congress prevents members from coming right out and calling each other "asshole," senators and representatives constantly say as much in elaborate false displays of courtesy. When a congressman uses a phrase like "with all due respect," "my distinguished colleague," or "what the junior senator from Montana fails to realize…," he is really saying "asshole." Drink.

Quarters

Players must drink every time Congress appropriates an additional quarter-billion dollars.

The Yeas Have It

Players form two teams, the "Yeas" and the "Nays." As a congressional vote is being tallied, players drink each time a new "yea" or "nay" is cast for their respective side. Be warned, this game is only to be played during highly contested votes or sparsely attended sessions. With 435 congressmen, a landslide will lead to alcohol poisoning. (Bonus: Make the other team drink if you can identify the Vivaldi movement playing over voting footage.)

Hi Ted!

Senator Edward Kennedy (D-MA) is one of the lions of the Senate, and as a 42-year veteran chairs several key committees. When the camera cuts away to one of his frequent eye-rolls or "naps," players drink a shot. A wheeze, snort or any form of gaseous emission means the person to your left drinks. If the camera catches Kennedy drinking, players must finish their remaining beer, another beer, then run around pantsless.

Booknotes

Drink heavily through an entire episode of "Booknotes."

Zoom, Schwartz, Kucinich

The name of this elaborate game changed following Dennis Kucinich's (D-OH) 1985 electoral victory over rival Kenneth Profigliano (R-OH).

C-SPAN

(Continued from page 63)

free. The Speaker of the House would also be third in line for the presidency, though as many an ambitious speaker has noted, it's not a very fast-moving line.

A Congressional Glossary

Quorum:

The minimum number of law-makers needed to enact legislation. Similar in concept to the Hebrew minyan (10), the Argentinian tango (2), or the number of people needed for it to officially count as an orgy (6).

The Sausage of Governance: How Laws Are Made

The size and makeup of Congress having been decided, it was time to lawmake! Now, the process of creating and enacting legislation is far too complicated to be covered in a book – even this book, which is ostensibly written by experts and dedicated to doing just that. Interested readers should refer to the definitive work on the subject, *Schoolhouse Rock* (Dorough, 1973), for a more detailed, catchier treatment.

But, put very briefly, a piece of proposed legislation is known as a bill. Each year, members of Congress sponsor thousands of bills, or at the very least scribble their names onto other people's bills for partial credit. These bills then become laws…or not.

Of course, that's not the entire story. After a bill's sponsors have tweaked and massaged it to their liking, the bill heads to the appropriate committee, like the **Appropriations Committee**. That's a good committee. Bills dealing with national security are sent to the **Intelligence Committee**, economic policy bills head to the **Treasury Committee**, while the **Itty Bitty Titty Committee** sits and waits for bills that never come.

Committees are where members of both parties consider the bill, and then mark it up with additions, deletions and haikus.[5] The Senate Appropriations Committee or the House Ways and Means Committee also review most bills. These committees are concerned with the financial implications of each bill and generally compete in a game to see which chamber has the balls to drive the national debt higher. It's called "deficit chicken," and it's even more fun when you're drunk.

Once out of committee, a bill then travels to the floor for a process known as **floor action**, which is 70-75% less hot than it sounds. The bill's backers are "given the floor" to describe its benefits, while the bill's critics are expected to sit quietly and limit dissent to eyerolls and muffled "homosayswhats?" Increasingly, debaters make their points with C-SPAN's two cameras in mind, leading to a dramatic growth in the use of misleading charts (see misleading chart). All legislative speeches and documents are then entered word-for-word into *The Congressional Record* to preserve the nation's wealth of pompous bullshit for future generations.

(Continue on page 69)

[5] *Re: Lockheed Martin:*
C-130 flies well but
Exceeds the budget.
(Senate Armed Services Committee minutes, 6/5/02)

A Congressional Glossary

Pork:
Unnecessary government spending to enrich one's constituency. Like a kickback, only legal.

Example:
*"The $3,000,000 grant to the Iowa Swine Farmers' Association for a new 'Pig-a-tarium' is government **pork** on no fewer than two levels."*

Growth in Misleading Charts

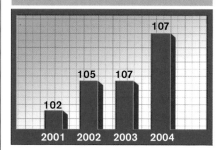

Drastic increase in # of misleading congressional charts, 2001-2004.

Senate Color by Numbers

The United States Senate is a deliberative body drawn from the ranks of the very people it serves. As the nation grew in ethnic and cultural diversity, the Senate responded by getting bigger. Here's a fun, comparative color by numbers of the original Senate (1789) and the most recent incarnation (2004). And remember, kids, stay inside the lines or risk censure!

Key:
1 = White

(Continued from page 67)

Once a bill has been widely debated and minds have been made up as to its efficacy, it's amendment-sneakin' time. For example, a representative might take an important $2 billion airline-security bill on the verge of passage and attach a $75 million rider appropriating funds for his home district to build an interactive corn museum. In the lingo of Washington, such magnanimous expenditure is known as **pork**. You might think the phrase derives from the piggish greed its practitioners display by subverting fiscal responsibility in the name of self-interest, but in reality it's a harmless reference to the benign plantation practice of distributing rations of salt pork to slaves from wooden barrels.[6]

Once one house approves a bill, it is referred to the other, which repeats the committee-debating-vote process. The two chambers then reconcile their versions of the bill in one last round of compromise and underhanded patronage. The bill is now ready to be sent to the **lobbyists**.

For if a bill is finally going to become law, it's going to have to pass lobbyist muster. At rates of only $300-$500 an hour these professionally concerned private citizens can assist our representatives in any last minute changes in language, content or intent necessary to insure their reelection funds. Lobbyists even help expedite legislation by touting its benefits to members whose votes are needed. In many ways, lobbyists are the cheerleaders of Capitol Hill—sad, soulless, clandestine, unfuckable cheerleaders (see pages 70–71).

Now that the statute no longer forbids dumping mercury into kiddie pools, the bill has passed lobbyist muster and is ready for the president's signature. Arduous? Yes. But it's this magical process of lawmaking that helps turn "Thou shalt not kill" into "Within the special maritime and territorial jurisdiction of the United States, any unlawful killing of a human being with malice aforethought, perpetrated by persons lying in wait, or any other kind of willful deliberate malicious and premeditated killing or committed in the perpetration of an attempt to perpetrate any arson, escape, murder, kidnapping, treason, espionage, sabotage,

(Continue on page 74)

---

[6] Good times.

A Congressional Glossary

Rider:
An amendment, often unlikely to pass on its own, attached to another unrelated bill that is heading for passage.

Example:
Congressman A: *"Gee, I don't remember voting to give the FBI unlimited wiretapping freedom on all Americans."*

Congressman B: *"That's because I buried it as a **rider** in the Farm Bill! Ha ha ha ha ha!"*

Congressman A: *(Weeps softly)*

Meet Your Lobbyists

The Environmental Lobby
(Greenpeace, Sierra Club, et al)

Money Given in 2000: $2,031,319
Represents: Tree huggers, air snugglers, flower fondlers, grass gropers, forest fingerbangers
Recipients of their largesse: Anything with birkenstocks and/or gorp
Stated Agenda: Protecting the environment
Hidden Agenda: Bothering people on the street when they're late for work

The Gun Lobby
(The NRA)

Money Given in 2000: $4,086,245
Represents: Deer hunters, beer hunters, queer hunters
Recipients of their largesse: Rep. Tom Delay (R-TX), emergency rooms
Stated Agenda: Keeping armor-piercing bullets on the street, where they belong
Hidden Agenda: Providing black people with enough weapons to wipe each other out

NAACP

Represents: African-Americans less radical than Louis Farrakhan, more radical than Hootie
Recipients of their largesse: The numerous black senators and representatives who…okay, friendly white people
Stated Agenda: To be the only organization left in America still using the term "colored people." Seriously, colored people? Even in the fifties they used "Negro."
Hidden Agenda: Propagating myth of Wayans brothers' talent

The Labor Lobby
(AFL-CIO, et al)

Money Given in 2000: $90,152,281, more than half in the form of goods that "fell off the back of a truck"
Represents: The working man and woman (Monday-Friday 8-4, off weekends and holidays)
Recipients of their largesse: Rust Belt Democrats who enjoy posing on forklifts
Stated Agenda: To keep the working man from getting screwed
Hidden Agenda: To keep the working man from working

The Pharmaceutical Lobby

Money Given in 2000: $26,707,861
Represents: Multi-billion dollar pharmaceutical corporations who have nothing but your health and best interests at heart
Recipients of their largesse: Democrats, Republicans, Independents…who wants a Zoloft? You'll feel better!
Stated Agenda: Eternal sunshine of the spotless mind
Hidden Agenda: Clck hree now 4 free info on ci_ali s , n—exi---ium, and vi-a_ga!
Side Effects: Dry mouth, chest pain, rash, indigent elderly and, of course, diarrhea

Big Tobacco

Money Given in 2000: $8,610,638 (in Camel Cash)
Represents: The fine people behind Kent, Kool, Benson & Hedges, Salem, Virginia Slims, Lucky Strike, and yes, you hippie jackasses, American Spirit
Recipients of their largesse: Only the cool senators
Stated Agenda: Ensuring that from the moment you emerge damp and steaming from the womb to the moment you leave this world, you're unable to go more than a few minutes without a hit of sweet, sweet nicotine, thereby aiding the tobacco industry's subsidiary, Big Oncology
Hidden Agenda: Lebensraum for Marlboro Country

While all Americans are equally represented in Congress, some groups deserve extra equal representation. For them, there are lobbyists, a group of noble souls who dedicate their lives to the agenda and causes they're paid enormous amounts of money to feel passionately about. By donating money to and putting in "face time" with members of Congress, lobbyists give support and comfort to such groups as energy conglomerates, retail giants, the Saudi royal family – you know, the voiceless. On these pages, a listing of some of these unsung heroes of American government.

The Christian Coalition

Represents: Your cousins you hate in Wisconsin, *Left Behind* readers
Recipients of their largesse: Suspiciously well-groomed Republicans
Stated Agenda: One nation under a very specific God
Hidden Agenda: See Book of Revelations

Pro-choice Movement
(Planned Parenthood, et al)

Money Given in 2000: $2,883,891 (not including free Congressional STD tests)
Represents: Human beings not currently living off a placenta
Recipients of their largesse: Pro-choice politicians, pro bono attorneys, pro athletes (especially NBA)
Stated Agenda: Non-stop, consequence-free, underage, non-parental consented fucking
Hidden Agenda: Mandatory abortions

Hollywood (The MPAA)

Money Given in 2000: $37,936,084 (mostly in back-end points)
Represents: Jewish homosexual limousine liberals who hate America
Recipients of their largesse: Howard Dean, Al Gore, Gary Hart – winners all!
Stated Agenda: Reminding politicians the constitutional guarantee of freedom of expression also protects Sharon Stone beaver shots
Hidden Agenda: A Baldwin in the White House by 2016

The Retired Lobby
(AARP)

Money Given in 2000: $102,479,744
Represents: "Active adults," "ladies of a certain age," "distinguished gentlemen" and other euphemisms for useless old people
Recipients of their largesse: Anyone who will listen
Stated Agenda: Preserving the dignity of the elderly
Hidden Agenda: "That cocoon is out there in someone's pool, and by Christ, we are going to find it!"

The Legal Lobby
(American Bar Association/ABA)

Money Given in 2000: $112,188,449 but only on a contingency basis
Represents: Themselves...and very well, we might add
Recipients of their largesse: Let's see, who amongst our nation's lawmakers might have interest in the law...
Stated Agenda: Objection! Our stated agenda is not on trial here!
Hidden Agenda: Quantifying the precise monetary value of every aspect of the formerly mysterious and awe-inspiring experience that is life

North American Man-Boy Love Association (NAMBLA)

Money Given in 2000: $0 (for some reason, all checks returned)
Represents: Membership undisclosed
Recipients of their largesse: None, see above
Stated Agenda: The legalization of sexual relations between adult males and young boys
Hidden Agenda: Dude, did you read the *stated* agenda?

Know Your Bureaucrats

Bureaucrats aren't elected. But these government employees fill an important role in the democratic process: they turn "policy" into practice. Or, at least, into "directives." Those directives then get turned into "memos." The memos are quickly forgotten by most bureaucrats, at which point they become "stern talkings-to." And the stern talking-to is the final stage in the life cycle of the people's government. Let's meet some of the people who have the privilege of working for America.

NAME: Dylan Barnes
JOB: Assistant Ecologist
AGENCY: Environmental Protection Agency
YEARS TO RETIREMENT: 42
QUOTE: "Save the Earth – it's the only one we've got."

NAME: Walter Phipps
JOB: Appropriations Director
AGENCY: Bureau of Prisons
YEARS TO RETIREMENT: 5
QUOTE: "Free your mind. 'Cause your ass ain't going anywhere."

Dylan sees working at the EPA as a chance to "really make a difference" in the future of his favorite species, the Yellowstone River cutthroat trout. A graduate with honors from the University of Colorado, Dylan has "lots of ideas" for lowering the levels of sulfites and increasing the mean rate of flow in the Yellowstone drainage. He's tried to share his vision with his Assistant Director on numerous occasions by filling out the required W95/34-A Meeting Request Form, but the paperwork is still pending approval. In the meantime, his supervisors have ordered him to collect specimens of the Greater North American Snipe. After several nocturnal trips into the field, Dylan has yet to encounter any. He suspects the species may be endangered.

Walter Phipps's government career was born out of his passion for civil rights. In 1967 he took a job with the Department of Housing and Urban Development. He was proud to oversee construction of the Clear Springs low-income apartments outside Detroit, viewing it as a step toward greater social justice. Twelve years into his government service, Phipps saw an opportunity to "jump two pay levels" by transferring to the Department of Transportation. There, he directed a project that "greatly eased Detroit's traffic congestion" by demolishing the Clear Springs apartment complex to make way for a freeway bypass. In 1995, Phipps left the DOT to take a still higher-paying position with the rapidly expanding Federal Bureau of Prisons. Today, he boasts, "I'm housing more brothers than I ever did at HUD."

NAME: Leslie Turow
JOB: Clerical Assistant
AGENCY: Amtrak
YEARS TO RETIREMENT: 7
QUOTE: "It's tough to soar with the eagles when you work with turkeys. Just kidding, Mike!"

NAME: Howard Brown
JOB: Classified
AGENCY: Classified
YEARS TO RETIREMENT: Classified
QUOTE: "The rooster is in the hayloft. Repeat—the rooster is in the hayloft."

NAME: Wilford McLellan
JOB: Co-Regional Assistant General Manager's Assistant
AGENCY: Department of Veterans Affairs
YEARS TO RETIREMENT: 3
QUOTE: "Three years to retirement."

Leslie's posting in the Office of Fuel Procurement requires her to assist the Office Director in keeping Amtrak well-supplied with coal. While "absolutely zero" of the line's trains actually runs on coal, the company has been required to purchase coal for decades due to a little-noticed law authored by legislators from Pennsylvania and West Virginia. With no coal-burning locomotives to consume the fuel, much of Leslie's time is spent re-selling the coal that Amtrak buys, usually back to the same coal companies that sold it to them, often at a steep discount. While the process sounds inefficient, Leslie is hard at work on a plan to streamline it. "Next year, they won't even have to deliver the coal," she says. "We'll just cut them a check."

Howard Brown, known affectionately to his coworkers as "The Condor," began working for a branch of the United States government in 1982 after a psychological evaluation deemed him suitable for the rigors of certain types of bureaucratic work. Proving both dedicated and efficient, Brown was sent abroad on a number of assignments where he worked as "a troubleshooter...of sorts." Brown's job took him to exotic locales—so many that he has difficulty recalling any of them specifically, particularly when under oath. After suffering a work-related injury "somewhere in the Southern Hemisphere," Brown was reassigned to an administrative position at a nondescript office building in northern Virginia. Today, this modest servant continues to be reluctant to discuss his achievements. "That's about all the time I have," he says. "Mr. Johnson here will show you out."

Wilford McLellan began work for the VA in 1972, overseeing the agency's then state-of-the-art OMNIVAC computer system. The machine is still in use today, occupying the entire fourth floor of the agency's headquarters in Washington, D.C. "She runs pretty hot," Wilford observes, sliding a punch card through the computer's input slot. Though advanced for its time, OMNIVAC possesses 1/32,000th the processing power of a modern PC. Attempts to modernize the VA's record-keeping system have faltered, and Wilford admits he's been less than cooperative. "How do you even get inside those new machines?" he asked. "This one here's got a front door."

(Continued from page 69)

aggrieved sexual assault, or burglary or robbery or perpetrated from a pre-meditated design unlawfully and maliciously to effect the death of any human being other than him who is killed is murder in the first degree."[7]

The Modern Congress: Representin'

Lawmaking is tedious and never-ending. If not for the good salary and godlike sense of ultimate power it would hardly seem worth it. But law-making is not the only power the Constitution grants Congress. Article I, Section 8 also embues in Congress the power to "lay and collect taxes, duties, imposts and excises to pay debts." Congress also acts as a check and _____[8] on the government's other branches. Congress has the final approval over presidential appointments, to say nothing of treaties and the ultimate ability to declare war. Add to that the congressional responsibilities for weights and measures, raising and maintaining militias and navies, punishing piracy and printing money, and it's no wonder these workhorses are in session almost a full 120 days of any given year.

Yes, when not running for re-election or raising money to run for re-election or spending money in the interest of their re-election, Congress is doing the people's business. Sometimes, congressmen even return to their districts and states to "rap" with the people. This practice is excruciatingly awkward for both sides.

>>Fig. 4.3

John F. Kennedy (1917-1963), whose idealism and/or sexual escapades inspired a generation.

But remember, Congress is us, and we are congress. Our representatives are men and women drawn from all echelons of American society – lawyers, doctors, former athletes, lawyers again, businessmen, moguls, magnates, pooh-bahs, VIPs, and Gopher from *The Love Boat*. Why do they serve? Some are moved by the words of the

(Continue on page 77)

---

[7] Federal statute # 1111.

[8] If you can't fill in the blank with the word "balance" by now, you are clinically retarded.

The Congressional Cafeteria *An Appetite for Politics*

For a brief moment in February 2003, the nation's eyes turned to the House cafeteria's menu board, when legislators decreed "French fries" would henceforth be known as "freedom fries"—a move we now know was instrumental in winning the War on Terror. But this was not the first time the menu at the Congressional Cafeteria has been changed. Indeed, to pick up the menu today is to hold a window into the history of our great nation as reflected through the prism of institutional food.

All prices at the Congressional Cafeteria have meaning in American history. 435 is the number of members in the House of Representatives. It is also the weight in pounds of Speaker of the House Dennis J. Hastert (R-IL).

Formerly "French Onion Soup," the name was changed after a minor diplomatic squabble between Dwight Eisenhower and Charles De Gaulle. (Did you really think 2003 was the first time we were pissed off at the French?)

Cafeteria Menu for the 108th Congress of the United States of America
"The Yum's have it!"

❧

Appetizers $4.35
Legal Tenders
Freedom Onion Soup
The Federalist Poppers
Cajun Shrimp

In negotiating the Louisiana Purchase with Napoleon, Thomas Jefferson not only acquired millions of acres of land, but also the Emperor's killer secret recipe for Cajun shrimp. Napoleon rued the day he gave away the recipe. As for Louisiana, eh.

These dishes honor the surprising number of Supreme Court justices whose names happen to resemble types of sandwiches. One striking omission from the list: early 19th century Chief Justice Thomas W. Turkeyclubonryenomayo.

*

"Supreme Sandwiches" $14.92
The Warren Burger
The Ruth Bader Ginsburger
The Felix Frankfurter
The Smoked Salmon P. Chase
The Hugo L. Blackened Chicken Sandwich

(Supreme Sandwiches come with choice of Freedom Fries, Oliver Wendell Homefries or Hash Browns v. Board of Education and Ketchup)

The year Columbus discovered the poblano chile.

For its first century and a half, the Congressional Cafeteria featured a condiment known, in an unfortunate coincidence, as "Nazi Sauce." The name was changed to "ketchup" shortly following the discovery of Auschwitz.

We hold this price to be self-evident.

*

Entrees $17.76
"Pardoned" Turkey
Freedom
Bison-tennial ($2 surcharge)
Repeal-and-Eat Shrimp
Chicken à la Leader Who Is
Democratically Elected by the Colonies in Accordance
With the Principles of Self-Rule

(All entrees come with choice of green salad or Yankee Bean Soup, and mixed plate)

Each Thanksgiving, the president "pardons" one lucky turkey. What people don't realize is that due to the "separation of powers" the pardon only applies to the executive branch. The turkey is immediately handed over to the House of Representatives for what can only be described as a brutal ritual of slaughter.

Not, as you might suspect, a renamed French dish, but rather fresh, free-range freedom, grilled and garnished with cilantro.

It was only in 1954—following the Supreme Court's landmark decision on segregation—that the cafeteria allowed black beans and white rice to share the same plate.

*

Dessert $5.00
Apple Pie
Remember the à la mode!
($1.00 extra)
Impeach Cobbler
"Kaiser Wilhelm Is a Douchebag" Chocolate Cake

*

Emboldened by their victory in the American Revolution, Congress struck yet again at the British monarchy, renaming the traditional dish of Chicken à la King.

$5.00 commemorates what is widely considered to be a reasonable price for dessert.

Drinks

The Congressional Cafeteria is pleased to offer a wide selection of premium alcoholic beverages. A beer and wine list is available upon request for the pussies. The Congressional Cafeteria regrets it does not serve non-alcoholic beverages, though the chef can prepare a de-whiskeyed cup of Irish Coffee with a half hour's notice.

Gordon Senatorial
Consulting L.L.C.

1427 K Street,
Suite 304
District of Columbia

"How To Filibuster" *

Or,

"Making the Most of Your Time On the Floor** Once You Have Obtained Over 40 Signatures From Fellow Senators, Breaking to Yield Only to Like-Minded Colleagues (Who Must Make Comments Only in the Form of Questions) Until You Are Possibly Struck Down By Cloture Rules (Passed in 1917 ¥, Updated in 1979µ and 1986) Where a Three-Fifths Majority (60 Senators) Can Effectively Cut Off a Filibuster by Limiting Debate On a Bill to One Hour and Not Be Swayed By The Opinions Of Men Like President Woodrow Wilson _ (served 1913-1921) Who Once Condemned the Practice As The Work of 'A Little Group of Willful Men, Representing No Opinion But Their Own,' A Remark Directed at Robert "Fighting Bob" LaFollette ☺, Who Appears in the First Paragraph of This Article Anecdotally As A Way of Putting a Human Face on A Complicated, Yet Important, Senatorial Practice (It Does Not Happen In The House)."

**by Phillip "Philibuster" Gordon
President of Gordon Senatorial
Consulting L.L.C.
1427 K Street, Suite 304
District of Columbia
BS Georgetown University 1979
MBA Yale School of Business 1983
Authorized Lobbyist 1991
Lobby Number: 34876-908777US14**

* Quotes denote title is from an essay of a larger piece, *Diapers and Lozenges: How To Win the War For Long-Windedness* (copyright 2003), as opposed to a "standalone" work, in which case our title would then have been italicized, as we see above in the title *Diapers and Lozenges: How To Win the War For Long-Windedness.*

** By "floor," we refer to the portion of the chamber where one does his/her speaking. Not literally "on the floor," although in 1931, Huey Long's filibuster contained him doing a tableau vivant entitled *"A Salamander At Rest"* that saw him lying very still on the carpet for several minutes. It was excellent and thought-provoking. ¥

¥ Overheard statement by young, effete page named Geralde (he added the "e" upon acceptance to the program). His surname is lost to history.

¥ Passed during the administration of Woodrow Wilson (this note refers to the above mention within the "title" of our essay about the year 1917. If you went to the above footnote concerning the "two astericks" footnote, about an effete page named Geralde, we apologize for the confusion. Please note that it was a footnote to a remark within the footnotes section of our piece. Geralde was a page in the summer of 1931. While we know little about him, we know for a fact that he had nothing to do with the cloture rules of 1917.)

µ During the Carter administration, where Senators were given preference in offering amendments to a measure under cloture if they had previously offered fewer than two. (We hope that you are back on track with your footnotes. ☺)

_ See ¥, the second one. Which will herein be referred to with an ® The ® is now about the administration of Woodrow Wilson. (If there is any further mention of Geralde, and his enthusiasm for the "performance elements" within the filibusters of Huey Long, that will be noted with the previously used ¥ symbol.)

☺ Indicates author's fondness for the nickname of Robert "Fighting Bob" LaFollette. (In body of piece, not in the footnote before the above footnote. That smiley face was an attempt to smooth things over, if you will, for any confusion over the matter of the 1917 cloture rules and the possible role of Geralde.)

There are many glorious, wondrous, inspiring tales of the filibuster—I am reminded of a page boy named Gerald.¥

(continues on page 459)

(Continued from page 74)

late John F. Kennedy, "Ask not what your country can do for you, ask what you can do for your country." Others are inspired by the amount of tail that kind of talk used to get the late president. Still others entertain Mephistophelian visions of unlimited power over the affairs of men.

Ultimately, though, all are active participants in the lawmaking body that forms the bedrock of our Republic. They give voice to the nation's millions and through legislation shape the way we live. Indeed, the rules mandated by Congress define our very society and, in a larger sense, who we are as a people.

And *that* is why pot is still illegal. ◑

Were You Aware?

56% of congressmen believe in angels, and an additional 28% "want so very badly" to believe.

Writing Your Congressman

The old-fashioned pen-and-paper letter remains one of the bulwarks of representative democracy. It is personal. It is tangible. And it shows you care enough about an issue to spend five, maybe ten minutes expressing your opinion—an investment of time that, by contemporary standards, makes you Cesar Freakin' Chavez.

However, there are steps you must take to ensure your letter will be taken seriously.

- ■ Avoid lengthy manifestos, and try to stay on topic.
- ■ Use facts and figures to back up your point.
- ■ Refer by number to the bill or proposal you are addressing.
- ■ If at all possible, avoid using the word "twat."

Also, be advised that congressional staffers are directed to count exclamation points. Though your anger may be profound, anything more than six at the end of a sentence looks silly. Here is an example!!!!!! See? It's ridiculous.

Still confused? To the right is a template for you to follow the next time you have a request for your servant in Washington.

"Stardate" is NOT appropriate

DATE

Representative or Senator's Name
Representative or Senator's Address
That Domey Thingy
Washington, DC [ZIP TK]

Dear Honorable **(for senators)**/Distinguished **(for representatives)**/Abby **(for advice-seekers)**

As a concerned citizen of your **district/state/household**, I kindly **request/urge/demand/insist/order** you at gunpoint to **co-sponsor/condemn/remain ambiguously silent on** the legislation that Representative Elder Centrist Democrat and Senator **Moderate Republican You've Never Heard Of** have introduced to **increase/decrease** spending for _____.* ____

I am not ordinarily moved to write, but **I have a child affected by/vaguely remember a TV report about/have nothing better to do than write a letter concerning** this issue. I supported you through all **five elections/three scandals/two convictions** and would be extremely disappointed to have to **vote against/stalk/cuckold you.**

Thank **you/your unpaid intern** for hearing me on this important issue.

Respectfully/Disrespectfully/Suck it,

Your Name/Pseudonym/"X" mark

> *Insert pet cause/thing that will negatively affect you financially here.

If this is your third or fourth attempt to reach out to your congressmen you might want to pepper the above template with such statements as...

I am increasingly disappointed you **haven't taken the time to answer/don't give a shit about/spend untold hours mockingly reading aloud to your slack-jawed lackeys** my previous letters. Please be advised that I live in your district and I **vote/plan on registering to vote this time/will wake up on Election Day** with every intention to vote but, like Joyce's Leopold Bloom, will find my day inexorably pulling me in every direction but the one toward which I intended to go.

(Think you're ready to write your own? Just remember, congressional aides scan letters for key phrases, like "the signals you are transmitting into my body" and "I dare you to step onto my compound." Use of these will assure your missive winds up on a completely different kind of "priority scale.")

Discussion Questions

1. If "con" is the opposite of "pro," then isn't Congress the opposite of progress? *Or did we just fucking blow your mind?!?*

2. What does "bicameral" mean? Are any of the girls in your class "bicameral?"

3. Which would you rather see getting made: sausage or laws?

4. In *Star Wars: Episode II*, Chancellor Palpatine convinces the Galactic Senate to grant him emergency powers in order to squelch the Separatist movement's droid army, led by Count Dooku. But Palpatine ultimately abuses his authority, disbanding the Republic and appointing himself the lone ruler of a new Galactic Empire. Could it happen here?

5. How are you enjoying the book so far? Be honest.

6. Remember that old *Schoolhouse Rock* cartoon about the bill who sings a song about how he becomes a law? Hey, and what about the Snorks? Remember them?

>>Fig. 4.4

The ABC television network wanted an exorbitant sum of money ($1000) for use of a tiny postage-sized image of the "Bill" from Schoolhouse Rock, *forcing* Daily Show *writer Eric Drysdale to draw this virtual facsimile in less than five minutes. Drysdale was not compensated.*

Classroom Activities

1. Take construction paper, trace your hand, and make a Turkey of Congress.

2. Ask your students to choreograph an interpretive dance or compose a tone poem that represents the spirit of their favorite piece of legislation currently under consideration by a Senate subcommittee.

3. Find out each representative's "porn name" by adding the name of the largest city in their district to the name of their state flower! (Example: Ben Chandler, D-KY = "Frankfort Goldenrod")

4. Help the children make their own "mace"—the ebony and silver rod on the House rostrum symbolizing the authority of the House—out of paper towel rolls and elbow macaroni. Explain to the children they have just made useless representations of something that is itself useless and symbolic. Shame them.

5. Have fun with the gerrymander! On the right are five congressional districts in rural Texas that have experienced a sudden upswing in minority population. Using only three straight lines, can you re-draw the boundaries to consolidate white power in four of the five districts? If you can, please contact the office of Rep. Tom Delay (R-TX).

Texas Congressional Districts

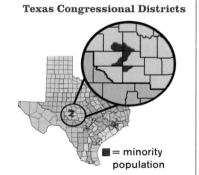

■ = minority population

"**Jesus, talk about a sausage-fest.**"

—*Sandra Day O'Connor, 1981*

Chapter 5

The Judicial Branch: It Rules

Having discussed the executive and legislative, we arrive now at the judicial branch. If, as mentioned in Chapter 2, the Constitution is the nation's owner's manual, then the judicial branch is America's helpful 24-hour tech support, always available to explain how things should work. And like any good tech support, it costs extra, takes forever to reach, and you don't understand their instructions half the time anyway.

The judicial branch is charged with interpreting the Constitution and in any discussion of the United States government is always mentioned last. There is no shame in that. The judicial branch is up against some very strong branches. Who wouldn't want to be president? Even Congress, with lawmaking powers and a short work year, has a certain elegant simplicity and glamorous appeal. This is not to insinuate people feel the judicial branch is an *un*important part of our government, just that it is the *least* important. And that is exactly how the judicial branch likes it. Flying under most people's radar allows the judicial branch to quietly control all aspects of your life. From your morning hardcore pornography masturbation

>> Fig. 5.1

Without her blindfold, many believe Justice would see much better.

session, to your lunchtime abortion, right up through your twilight neo-Nazi march through a predominantly Jewish/black community, the judicial branch is there to make sure everything you say can and will be used against you in a court of law…under God.

At the top of the judicial branch is the Supreme Court. Unelected by the people, its proceedings are not televised. Justices rarely comment publicly or give on-the-record interviews. Not one has ever appeared on *Leno*. It may seem odd—undemocratic, even—that a small group of unelected

>> Fig. 5.2

Placing one hand on this book and raising the other makes you physically unable to lie.

You Make the Call!

Is a Monkey Your Uncle? (1925)

A Tennessee high school teacher stands accused of teaching evolution in his classroom, breaking a state law banning Charles Darwin's theories from public schools. But does a law endorsing a religious viewpoint (Creationism) violate the Constitution's separation of church and state?

The Verdict: Irrelevant!

This case rests solely on whether the defendant had violated a state law—not whether that law was constitutional. The teacher was found guilty and fined $100.

Tennesseans supporting the law celebrated the "defeat of evolution" by grunting happily and hurling feces.

individuals can shape public policy, far from the public's eye,[1] but the Court's peculiar insularity is by design. The justices' rarefied position provides them with a buffer from the winds of public sentiment and the demands of political expediency. They are thus free to base decisions entirely upon their interpretation of the Constitution. Interestingly, the interpretation of the word "interpretation" has itself evolved over the years, and now means "the political beliefs of whoever appointed you."

Below the Supreme Court, district and federal appellate courts form an elaborately structured hierarchy of justice so vast and multi-layered it is quite possible you can be found "innocent" and "guilty" at the same time, and be named a bankruptcy court judge in the bargain.

So who are the people who make up the judicial branch? Why are they vested with the authority to make laws? And just who the fuck do they think they are? These questions and more will be answered as we examine the origins of the judiciary and "peek beneath the robes" of the men and women who serve there, deepening our constitutional understanding and maybe, just maybe, getting a glimpse of their genitals (see page 99).

The Justices: Who Are They to Judge?

The highest court in the land is called the **Supreme Court**, proving that while justice may be blind there's nothing wrong with her ego. And though the moniker may seem more appropriate for an omnipotent group of superheroes than nine withered octogenarians, a position on the Court is very prestigious. The process for selecting a chief justice and eight asso-

---

[1] If you find this genuinely surprising, you may want to go back and reread the last chapter's section on lobbyists.

ciate justices is complex, as each receives a lifetime appointment. A justice only leaves the bench via retirement, incapacitation or removal by impeachment. They cannot be fired, laid off, downsized or out-sourced. Additionally, the only way to kill or wound a justice is with a diamond-tipped bullet from the anvil of Hephaestus.[2]

>> Fig. 5.3

Upon appointment, new justices are given their very own "stretch" gavel.

The president is responsible for nominating candidates to the Supreme Court. When selecting a nominee, presidents take into account a wide range of criteria: a lifetime of public service and scholarship, a thorough understanding of the day's political and social climate, and perhaps most importantly, minority status equal to or greater than the court member being replaced. The federally recognized value chart is as follows:

White man < white woman < black or latino man < black or latino woman < any Eskimo

Diversity has become a consideration because for the first 180 years of its existence, America's highest judicial body was comprised exclusively of white males.[3] Then, in 1967, President Lyndon Johnson made Thurgood Marshall the "Jackie Robinson" of the Supreme Court. Marshall went on to bat .312 and steal 45 bases as he led the '68 Court to the National League pennant. (Sadly, the Court lost the World Series 4-3 to the Detroit Tigers.) Today, the Court has achieved a moderate level of diversity with two women, one African-American, and one homosexual.[4] Ultimately, it is left to the president's discretion to choose a nominee. And whether he selects a good friend or merely a long-time acquaintance, a president must ask himself one critical question: "Will this person only make decisions I agree with?"

(Continue on page 87)

[2] Vulcan, son of Hera, D-Athens.
[3] Surprised?
[4] Hint: it rhymes with "Palia."

America's Court System

The United States legal system is a complex hierarchy of court divisions designed to allow for the swift and equitable administration of justice. This chart, however, is in no way an endorsement of said system, or a repudiation of the virtues of vigilante, or "street," justice.

U.S. Court of Appeals (12th Circuit)

The Supreme Court's farm system, but with fewer Dominican players and more assholes from Yale.

District Courts
94 districts nationwide handling everything from massive corporate fraud (boooooring!) to transporting a minor across state lines for sexual purposes (jackpot!).

Territorial Courts (U.S. Virgin Islands, Puerto Rico, Guam)
Where U.S. citizens learn federal drug statutes aren't suspended just because they're on vacation.

U.S. Tax Court
The place to argue that the bubble-jet printer on your kitchen counter constitutes a "home office."

Court of Public Opinion
Judgment is harsh, verdicts are swift, but can be easily reversed via 20-minute sit-down with Diane Sawyer.

Racquetball Court
Goggles required. Hasn't been used since the early '80s.

Mom and Dad
Arbiter of all curfew, allowance, and homework-completion related matters. Frequently Draconian; often arbitrary, citing legally questionable precedent of "because I said so." Jurisdiction confined to "under their roof." God, you hate them. Hate them, hate them, hate them.

The Supreme Court

U.S. Court of Military Appeals

For soldiers who got nowhere else to go...who got nowhere else to go!!!

Court of Appeals for the Federal Circuit (13th Circuit)

A 12-judge panel which hears appeals from the lower courts. Its judges are a heartbeat, stroke or onset of senile dementia away from the Supreme Court.

Courts of Military Review
This is the *JAG* one.

U.S. Court of Veterans Affairs
Looking for the world's most depressing court experience? You've found it!

U.S. Claims Court
If you're injured by government agents during a raid on your counterfeiting operation, this is where you sue them for millions.

U.S. Court of International Trade
Have you been wronged by a freighter ship with a Liberian registry? We want to help!

Small Claims Court
Where the pathetic sue the desperate over the mundane.

Food Court
The Honorable Theodore G. Sbarro presiding. Verdict: Coronary thrombosis!

Frank McCourt
Handles immigration issues with warmth and passion. Makes a great gift.

Objection! America's Most Controversial Supreme Court Nominees

Though most Supreme Court nominees win easy congressional approval, every now and then the president tries to sneak in a kook. Below, a partial list.

Robert Bork

Nominated by: Ronald Reagan (1987)
Reason why controversial: Ultra-conservative ideology
How conservative was he?: So conservative, he ruled *against* abortion in the landmark case *Rosemary v. Baby*.
Worst decision: Wearing an "I supported Nixon during Watergate!" T-shirt to confirmation hearing.

Douglas Ginsberg

Nominated by: Ronald Reagan (1987)
Reason why controversial:
Admission of past marijuana use
Things feigned by critics: Surprise, moral outrage
Famous quote: "Have you ever really looked at the precedent set by 1870's *Hepburn v. Griswold*? I mean, *really* looked at it?"

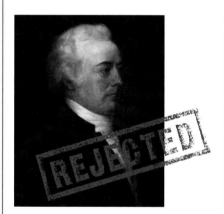

John Rutledge

Nominated by: George Washington (1795)
Reason why controversial: History of mental illness
How crazy was he?: Believed CIA had implanted mind-control chip in brain—163 years prior to invention of either. Also, ate gavels.
Nickname: Crazy Johnny

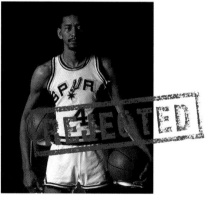

George "The Iceman" Gervin

Nominated by: Jimmy Carter (1978)
Reason why controversial: Lack of judicial experience
Reason for nomination: Gervin represented Carter's attempt to fundamentally alter the make-up of the Court by adding size, athleticism, and a patented "finger roll" to a body previously devoted to maintaining the integrity of the Constitution. Ultimately, the vacancy was filled by Ruth "Chocolate Thunder" Ginsberg.

Floyd Burnington

Nominated by: Calvin Coolidge (1926)
Reason why controversial: Member of KKK
In his own words: "I didn't say they were monkeys, I said they *reminded* me of monkeys."
But some of his best friends were: Actually, they were all white.
Fun Fact: Burnington went on to serve a distinguished 9-term career in the U.S. Senate.

(Continued from page 83)

Once nominated, a candidate goes through a **confirmation process** overseen by the Senate. In recent years, this process has grown noticeably politicized, with Judiciary Committee members attempting to learn in advance how a nominee might rule on various hot-button issues. These are called "litmus tests," because "abortion tests" sounds creepy.

The judicial philosophies held by the nine justices go a long way towards determining the decisions they hand down. For our purposes,[5] these philosophies can be casually oversimplified into two main categories.

>> Fig. 5.4

Until 1943, Supreme Court nominees were wrapped in litmus paper and dipped in acid to determine their worthiness for the Court. Later Courts were less literal-minded.

1. A **judicial activist** sees the Constitution as a living document that can be adapted and re-interpreted to protect the needs of a changing society, such as "marriage between sodomites" and "impulse abortions."

2. A **strict constructionist** interprets the Constitution according to the language and original intent of the text at the time of its writing, in much the same way as a fundamentalist views the Bible. Fortunately for strict constructionists, they have been endowed by God with the superhuman gift of being able to read the minds of people who died 200 years ago. Naturally, they use this power only for good.

A Court is very often a reflection of its chief justice. For example, the Warren Court, under Chief Justice Earl Warren, is remembered for taking "activist" stances in cases involving civil rights. Its landmark decisions include *Brown v. Board of Education* (1954) and *Miranda v. Arizona* (1966), names that, even today, most high school students can easily recall for testing purposes. In contrast, the midnineteenth-century Taney Court,

(Continue on page 91)

---

[5] Financial gain.

>> Fig. 5.5

As chairman of the Warren Commission, Earl Warren determined that President John F. Kennedy died of a self-inflicted gunshot wound.

The Supreme Court All-Time All-Star Team

It's the ultimate water-cooler conversation: If you could field an all-time Supreme Court team, using any nine judges from the history of American jurisprudence, who would you pick? The following subjective list is meant only to provoke debate and discussion.

Court Tenure: 1967-1991

Thurgood Marshall

"And to think they said I lacked the buoyancy to be on the Supreme Court."
—Remarks upon retirement (1991)

In 1967, Marshall broke the color barrier when Lyndon Johnson named him the Court's first African-American justice. Marshall was uniquely qualified for the position, having spent ten years as a star appellate court judge for the Chattanooga Bluerobes of the Negro Justice League. He spent a quarter of a century championing civil rights and social justice. Fortunately, upon retirement in 1991, he was replaced by Clarence Thomas, who soon undid all the damage.

Court Tenure: 1799-1829

Bushrod Washington

"Hey, you know who'd have an interesting opinion on this? My uncle, George Fucking Washington, that's who."
—McCulloch v. Maryland (1819)

Bushrod Washington makes the list for the same reason he made the Supreme Court in the first place: his uncle, George. Washington. Bushrod parlayed having a famous uncle into a three-decade-long undistinguished judicial career. He was once described as "a short, untidy man who liked snuff and suffered from ill health," and that was in his own autobiography. His appointment marked the last time in American history anyone was given a high-level government job simply because of family connections.

"But beefsteak is delicious!"
—U.S. v. Beefsteak, 1925 (dissenting opinion)

Taft served as both president of the United States and chief justice of the Supreme Court – a remarkable feat unmatched in U.S. history. Taft also weighed 320 pounds, making him the heaviest to serve either position. Guess which distinction people brought up more.

Court Tenure: 1921-1930

William Howard Taft

Court Tenure: 1941-1942

James F. Byrnes

"zzzzzzzzzzzzzzzzzz zzzz."
—Chaplinsky v. New Hampshire (1942)

Byrnes's 16-month tenure still stands as the shortest in history. The Franklin Roosevelt appointee found the deliberative, insular life of a justice too dull and uneventful, once describing the United States Supreme Court as "the place where fun goes to die."

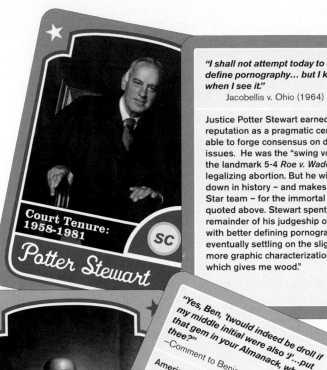

"I shall not attempt today to further define pornography… but I know it when I see it."
Jacobellis v. Ohio (1964)

Justice Potter Stewart earned his reputation as a pragmatic centrist able to forge consensus on divisive issues. He was the "swing vote" in the landmark 5-4 *Roe v. Wade* ruling legalizing abortion. But he will go down in history – and makes the All-Star team – for the immortal words quoted above. Stewart spent the remainder of his judgeship obsessed with better defining pornography, eventually settling on the slightly more graphic characterization, "that which gives me wood."

Court Tenure: 1958-1981

SC

Potter Stewart

"The most stringent protection of free speech would not protect a man in falsely shouting fire in a theater and causing a panic."
–Schenck v. United States (1919)

Holmes's famous dictum on the limits of free speech was shaped by personal experience. On March 7, 1847, the six-year-old attended the Boston Lyceum Theatre's world premiere of the new musical comedy, *Hey, Everybody, There's a Fire in the Theater…We're Not Kidding.* The show closed after six minutes, leaving 438 dead. Among the survivors: a future Supreme Court justice with a healthy respect for the limits of free speech… and a bitter hatred for musical theatre.

SC

Court Tenure: 1902-1932

Oliver Wendell Holmes

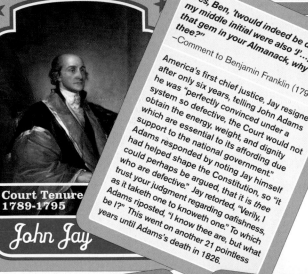

"Yes, Ben, 'twould indeed be droll if my middle initial were also 'j'…put that gem in your Almanack, why don't thee?"
–Comment to Benjamin Franklin (1792)

America's first chief justice, Jay resigned after only six years, telling John Adams he was "perfectly convinced under a system so defective, the Court would not obtain the energy, weight, and dignity which are essential to its affording due support to the national government." Adams responded by noting Jay himself had helped shape the Constitution, so "it could perhaps be argued, that it is *thee* who are defective." Jay retorted, "Verily, I trust your judgment regarding oafishness, as it taketh one to knoweth one." To which Adams riposted, "I know thee are, but what be I?" This went on another 21 pointless years until Adams's death in 1826.

Court Tenure: 1789-1795

John Jay

"Don't pee on my leg and tell me it's raining."
–Tony Z's Quik-Park v. Kwanesha (1997)

During her long, distinguished television/judicial career, Judge Judy has effectively translated the nuanced complexities of the law into the harsh, guttural language of daytime TV. But perhaps more significantly, her nasal voice and constant nagging put the "Jew" back in the judiciary.

"Enough judging for today! Who wants to buy shoes?!"
–Hartford Fire Insurance Co. v. California (1993)

O'Connor broke the Court's gender barrier with her appointment in 1981 by President Ronald Reagan. Her arrival heralded a new age of sexual tension in the hallowed halls of justice. A shameless flirt, O'Connor is not above using her feminine wiles to get what she wants: a strict interpretation of the Constitution limiting, but not crippling, federal power over the states. And she doesn't care who she has to blow to get it.

Court Tenure: 1981-present

SC

Sandra Day O'Connor

Syndication Tenure: 1996-present

SC

Judge Judy Sheindlin

Landmark Supreme Court Cases

Though the Supreme Court decides dozens of cases each year, only a handful of decisions are familiar to the general public. Here are a few of these landmark decisions.

Marbury v. Madison (1803)

Established the principle of "judicial review"—that the Supreme Court has the power to declare laws unconstitutional. Before that, the Court only had the power to check laws for spelling and punctuation.

Dred Scott (1856)

The Court finds that Dred Scott, a fugitive slave, is not a person but property, and therefore is entitled neither to file suit in a federal court nor to remain free in the North. Not the verdict Scott was hoping for. Historians agree the Court battle sapped him and when he went back to being a slave, his heart just wasn't in it.

Dred Scott thought he was running away from slavery. What he was really running away from… was himself.

Plessy v. Ferguson (1896)

The Court upholds segregation and the constitutionality of the "separate but equal" doctrine. The ruling was intended only to keep Plessy, a notorious womanizer, away from Ferguson, whose wife was quite comely. However, in one of the wackiest mishaps in judicial history, it was used to keep an entire race of people down for half a century.

Brown v. Board of Education of Topeka (1954)

Again with the black people. Only this time, there's a twist: The Court overturned the *Plessy* ruling, declaring the establishment of separate public schools for black and white students inherently unequal. This landmark verdict paved the way for integration, the Civil Rights Movement and the Beastie Boys.

Adam Horowitz, Mike Diamond, and Adam Yauch, direct beneficiaries of Brown v. Board of Education.

Roe v. Wade (1973)

Abortion lovers rejoice! The Court rules that the right to privacy protects a woman's decision to have an abortion and the fetus is not a person with constitutional rights, thus ending all debate on this once-controversial issue.

Miranda v. Arizona (1966)

The Court rules suspects must be informed of their legal rights upon arrest. The resulting "Miranda Warning" safeguards defendants from abuse and self-incrimination. It also requires the two police officers handling a suspect's interrogation to adopt diametrically opposed attitudes toward that suspect, with one taking a more benevolent approach while the other, perhaps a loose cannon with nothing left to live for, takes a more malevolent tack.

Godzilla v. Megalon (1973)

In a rare foray into international law, the Court agreed to settle a dispute between two giant monsters rampaging through the Japanese countryside. In a 7-2 decision, the Court found Megalon's emission of lightning from his horn-like appendage did not constitute a violation of Godzilla's civil rights. Frustrated by the decision, Godzilla and attorney Melvin Belli destroyed Tokyo.

The plaintiff.

Roe v. Brown (1978)

Due to public demand, the winners of *Roe v. Wade* and *Brown v. Board of Education* go head-to-head in an elimination match televised on *ABC's Wide World of Sports*. The right to have an abortion was upheld 8-1 over the right to desegregated public institutions. Chief Justice Warren Burger later called his participation in this event "the most regrettable incident in my entire career."

Bush v. Gore (2000)

The Court votes 5-4 to stop the recount in the disputed Florida election, effectively handing George W. Bush the presidency. In a remarkable coincidence, each justice's decision aligns exactly with his or her party affiliation—an accidental synchronicity a lonely, unemployed Al Gore muses on each and every evening as he cries himself to sleep.

William Rehnquist (right), a Republican, was lucky enough to vote for George W. Bush twice. The second time counted more.

(Continued from page 87)

under Chief Justice Roger Taney, slanted more conservative, perhaps because it leaned towards states' rights...or maybe it was their slaves that gave it away. (Said Taney famously, "What? These robes aren't gonna clean themselves.") The Taft Court, under Chief Justice William Taft (1921-30), was known for its indecisiveness. In ten years the Taft Court rendered only one decision, finding for It in the case *Eeny v. Meeny*.

You Make the Call!

Murder, He . . . Committed?!? (2004)
A man stands accused of murdering his wife in a crowded shopping mall. Eight eyewitnesses confirm they saw the man commit the crime. The act was captured on three surveillance video cameras. The man's fingerprints are on the weapon. He signed a confession admitting guilt in the case. Guilty or not guilty?

The Verdict
Depends. I mean, does he have any "recalled memories" concerning childhood abuse? Was his wife abusing him? Have his body and spirit been abused by a preponderance of sugary, easy-to-obtain foods? Oh, and request to have his signed confession ruled inadmissible pending investigation whether your client was properly Mirandized. Besides, when society fails one of us, aren't we all guilty?

How Do You Get to the Supreme Court? Practice (Law), Practice (Law), Practice (Law)

How does the Supreme Court decide what cases to hear? Clearly, it cannot come running every time a fat guy sues a hamburger joint. Do you think they have that much time on their hands? They do not. Do you think the Court is loafing? There is already a pending lawsuit regarding your careless accusations. They are but nine feeble old people, up against Americans, the most litigious people in the history of the planet. No, the Supreme Court only gets involved in the most difficult, important, and seminal cases. And if you are fortunate enough to find yourself in an intractable and tragic situation you too could join the exalted ranks of a Roe, Miranda, or Nixon. But before you get there, you must travel a long and perilous legal trail. Bring gorp.

"The Supreme Court is but nine feeble old people, up against Americans, the most litigious people in the history of the planet."

(Continue on page 93)

So You Want to Be a Precedent

By Stephen Colbert

Let's face it, nobody wants to die, least of all me. Thankfully, I have achieved the immortality of celebrity, whereas if you paid for this book you're probably not famous or else we would have given you a copy just to make sure it showed up at the "right" parties, if you know what I mean, which again, you probably don't. My point is, the Wolf of Oblivion will soon be lapping his Eternal Tongue at your door, and none of your pleading will save you from the hungering darkness.

On the bright side, there is a way for your name to live forever in the annals of legal history. It's called being a **precedent**, and if a no-name like Roe (not her real name) or that asshole Wade can do it, so can you!

It's easy. First, have something awful happen to you, like getting arrested without being read your rights, not being allowed to go to school due to your race, or picking up a cup of coffee that's a tad too hot. But—and this is important—you can't have one of those. They've already been precedented. "Is 'precedented' even a word?" you may ask. Well, it is now, Noah-fucking-Webster. I just precedented it.

So, not only must it be something awful, but it has to be *uniquely* awful and constitutionally interesting. Then you're in business! As of this writing, gay marriage is very hot. Unfortunately for you, a slew of gays (and "slew" is the correct term for more than one homosexual) have a head start on that one, so just marrying a gay man probably won't cut it. You might have to marry two gay men. Or if polyhomolygamy's been done, make one of the gay men a transgendered monkey who's in a coma, and you want the right to pull the plug as one of its husbands... and heal it with prayer in our public schools.

Nobody said this was going to be easy. Think of yourself as a pioneer of suffering, and brace yourself for the excruciatingly slow turning of the wheels of justice. Remember: There were countless fugitive slaves, but only *one* – Dred Scott – had the patience to endure the vicissitudes of America's legal system. But it was all worth it when he made it to the highest court in the land and was told by the chief justice that he was a) wrong and b) not a man, but a piece of property.

His true reward, however, would come years later, after he was dead and it was of no use to him. For his case was a precedent, and today it is discussed by historians, memorized by high-school students, and joked about by assholes like myself.

Care to join him?

Stephen Colbert is the Chief Defender of International War Crimes at the World Court in The Hague. He is personally unpleasant.

Enter the Lower Courts

Seriously, enter the **lower courts**. These exist to ease the burden on the Supreme Court, to lessen the load on their fragile, osteoperitic, uncomfortably hunched backs.[6] These courts are called "lower" courts because they're "lower," or "worse."

It all starts with the **U.S. district courts**, the first stop whenever someone decides to "make a federal case" of something. Judges in these courts can barely read, and instead of gavels bang their thick skulls against their desks to bring the court to order. It is not unusual for a district court judge to throw his sandwich at a lawyer he dislikes.[7]

In addition to the federal court system, all 50 states have their own supreme and lower courts, employing a total of 53,545 bailiffs, 73,143 stenographers, 48,734 sketch artists, and 3 public defenders.

Thus, it is no surprise many cases brought before district courts are unsatisfactorily resolved. These cases move to the next step, the **U.S. court of appeals**, a.k.a. "The Court of the Sore Loser." There are eleven U.S. Courts of Appeal, and while not the highest court in the land it is considered the most sarcastic. Requests to these courts are met with "Wow, *great* motion. You must have gone to a really good law school." Finally, if a litigant feels he did not get the result he desired from the huge dicks on the appeals court, it is on to the Supreme Court … *if*, and this is a big if, the Supreme Court feels like it.

For the Court to take on a case, at least four of the nine justices must agree to hear it. Lawyers discover whether or not their case made the Court's docket when they show up and start making their arguments. If the Court

(Continue on page 96)

---

[6] Here, hyperbole is used to convey the justices as almost comically old.

[7] Individual district court experiences may vary.

Were You Aware?

Transcripts of every case argued before the Supreme Court are available for free on the internet, whereas transcripts for the Judge Mills Lane Show *cost six dollars by check or money order.*

Inside the Supreme Court

Cameras have never been allowed inside the Supreme Court, and those who have entered its hallowed halls must take a sacred oath not to reveal what they have seen. Nevertheless, a handful of scattered eye-witness accounts and sketched interpretations have emerged over the years, offering Americans a tantalizing glimpse into the most mysterious of the three branches of government.

Account Number One (Philip A. Simon, paralegal, 1931)

"The interior chamber is near dark. In the middle of the room, the justices float in a huge tank of brine. Their decisions and dissents are issued in whale-song and hastily recorded and interpreted by clerks."

Account Number Three (Brian Hicks, attorney, 1999)

"All I know is, everybody was fucking. Everybody. It was nine heads and 36 tangled limbs intertwined in a writhing, whirling dervish of group sex. Some guy – a clerk I can only assume – was twanging a sitar off to the side. Once in a while Scalia would break off from the orgy to cut hunks off a giant brick of hash with a Bowie knife. Then he remounted Ginsburg."

Account Number Two
(Theodore Williams, former janitor, 1952)

WHEN THEY HIRED ME, THE FIRST THING THEY TOLD ME WAS 'KEEP MY EYES ON THE FLOOR AND CONCENTRATE ON THE DROPPINGS.' BUT ONE TIME I LOOKED UP AND SAW NINE HAIRY BIPEDS LOPING INTO A LINE OF CURTAINS.

Account Number Four
(Anonymous attorney, c. 1973)

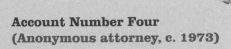

"It was kind of scary. They had curtains strung up to create dark little corridors, and a strobe light blinking somewhere. I was taken aback to hear that 'Rock and Roll Part II' song as the Justices entered. One justice, I think it was Thurgood Marshall, was wearing a skeleton mask. He made me put my hand in a box. I thought it was full of macaroni, but he told me it was 'Frankenstein's brains.' I got scared and ran out before I had a chance to argue. And that's how I lost Roe vs. Wade."

Account Number Five
(Anonymous Law Clerk, 1982)

It was the only time in my adult life I had the misfortune to experience a 'purple nurple.' I left the law ~~dating~~ shortly there after.

(Continued from page 93)

has decided *not* to hear them, the justices turn to one another and say, in an exaggeratedly theatrical manner, "Do you hear something? I thought I heard something. Hm. It must be flies buzzing around or something. Lalalalalalala."

Arguing Your Case: Let It Plead

Oral argument before the Supreme Court is limited to a half-hour per side.[8] While this may seem short, it is generally assumed the Court has familiarized itself with the details of the cases. (Also, David Souter has the attention span of a goldfish.) Lights on the Court's lectern warn lawyers when their half-hour is almost up: A white light means a lawyer has only five minutes left,[9] while a red light indicates his time is up, and he may only complete the sentence he is saying. A blue light indicates there is a special in aisle seven. Sometimes these specials offer litigants up to fifty percent off future writs.

>> Fig. 5.6

Cases are often said to be "on the docket," but few know what a docket looks like. Above, an example.

After hearing oral arguments, each justice retires to chambers to formulate a decision based upon his or her interpretation of the Constitution – or, in the case of Clarence Thomas, Antonin Scalia's interpretation of the Constitution. The majority then writes its decision. Justices who disagree are free to issue dissenting opinions, which have no legal bearing but serve as a nice on-the-record "Fuck you" to the other justices.

It is as simple – and profound – as that. Once the justices issue a decision, their word becomes law of the land. Schools are desegregated, abortions legalized, penises inserted into the anuses of our choosing. These nine wise men and women, guided only by their consciences, their study of the law, their political affiliations, their obedience to the president who appointed them, their personal distaste for the litigants

(Continue on page 100)

---

[8] Anal argument is capped at 30 seconds.
[9] Unless the white light is large and all-encompassing, in which case the lawyer is dead.

If I Were a Supreme Court Justice

By Ed Helms

When I read earlier in this chapter how the job of Supreme Court justice is a lifetime gig, I immediately realized it's the perfect job for me. Plus, I'm pretty interested in the law.

A Supreme Court justice is the custodian of our legal integrity and must lead by example. That is why I would start all my remarks with, "For example…"

For example, if I were a Supreme Court justice, I would make it illegal to break the law. Just seems like a no-brainer, people.

I would approach every argument with an open mind. Too often, Supreme Court justices let their ideologies determine the outcome before they've heard the arguments. Also, I would let my faith completely inform my decision-making. I mean, let's be honest, there really is only one Judge. His name is Jesus Christ, and he cries when babies die.

Justice Ed Helms, however, would make it a point to be the most unpredictable judge on the bench. "Swingin' Ed Helms," they'd call me, because I could go either way on any case…

and also because I'd use my position to get ungodly amounts of high-class trim.

Another thing I would do as an "active" judge is revisit poor decisions the Court has made in the past. In *United States v. La Vengeance* (1796), the Court granted the federal government maritime authority over inland waterways. That's bullshit! I firmly believe the government should not have this authority at *any* time, let alone maritime.

Also, I would order the immediate death of Roger Simpson. The one who lives at 1310 North Seventh Ave., Apt. 12A, Oroville, CA. He knows why.

For a closing argument, let me just say this: Vote Ed Helms for Supreme Court Chief Justice.

Ed Helms is a Fifth District Circuit Court judge representing the northern Great Plains.

Were You Aware?

The average Supreme Court justice spends 53 hours of his or her life engaged in the following exchange at parties:

Partygoer: *"So what do you do for a living?"*
Justice: *"Uh, I'm in law."*
Partygoer: *"Really? So you're a lawyer?"*
Justice: *"Well, kind of. I'm a judge."*
Partygoer: *"Really? What kind of judge?"*
Justice: *"Actually, I'm a Supreme Court justice."*
Partygoer: *(awed silence)*

Dress the Supreme Court

Below are the nine current justices of the United States Supreme Court. They are naked. Restore their dignity by matching each justice with his or her respective robe.

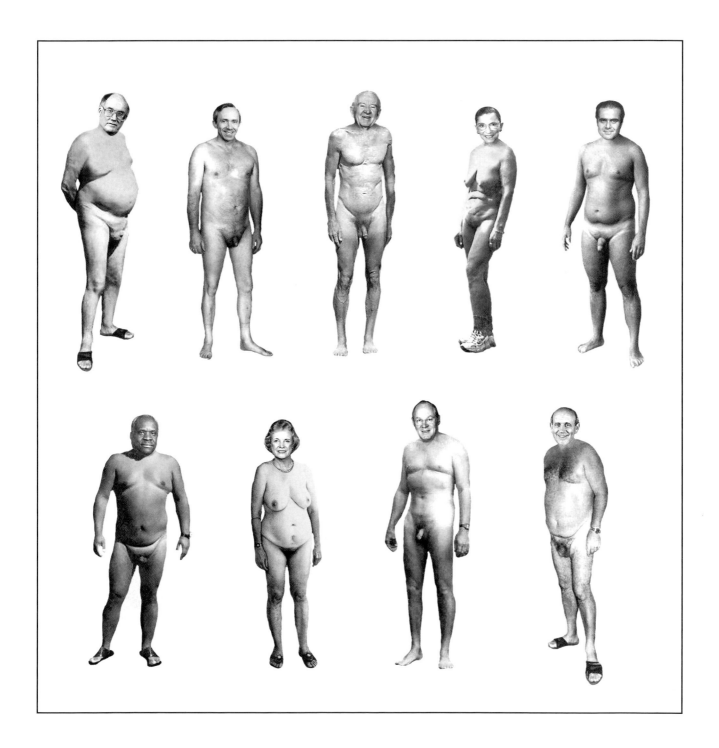

(Continued from page 96)

before them, their accumulated lifetimes of prejudices and preferences, mood swings, affections and animosities toward their fellow justices, and—of course—the occasional coin toss, make fundamental changes to the function and interpretation of the Constitution. The matter that has come before them is settled for good.

Until, of course, a justice dies or retires and is replaced by a new appointee. At that point, all legal matters are once again subject to review, the 5-4 ruling of yesterday becomes the 4-5 ruling of tomorrow…and what do you know, it's back into the closet with the buttsex. ◐

You Make the Call!

Bibb v. Navajo Freight Lines (1959)
An Illinois statute, applicable to interstate motor carriers operating under certificates of public-convenience and necessity issued by the Interstate Commerce Commission, requires trucks operating on that state's highways to be equipped with a specified type of rear fender mudguard. That mudguard, however, differs from those permitted in at least 45 other states. Would nationwide adoption of the Illinois mudguard—which would necessitate the welding of a new mudguard into place at the Illinois state line, thus interfering with shipping companies' interline operations—violate the "commerce clause" (Art. 1, § 8) of the Constitution?

The Verdict
It doesn't matter what your answer is. If you've read this far, congratulations! You are now a federal judge!

Discussion Questions

1. How many of the nine Supreme Court justices can you name? How many of the nine members of *The Brady Bunch* can you name? What does that say about you?

2. Ginsburg or O'Connor? Or, if you are female, Scalia or Stevens?

3. At what point during a typical Supreme Court hearing is it most appropriate to leap to your feet and shout, "*I'm* out of order?!? This whole *court's* out of order!"

4. Name five differences between a gavel and an ordinary hammer (see Fig 5.7).

5. If the current justices of the Supreme Court were a baseball team, which position would each one play? What position would each play if they were a cricket team, not counting the wicketkeeper and bowler? Which justice, past or present, do you think would make the best deep mid-wicket?

6. Separation of church and state is one of the fundamental principles of our government, yet court witnesses are required to swear on *The Bible*. Justify this.

Classroom Activities

1. Using felt and yarn, make a hand puppet of Clarence Thomas. Ta-da! You're Antonin Scalia!

2. Have the entire class dress up in black robes and put white wigs on. Observe how much easier it is to get serious work done.

3. Make a God's eye from popsicle sticks and yarn, then teach your students about the one true Judge: The Lord! (See Fig 5.8.)

4. Explain to the class that most Supreme Court justices decide cases along predictable ideological lines, but there are "swing justices" who could go either way, and are therefore fun to bet on. Start a bookmaking operation, collecting wagers from your students on which way the justices will vote.

5. While you're at it, start a death poll—many justices are on their last legs.

6. Make the judicial branch come alive for your students by conducting mock Supreme Court proceedings in the case of *Smelt It v. Dealt It.*

7. Have your students "re-argue" *Colgrove v. Green*, 328 U.S. 549 (1946), to determine if, as Colgrove argued, the Illinois congressional districts "lacked compactness of territory and approximate equality of population." That'll teach the little shits for chewing gum in class.

>>Fig. 5.7

A hammer is to a gavel as a normal person is to a _____.

a. fireman
b. astronaut
c. queer
d. normal person with a gavel
e. a & c

>>Fig. 5.8

We are all sinners in the eyes of these popsicle sticks.

HUMPHREY IN '68

BECAUSE OTHERWISE IN FOUR YEARS NIXON'S GUYS WILL GET CAUGHT BREAKING INTO THE WATERGATE HOTEL TO SABOTAGE THEIR OPPONENTS, CAUSING UNPRECEDENTED SCANDAL AND USHERING IN AN ERA OF CYNICISM THAT WILL SHAPE POLITICS FOR DECADES TO COME. CALL IT A HUNCH. SO, TO REPEAT: HUMPHREY IN '68.

CREATE POLITICS-AS-USUAL!
VOTE WASHINGTON

CHESTER ARTHUR 18 IN 84

THE POLICIES WE WANT. THE MUTTONCHOPS WE NEED.

If I were a first born white male landowner I'd vote for the **Earl of Norfolk** Parliament in 1452

'tis *John Adams* whose candidacy *I approve of with great vigor*

VOTE NIXON IN '80
JUST KIDDING

MONROE THE DOCTRINE IS IN!

I SCHTUPPED PRESIDENT KENNEDY AND I VOTE

LIFELONG-DEMOCRAT RETIRED PALM BEACH JEWS FOR BUCHANAN

Undecided Voters For CANDIDATE

I CAST MY 5 SLAVES' 3 VOTES FOR **JAMES K. POLK**

Yo, fuck McKinley.

Catch the DUKAKIS magic!
Then, let us know where you found it.

Chapter 6

Campaigns and Elections: America Changes the Sheets

Now that you have read the first five chapters and assimilated every word into the fiber of your being—or have randomly opened to this page while taking a dump—you are ready to learn about **campaigns and elections.** In brief, campaigns and elections are democracy's vetting process. Democracy sounds good "on paper," but how do we know it won't explode when we start it? Campaigns and elections are where the idealism and elegant design of the American Experiment are set free, to see if they can survive in the wild.

Initially, the process of conducting campaigns and holding elections was conceived as a means to an end – the peaceful transfer of power. But more than two centuries of refinements have elevated the process to an end in itself. Indeed, it can be said campaigns and elections have become the most important part of the Democratic Cycle, easily crushing the overrated "governance of the people" (see Fig. 6.1). Today, *running* for office takes as much, if not more, time, energy and resources as *holding* it. Think that's an inefficient perversion of our political system? Run for office and change it!

Although the skills needed to woo voters are at times diametrically opposed to those necessary to govern them, the expensive and arduous process exists for a reason: to ensure that those who wish to govern are, if not the most qualified our country has to offer, at least the ones who want it the most. The ones who want it *so* badly they will endure any humiliation just to catch but a whiff of the aphrodisiac that is power.[1] As Nixon famously said of Hubert Humphrey, his opponent in the 1968 presidential

---

[1] Power being defined as "a junior, non-voting appointment to a congressional transportation subcommittee."

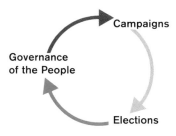

>>Fig. 6.1

Like the menstrual cycle, the democratic cycle is a highly regular occurrence that, while reassuring, is a bit of a nuisance.

election, "Yes, my opponent is wise; yes, he is honorable; but is he willing to kill anybody who stands in his way?" Nixon's subsequent triumph was proof of the system's central tenet: Campaigns and elections are the process in which democracy separates the willing from the able...and goes with the willing.

Running for Office: The Toughest Job You'll Never Love

Do you like babies? How about veterans? Can you feign interest in old people—and smile while touching them? How are you with handshaking? Backslapping? Palm-greasing? How do you feel about saying the same thing over and over again? Bus travel? Do you like being vilified on television? What about in print? Your spouse and children—do they enjoy being followed around, maybe having their backgrounds looked into? Chicken—can you stomach copious quantities of it in a sterile auditorium-like environment? Finally, do you like all those things enough to put up with them every day for the remainder of your professional life? If you answered "yes" to every one of those questions, congratulations!!! You're ready to enter the political arena.

And not a moment too soon. As our country has grown in size and stature, the scope of political campaigns has kept pace. The election cycle itself is fixed,[2] but everything else around it has expanded... sometimes grotesquely!

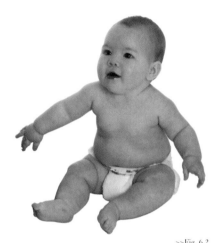

>>Fig. 6.2

On the campaign trail, you will grow to hate these things.

The Periodic Table of Elections	
Office	**Election Frequency**
Senate	Every six years
President, Governors	Every four years
Imperial Grand Wizard	Every three years
House of Representatives	Every two years
Prom King/Queen	Every year
Employee of the month	Dodecennially
American Idol	Weekly (Jan–May only)

2 As are many elections. See for instance Kennedy, John F., 1960, Illinois, "Project Giancana."

The most significant change to campaigns over the years has been cost. And while if you are considering a run for office you no doubt have an impressive personal fortune, only the rarest breed of politician can foot the bill on his own.[3] So that means fundraising, and lots of it.

(Continue on page 107)

Breaking Down a $2,000-a-plate Fundraiser

Political fundraisers take many forms, but the most common is the dinner. Supporters gather in a crowded auditorium or banquet hall to eat chicken. If they're lucky, the candidate will breeze in at the end to spend five minutes pumping hands and slapping backs before jetting off to another fundraiser. This experience costs $2,000. Where does that money go?

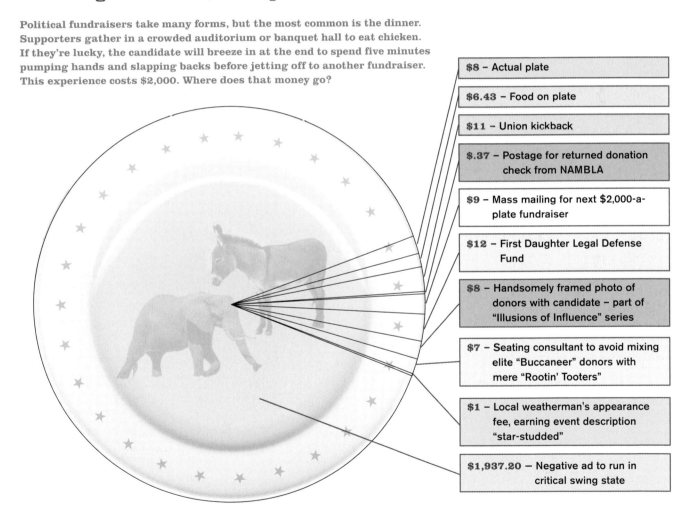

$8 – Actual plate

$6.43 – Food on plate

$11 – Union kickback

$.37 – Postage for returned donation check from NAMBLA

$9 – Mass mailing for next $2,000-a-plate fundraiser

$12 – First Daughter Legal Defense Fund

$8 – Handsomely framed photo of donors with candidate – part of "Illusions of Influence" series

$7 – Seating consultant to avoid mixing elite "Buccaneer" donors with mere "Rootin' Tooters"

$1 – Local weatherman's appearance fee, earning event description "star-studded"

$1,937.20 — Negative ad to run in critical swing state

---

[3] Such as billionaire Steve Forbes, who twice ran for president despite not having a goddamn clue what he was doing. "Flat tax." Yeah, keep saying that and see if it sticks, dipshit.

Political Conventions: A Poor Excuse for a Party

Party conventions used to hold a place of prominence in American politics. Candidates were nominated and tickets formed over a dramatic week-long period full of suspense and back-room negotiations. Today, conventions feature balloons. Below, a schedule for a typical day at the Democratic or Republican National Convention.

TODAY'S CONVENTION SCHEDULE

7:15 am	Wake-up Call
7:16 am	Hair of the Dog
7:25 am	Adulterer Walk of Shame
8:00 am	Prayer Breakfast
9:11 am	Issues Breakout Forums, third-floor convention rooms. Please sign up. Please?
11:30 pm	"I'm Representing My State, Yo!" An Awkward Young Delegate Roundtable
11:45 am	Tour of Host City (two-block police-protection radius around convention center only)
12:45 pm	Audition for role of "Black Guy on Dais."

1:00 pm	**CONVENTION CENTER PROGRAM BEGINS**

1:15 pm	Person with disease gives speech
2:00 pm	Disabled person with small business gives speech
2:45 pm	Disabled person fights person with disease; Winner gets to recite the Pledge
3:15 pm	"Local Open-Container Laws and You": An Overview and Discussion
3:30 pm	"Ladies and gentlemen, the Capitol Steps!"
3:31-3:40 pm	Sudden, overpowering sensation of hopelessness
5:15-6:00 pm	"How Many Is Too Many Balloons?": A Delegate Forum/Balloon Blow-up Session
6:30 pm	Armed Forces Color Guard*
6:45 pm	Hey, everybody, it's Rob Lowe/Gerald McRaney!
7:00 pm	Roll Call of the States
7:58 pm	The Waking Up of Wyoming
8:20 pm	Speech by red-faced Ted Kennedy/Pat Buchanan
8:45 pm	Senior campaign strategist dispatched to CNN skybox for Kennedy/Buchanan-related apology
8:50 pm	Speech by doddering former one-term president
9:15 pm	First introduction of "the next President of the United States"
9:30 pm	Second introduction of "the next President of the United States"
9:45 pm	Third introduction of "the next President of the United States"
10:45 pm	The next President of the United States begins speaking
11:00 pm	The next President of the United States cut off by local newscast
12:00 am	Lights Out
4:30 am	Entire hotel suddenly awakened by screams of fellow conventioneer who fears he may have just killed a hooker

*presented by Cheer Liquid Detergent with ColorGuard™

(Continued from page 105)

Savvy candidates know that without a powerful fundraising organization they will lose. "But I have a prescription for what ails our country and can lead…" Stop. You will lose. And raising money takes time, so plan on at least a year of non-stop solicitation to adequately compete. Don't worry, there will be plenty of time to come up with "core beliefs" and "policies" after you've been elected. Still doubt the importance of money in political races? Billionaire Ross Perot (see Fig. 6.3) received 19% of the presidential vote in 1992 despite being clinically insane.

Fortunately, candidates don't go it alone. Whether seeking city, state or federal office, they are undoubtedly running under the auspices of one of America's two political parties – **the Republicans** and **the Democrats.** (Yes, there's probably some state senator in Oregon who belongs to the Green Party, but face it: Hippie Q. McFreakington ain't going anywhere outside the greater Eugene area.) The Republican Party is the party of nostalgia. It seeks to return America to a simpler, more innocent and moral past that never actually existed. The Democrats are utopians. They seek to create an America so fair and non-judgmental that life becomes an unbearable series of apologies. Together, the two parties function like giant down comforters, allowing the candidates to disappear into the enveloping softness, protecting them from exposure to the harsh weather of independent thought.

>>Fig. 6.3

Billionaire Ross Perot's message of "gladrniaupra iweorna flinto" spoke powerfully to the nation's disembrained.

The Democratic Party's symbol, the donkey, represents the type of stubbornness that forces a town council to put a menorah up in the square alongside the Christmas tree even though the town only has five Jewish families.

The Republican Party's symbol, the elephant, represents the astounding memory of people who, if you say anything bad about them ever, file it away in a Rolodex of spite…and then trample you to death.

Were You Aware?

Despite candidates' constant assertions otherwise, only four of the 50 states are actually "great."

1.

2.

3.

4.

Above are those four states. To prevent a sudden and massive immigration crisis, we are leaving their names blank. Can you identify them by shape?

The parties provide candidates with the structure, financial support and enthusiastic placard-wavers critical for running a political campaign. In exchange, the candidate agrees to never take sides against the party. This agreement is typically signed in the blood of a candidate's first-born, though the party may make exceptions for those who promise to kill a hobo in front of them. Each party has a **platform**, a *prix fixe* menu of beliefs making up its worldview. The candidate can choose one of the two platforms, but remember – no substitutions. For example, do you support universal health care? Then you must also want a ban on assault weapons. Pro-limited government? Congratulations, you are also anti-abortion. Luckily, all human opinion falls neatly into one of the two clearly defined camps. Thus, the **two-party system** elegantly reflects the bichromatic rainbow that is American political thought.

From time to time in our history, there have been movements to create **third parties.** When introduced into a marriage, a third party can add a dash of spice and unpredictability to a relationship long loveless and dead. But as they say in electoral politics, "Two's company, three's a problem that must be undermined through legislative obstacles to their financing." Yet still they live. In 2000, the Green Party's Ralph Nader received thousands of votes that may have otherwise gone to Democrat Al Gore. Many say Nader's run cost Gore the presidency. Some egged his house. Still others crank called him at all hours of the day, saying "Thanks a lot, asshole." One man lit a paper bag filled with dogshit and placed it on Nader's front step. Ralph Nader wishes people would stop doing this, but to be fair, he is the one who tried to change the system.

>>Fig. 6.4

Of the three candidates in the 2000 election, Ralph Nader was second only to Al Gore in costing Al Gore the presidency.

The Campaign Trail: Learning to Hate the Land You'll Govern

>>Fig. 6.5

The necessary papers

Your party affiliation set and fundraising apparatus in motion, it is now time to dive headlong into the political fray by forming an **exploratory committee.** Exploratory committees are groups of one or more of your best friends whose job it is to tell you how much people like you. As it turns out, people like you a lot. The matter thus explored, you can file the necessary papers and declare your candidacy.

It is now time to develop the strategy that will win you the power you have craved since that beating in eighth grade. Step one is to define yourself. Distilling the ideas and intangibles of your candidacy into an easily digestible archetype can be meticulous and frustrating work. Thank God there are only two choices.

The Outsider. Outsider-dom is the strategy best suited to first-time candidates or veteran candidates who always lose. It reflects the distaste the public has for "politics as usual," and inside-the-beltway experts agree the outsider persona is the best choice for today's wanna-be insider. You won't want to use the word "outsider" too much in your campaign, however, so feel free to have your team of seasoned campaign managers, political operatives and speechwriters use synonyms like "grass-roots," "maverick," and "populist." Just make sure no one looks at your business cards and decides to use "billionaire financier." The important thing is, you know nothing about Washington and don't have a clue how the system operates.

The Insider. In the very likely event you are an incumbent, the whole outsider thing isn't going to work. Time for Plan B: running as "the guy with experience." This means you are a seasoned Washington veteran who has "gotten things done" and "risen above politics" to make the

(Continue on page 113)

>>Fig. 6.6

This Connecticut-born, Yale- and Harvard-educated multi-millionaire son of a former president ran as an outsider in 2000. Many experts still wonder how the fuck he pulled that off.

Third Parties: Rest in Peace

Your Campaign Team

The Seven People You Need to Put You in the White House

Chief Strategist

Crusty. Often best friend of candidate, either from college or youthful insider trading/real estate scandal. Soul rotting from inside out. Would make a very good president one day if not for crippling lack of likability.

Advertising Director

Madison Avenue refugee. Quit ad game to do something "real." Responsible for showing "human side" of candidate by filming him inside a classroom filled with young minorities, or on street shaking hands with grown-up minorities. Is himself fearful of minorities. Relies heavily on "minority wrangler."

Comunications Director

Finally, a place for a woman! Has unique ability to convert or "spin" any piece of remotely negative information into a positive. In short, she is a liar. But she is your liar. Try not to have sex with her.

Young Idealist

He's "jacked in." Doesn't talk about "Southern Voters"; instead, uses dynamic phrases like "New South." Eventually will become odious talking head for whichever news network offers nicest gift basket. Watch what you say around him—the notes he is taking will find their way into book form.

Pollster

A/K/A "The Sweaty Buzzkill." No one will meet him. He does not exist, because you, as a candidate, pay no attention to polls. Do not do anything until you talk to him first. The only person left on earth who seeks out "bicarbonate of soda" to cure gastrointestinal ills. (Make sure you have bicarbonate of soda!)

Policy Analyst

Finally, a place for a "woman of color." In charge of your "Health Care Initiative." Bugs you about going into more detail about your "Health Care Initiative." Doesn't understand no one gives a shit about her "Health Care Initiative." After your election, she will quit out of frustration for your lack of commitment to the "Health Care Initiative."

Opposition Researcher

Starts every sentence with "Back when I was in Black Ops…" Cites Nietzsche way too much. Does "research" on your opponent, which he then blends with "fiction" and "innuendo" to create "fact." Keeps dossier on own mother. Will offer to "take care" of "Young Idealist" after book comes out. Take him up on it.

(Continued from page 109)

type of tough, unpopular decisions that have gotten you re-elected to 19 consecutive terms in the House. You know everything about Washington and know exactly how the system operates. That doesn't mean you're out of touch – after all, Hootie & The Blowfish did play at your last rally, and, by all accounts, rocked. (If all else fails, remind constituents the defense plant 80% of them work at wouldn't be there if you hadn't snuck the appropriation into a cancer research bill.)

A third option is running as your own man. Good luck with that.

Now that you've defined yourself, it is time for the more important task of defining your opponent.[4] Remember, labels stick, so make up a good one. It needs to be simple, easily repeatable, and able to latch on to the electorate's collective unconscious like a deer tick on a fawn. Here's a list of some pre-vetted favorites:

- **Draft-dodger**
- **Flip-flopper**
- **Liberal**
- **East Coast liberal**
- **West Coast liberal**
- **Tax-and-spender**
- **Womanizer**
- **Soft on defense**
- **Soft on crime**
- **Soft on fabric**

(Note: All the above phrases are typically used by Republicans to define Democrats. This is because Republicans are superior to Democrats with this political technique. In fact, Republicans are superior to Democrats with *all* political techniques.)

---

[4] The third and arguably most difficult task will be defining "eleemosynary."

During the brief period he spends in the voting booth, the average American male thinks about sex 473 times.

If the voting booth is a rockin' don't come a knockin'.

Try not to refer to your opponent with these more explicit labels that may reflect badly upon your character:

- **Major league asshole**
- **War hero**
- **Fagatini**
- **'Tard**
- **His Satanic Majesty**

Remember, when in doubt, your mike is open.

Now that candidacy has been established and opponents defined, campaign season begins in earnest. In most cases, this is a three- to six-month dash to Election Day. Depending on the office, candidates may first have to fight through a **primary**, which is like a general election except it's against people of their own party and no one votes. Primary or no, election season is a time when those who already hold office put aside their responsibilities to get out there and meet the people whose needs they are now "officially" neglecting. Imagine being a secretary at an office, and every two or four years taking six months off to re-apply for the same job. Wouldn't that make your office more efficient? Oh, also, you're getting paid during the time you take off.

Every campaign features a few common elements. All of them are necessary...one is important.

Meeting constituents

This is accomplished by interrupting potential voters at a diner. Ask them questions. Touch them.[5] Look at them...ah ah ah! Not...with disdain. Oftentimes these appearances are accompanied by a short distillation of exactly who the candidate is, written by someone else. These are called **stump speeches** because they are to oratory what a stump is to a tree.

---

[5] Handi-Wipes are recommended.

Endorsements

If a fellow politician, celebrity or respected media publication puts its support behind a candidate, voters will follow. This is the theory behind endorsements. It has yet to work. In fact, in some cases, endorsements may even *hurt* a candidacy. For example, Barbra Streisand. Anything she touches turns to shit.

Debates

One of the nobler political traditions, the debate dates back to ancient Greece and Rome, where the ability to defend one's position was seen as manifest proof of the rightness of that position. Then Nixon flop-sweated in '60. Since then, the debate has focused less on a mastery of the issues and more on base, rouge and eyeliner. A pancake effect can make a candidate look waxy, but an insufficient base may expose unsightly blemishes and pocked skin – character flaws no amount of rhetorical prowess can overcome.

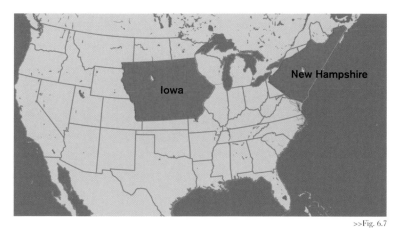

>>Fig. 6.7

By holding the first contests in the race for the presidency, Iowa and New Hampshire wield enormous power. This makes perfect sense given their size.

Advertising!

Now we're talking! Hectic campaign pace got you down? Your opponent seems to be right on too many issues? Buy some advertising time! It is the elixir to cure any ailing campaign. Whether a candidate is introducing him-

---

Which of these images should you not include in your campaign ad?

Waving American flag

Amber waves of grain

Your attractive but non-threatening wife and children

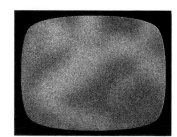

You teabagging a hooker

Your Stump Speech: Theme and Variations

	College Students	Farmers	NASCAR Dads	
"It's great to be here with all you…"	"…young people. Whoot, here I am!"	"…disproportionately influential primary voters."	"…child-bearing motorsport enthusiasts."	
"I grew up…"	"…the son of a hard-working brewery janitor and an immigrant bong-maker."	"…on a farm…well, not on a farm…what do they call those things they put up on fore-closed farmland? An estate. That's where I grew up."	"…in the backseat of a Formula F1 racer with a chrome moly tubing chassis, Aurora V8 3.5 liter engine, G-force radial slicks, custom rack-and-pinion steering, double-wishbone front and rear suspension and NLT sequential 6-speed transmission."	
"I'm reminded of my hero…"	"…Noam Chomsky."	"…John Deere."	"…Dashboard Jesus."	
"If elected…"	"…I will eat this bucket of worms." *(Hold bucket of worms aloft.)*	"…You will never be forced to sell your crops for money again."	"…I promise to focus on transportation safety measures, because there's a shitload of them we don't need."	
"My opponent says…"	"…he will draft you."	"…if he were passing through your region, and his car happened to break down, he would not hesitate to sleep with your daughters."	"…Richard Petty's a fag."	
"Thank you, and God bless…"	"…Stankonia."	"…the United States."	"…the U.S. of A!"	

self, re-introducing himself, explaining himself, defending himself, reinventing himself, or simply destroying his opponent, TV is the medium of choice. And here's the best part…there are no rules. Political advertising cannot be held to the same high truth standards of, say, a beer commercial. Try it. Refer to your opponent as Hitleresque! You've got nothing to lose but any chance of ever going to heaven!

Elections: Oh, Those Were Today?

It's finally Election Day. The day Americans celebrate their democracy. And while Election Day isn't a federal holiday, it is held on a Tuesday… for convenience.[6] On Election Day Americans exercise their fundamental right to

---

[6] Tuesday is considered the least important of all the workdays.

The countless speaking engagements a typical candidate must attend make it virtually impossible to write a new speech each time out. The stump speech, however, can be modified to tailor a message to a specific constituency. Below, some suggested variations.

Senior Citizens	CEOS	Chocoholics
"…GILFs."	"…Golden Circle Level contributors."	"…chocoholics."
"…at a time when bread – while costing considerably more than a nickel – was certainly not as expensive as it is now."	"…in a moral vacuum registered in the Cayman Islands."	"…in insulin shock."
"…Matlock."	"…Midas."	"…Count Chocula."
"… I will ask the FDA to make food softer."	"…I will be able to pay you back."	"…I'm going to have a hard time not eating chocolate, because I love it so much."
"…perhaps your grandchildren are not as precious as you think."	"…to tell you he'll be here in about five minutes, soon as I'm done."	"…chocolate is not delicious."
"…the United States of America."	"…Arnold Palmer."	"…the Oompah-Loompahs."

vote. Or not. 55-70% "vote" for the latter. It is perhaps a sign of the strength of our republic that so few people feel the need to participate. That must be the reason.[7]

Typically, voting is done in church basements or middle school gymnasiums staffed by well-intentioned volunteers whose naïve enthusiasm more than makes up for their blind incompetence. At their disposal: technology at least 50-75 years behind its time[8] – because if it was good enough for McKinley, it's good enough for us. With no national standard for conducting elections, states and municipalities are free to oversee them as they see fit. Ballots differ from state to state though common elements generally include a booth, a curtain and a disproportionate number of old people.

(Continue on page 120)

---

[7] Please say that's the reason.
[8] "Wow…this is the same lever and pully system as my cotton gin!"

Endorsements: Someone Likes You

Endorsements are the friendship bracelets of America's political school yard. And just like friendship bracelets, garnering endorsements requires a good deal of unrepentant ass-kissing. For a better understanding of endorsements and how they work, study the chart below:

Organization	How to Court	How They Help	How They Hurt
Firefighters Union	Refer to them repeatedly as "America's superheroes" (they really get off on that); roll eyes whenever someone mentions cops; pet the Dalmatian.	If you're standing next to them, why, you must be a hero, too! Also helpful if something's on fire.	Will probably bang your wife.
National Education Association	Sit up straight, don't slouch, keep eyes on own paper, and wipe that smirk right off your face, mister.	Control children and, therefore, the future.	They are a voracious, insatiable money pit.
The New York Times	Be a Democrat.	Shores up support among Lincoln Center season ticket holders.	Very few people have season tickets to Lincoln Center.
Z ROK 93.3	Participate in phone interview; don't back down when "The Mooch Man" asks you to slap scrotum against phone; be twelfth caller.	Will record catchy song parody incorporating your name and hot-button issue you're "too sexy for."	Surprise "concession" phone call from opponent might just be another "Thursday Morning Prank 'n' Spank."
Other Politicians	Implicit offer of position in your administration.	Will let you borrow old campaign bus.	Look inside yourself – do you really want to be surrounded with more of *that*?
Churches/ Religious Groups	Clap hands awkwardly to choir.	Members are "flock-like" in behavior, will vote however they are told.	If you cross them, they can have God kill you.
Veterans	Ask them what pin on hat represents, then nod politely for next three hours.	Just three of them magically transform any mundane situation into a patriotic photo-op.	Two words: "emotionally draining."

Negative advertising turns the spotlight on the other candidate in an attempt to lower his standing in the eyes of voters. Once seen as a last-ditch effort to salvage a flagging campaign, "going negative" has proven so effective, today's political candidates rely almost exclusively on it. Some say this cheapens the political discourse and turns people off to the entire process, but really, once you've portrayed a one-armed, no-legged war hero as a traitor to his country, what process is there to go back to?

The 5 Greatest Moments in Negative Advertising

1. Barry Goldwater Will Kill Us All (1964)

President Lyndon B. Johnson's 1964 "Daisy" ad ran only one time but made an indelible impression. Its image of a young girl counting flower petals before being vaporized by a mushroom cloud implied Johnson's Republican rival (Barry Goldwater) would lead the nation to nuclear war. In Johnson's defense, Goldwater's campaign itself also implied he would lead the nation to nuclear war. The conservative senator from Arizona was defeated handily by Johnson. The next year, Goldwater started a nuclear war.

2. Michael Dukakis: Friend of the Rapist (1988)

Horton Received 10 Weekend Passes From Prison

Seeking to portray Democratic opponent Michael Dukakis as "soft on crime," the campaign of George H.W. Bush produced the "Willie Horton" ad, suggesting that as governor of Massachusetts, Dukakis had personally requested a weekend furlough for convict Willie Horton, then driven him to Maryland, where he assaulted and kidnapped a young couple. As a result of the ad, Dukakis promptly replaced Horton as his running mate.

3. Grover Cleveland's Bastard Child (1884)

When supporters of James G. Blaine discovered his opponent Grover Cleveland had fathered a son out of wedlock, they distributed handbills featuring the above cartoon. Blaine lost anyway, giving presidents carte blanche for all eternity to have indiscriminate sex without political consequence (fellatio not included).

5. Caligula: Not So Bad (39 A.D.)

Widely recognized as a tyrannical megalomaniac who prided himself on cruelty and ruled through fear, Caligula was nearly undone by an underground smear campaign to depict him as a "pretty nice guy." Other sculptures and frescoes of the time libelously show him flying a kite and helping an old lady cross the Appian Way. An incensed Caligula immediately went into "damage control" mode by publically sodomizing a puppy.

4. Goody Proctor Is a Witch! (1692)

The Salem Witch Trials of 1692 marked the birth of negative advertising in America. Pamphlets outlining allegations of witchcraft, citing specific details of its practice, gave accusations a gravitas that standing in the town square pointing at passers-by and screaming hysterically "WIIIIIIIIIIIIIIIIIIIIIIIITTTTTTTTTTTCCCCCCCCCCHHHHHHHH!!!!!!!!" simply couldn't provide. But negative advertising proved short-lived in Salem society. Puritans soon grew ashamed of the evil practice and, as a sincere act of repentance, stoned the pamphleteer to death. Then, just to be safe, they drowned his family.

(Continued from page 117)

Given the intricacies of conducting an election, it is surprising so few have been disputed. This is largely because in most elections, margins of error are dwarfed by the differences in vote tallies. This was not the case, however, in 2000, when a hotly contested presidential race hinged on outdated equipment, poorly designed ballots and ill-prepared county supervisors. It laid bare a system in dire need of an immediate emergency overhaul. So look for that.

Then, just like that, the results you already know from weeks of internal and exit polling are in. Results usually go one of two ways.

You've lost. Thank your staffers. They could have worked harder, but now is not the time to tell them that. The next step is making the difficult phone call, through gritted teeth and crushed ego, to your opponent. Though over the past few days he has said things about you that in certain Middle Eastern countries would get his tongue cut out, you must offer your congratulations and pledge your support. You will spend the better part of the next three years working tirelessly towards his destruction, but keep that to yourself. Now go out there, failure that you are, and deliver a concession speech allowing you to exit the political arena with whatever is left of your dignity. The cameras are on; you are surrounded by loved ones and supporters; there is red, white and blue bunting that in your current mood can't help but strike you as temptingly flammable. It's been a good run. Good luck with your memoirs/consulting job/extended ski vacation/slow, depressing slide into obscurity. With any luck you'll at least be a historical footnote.[9]

Or,

You've won. Pop the champagne. You just got off the phone with your douchebag opponent, whose choked-back venom you couldn't help but chuckle at. Fuck him. Your junior communications director is massaging your balls while the deputy pollster works the shaft. It's good to be the king. Now go out there before the cheering throngs and tell them this is a time for unity. Make sure you throw in a couple of black people and someone in

(Continue on page 126)

[9] This could be you.

Of Course Your Vote Counts!

By Stephen Colbert

In every election, many people grapple with the nagging suspicion their vote doesn't count. As a citizen and someone who is always right, it is respectively my duty and my pleasure to tell them they are wrong. In fact, our democracy depends on every citizen recognizing the value of his or her vote.

And here is the value of that vote. In the most recent presidential election 105,360,260 people cast ballots. That means each person's vote counted .000000949%. I defy you to find a mathematician who will tell you that number is less than or equal to zero. Okay, so we can agree, your vote counts. It counts .000000949%.

Swish that around in your mouth for a while. How does it taste?

Taste like freedom? 'Cause to me it tastes like jack-all squat.

This brings up a related, better question than "Does your vote count?" Namely, "Does your vote make a difference?" To answer that, perhaps a more visual comparison would be illustrative. Imagine your vote as a deer tick. And the election as the continent of Asia.

Fig. 1 "Asia"   Fig. 2 "Deer Tick"

Do you notice the relative size of these two things? See how the deer tick appears in comparison with the largest continent on earth? This gives you a rough idea of the difference your vote makes vis-à-vis the entire electorate.

But there is good news. Due to the rampant (and growing) cynicism of people who feel their vote doesn't make a difference, voter turnout is steadily decreasing. Where this cynicism comes from escapes me, but it means that with each electoral cycle, the value of one vote increases. Now, it's difficult to imagine a day when the candidates running don't vote. So that's two votes right there. But, it is not difficult to imagine a day when only one other person bothers to vote. And oh, what a valuable vote that would be!

You're welcome.

Stephen Colbert has received the Werner Heisenberg Prize for Excellence in Theoretical Mathematics seven consecutive years, yet can barely feed himself.

Campaign Swag: Selected Items

While buttons and signs are the most common kinds of campaign memorabilia, they are hardly the only ones. Below are several priceless and rare artifacts spanning more than two centuries of American political history. They were purchased on eBay over a 10-minute period for $84.23.

Thomas Jefferson campaign tunic c. 1800

Theodore Roosevelt monocle shammy c. 1904

"Re-elect Herbert Hoover" bindle c. 1932

FDR "Action Cards" c. 1944

Jesse Jackson Yarmulke c. 1984

Cabbage Patch Mondale c. 1984

Silent Cal Ball Gag c. 1924

George McGovern 800-pound irregularly shaped object c. 1972

William Howard Taft Commemorative Dollop of Sour Cream c. 1912

VOTER REGISTRATION FORM

Dear Potential Voter:

Welcome to the democratic process! As you will see, registering to vote in the United States couldn't be easier. Think of this friendly form (FEC-V-22.a) as your gateway to American Democracy. Simply fill out the form below as best you can given your particular level of literacy. The government will not use the personal information you enter here for any purpose other than to register you to vote.[1]

By filling out this form, you attest that you are a United States citizen and that you will be 18 years old on or before Election Day. (If you will not be 18 on or before Election Day but could pass for 18 and need some quick cash, fill out form V-18, available in basement room B-05 after 7 p.m. Ask for Carlo.)

Enter your full name in this order:	Last	First	Middle	Nick	Sex: M ☐ F ☐

Address: Street | Apartment #

City	State	Zip	Key under: doormat ☐ fake rock ☐

Party affiliation: Democrat ☐   Republican ☐   Spoiler ☐

Why the sudden interest in voting?

Do you have some sort of a problem with the U.S. government?

Are you just doing this for the sticker?   Yes ☐   No ☐   *(If you want we'll just give you one.)*

Which square most resembles (that is, "looks like") your skin? *(Data collected for racial profiling only)* [2]   1 ☐   2 ▨   3 ▦   4 ▩   5 ■

If you checked boxes 2-5 may we purge you from the voting rolls?   Yes ☐   No ☐

I understand that the distance to my polling station will be in inverse proportion to my annual salary: Yes ☐   No ☐

You do realize that this also signs you up for the draft, right?   Yes ☐   No ☐   Maybe I don't need to vote ☐

If you are a Freemason, please enter the name under which your second "bonus" vote will be cast: _____   Is this an elderly polling place worker ☐ or a young first-time voter? ☐

DEPOSIT YOUR DNA SAMPLE IN THE ATTACHED VIAL. DO NOT CONTAMINATE THE VIAL.

	Date	SS#

Signature X _____
☐ *Please dot your "i" with a heart in this box, if applicable.*

Bank card PIN#	Credit card #	expiration date	ppv1 security code

[√] From time to time the government may choose to share your personal information with select marketers offering products and services of interest to our citizens. Uncheck this box if you don't want your information shared.

---

[1] And for various other purposes.
[2] If you checked a box other than 1 (white), please fill out a requisition form for additional forms GV8-322, GV8-327, GVX-J95 and GVP4-68-J1. Please anticipate 3-6 weeks for a reply. Don't contact us, we'll contact you.

The Campaign Bus

A critical weapon in any candidate's assault on democracy, the modern campaign bus serves as mode of transportation, place of residence, headquarters, and smelly bus.

Worst seat on bus. Reserved for staff member who completely fucked up VFW Pancake Breakfast in Des Moines. How do you not bring spatulas?!?

Lavatory. Popular among members of "Four-Feet High" Club.

Decorative tail fin

Candidate's child. It was either this or rehab.

Independent Documentary Filmmaker. "Actually it's digital video, but the quality's gotten so good you can make a movie for like 2000 bucks if you edit it yourself, which I'm gonna do on my Mac, jam in time for next year's Sundance…"

Blitzer

Coffee maker

Reserve coffee maker

Intravenous caffeine dispenser

Carpet stain (semen). Left over from when bus was used by "Rock the Vote."

Extra power supply for coffee maker

Tire spike release valves. To keep Michael Moore at safe distance.

24-inch "Spinning" alloy wheels. Available for "urban" campaign stops.

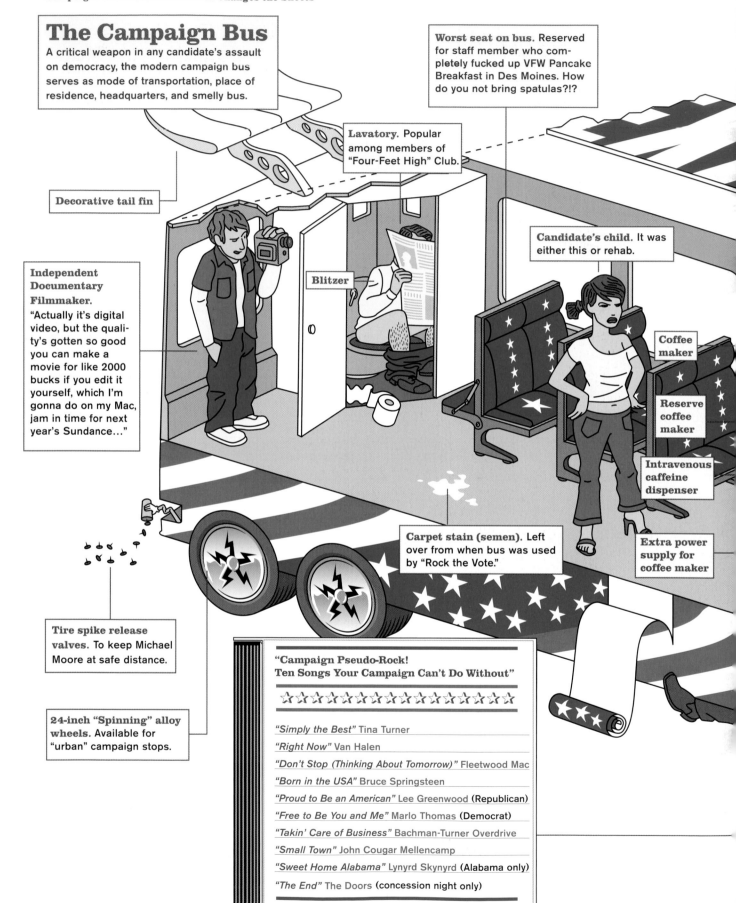

"Campaign Pseudo-Rock! Ten Songs Your Campaign Can't Do Without"

☆☆☆☆☆☆☆☆☆☆☆☆☆☆☆☆☆

"Simply the Best" Tina Turner

"Right Now" Van Halen

"Don't Stop (Thinking About Tomorrow)" Fleetwood Mac

"Born in the USA" Bruce Springsteen

"Proud to Be an American" Lee Greenwood **(Republican)**

"Free to Be You and Me" Marlo Thomas **(Democrat)**

"Takin' Care of Business" Bachman-Turner Overdrive

"Small Town" John Cougar Mellencamp

"Sweet Home Alabama" Lynyrd Skynyrd **(Alabama only)**

"The End" The Doors **(concession night only)**

Naming the Bus

History has proven you can't go wrong with some combination of the following words:

 **TOUR** **REAL** **STRAIGHT TALK** **PEOPLE** **TRUTH**

Be sure to tag it with:

EXPRESS

No one wants to come out to see the

Real Truth Straight Talk People Tour *Local*

Design is equally important. Color and font choices are endless and must be narrowed down. Specifically, narrowed down to big block lettering on a red, white, and blue background. And if you think the logo can have too many stars and/or stripes … think again, Mr. Also-Ran!

Multi-media Communications Area. Phones, fax machines, computers, and up to six (6) 13-inch televisions to monitor all leading news sources. $12.95/mo. additional charge for HBO or $1.00/mo. for Starz/Showtime/Sundance package.

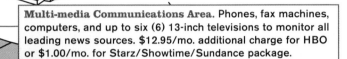

Secret Service Agent

Jets game

Driver. Preferably mixed race. Candidate must call driver by first name to show connection with "common man."

CD player

Keanu Reeves

Eco-friendly sticker. (For show only.)

"Candidate Simulator." Waves from tinted window when candidate takes private jet instead.

OnStar Navigation System. "On Star. May we help you, Mr. Next President?"

(Continued from page 120)

a wheelchair behind you to prove you meant all that crap about inclusion. Enjoy the evening. Tomorrow, you wake up an office-holder-elect, and the real work begins.

Running for re-election. ◐

>>Fig. 6.8

The long, grueling ordeal that is a modern campaign climaxes when the victorious candidate stands up on the podium, looks out at his supporters, and realizes he's forgotten why he ran in the first place.

Do You Have "It"?

To truly succeed in public office, a politician needs an indefinable quality above and beyond intelligence, dedication and any grasp of the issues. The French call it "je ne sais quoi." Americans, who aren't pretentious snobs and don't need fancy words to make them feel all cool, call it "It."

Do you have "It"?

		Yes	No
1.	Do people from different ethnic and socioeconomic backgrounds feel comfortable with you, even when you neither know nor care about them?	○	○
2.	Can you express strong emotion on cue?	○	○
3.	Do you have disciples?	○	○
4.	Do strangers offer you sex with little or no coaxing?	○	○
5.	Does your portrait look good framed and hung over a bureaucrat's desk?	○	○
6.	In school, did you have few true friends but dozens of student council campaign volunteers?	○	○
7.	Have your children written memoirs casting you as an emotionally unavailable enigma?	○	○
8.	Do people feel like they are the only ones in the room when you are speaking to them?	○	○
9.	Do rooms feel like they're the only ones in the house when you are in them?	○	○
10.	Are you able to pass off glaring defects of character as lovable quirks?	○	○
11.	When you play tag are you often "It"?	○	○
12.	Is your hair flecked with enough grey to make it seem like you've been around the block, but not so much to make you "Medicare-y"?	○	○

If you answered "yes" 1 to 4 times:	If you answered "yes" 5 to 8 times:	If you answered "yes" more than 9 times:
You have insufficient "It." But leave your name and maybe you can stuff some envelopes or something.	You possess enough "It" to be a moderately successful city-level administrator and/or local news anchorman.	You are "It" rich. Assemble an exploratory committee and weigh your options.

Were You Aware?

Before 1920, women used to call Election Day "Stay Home and Cook Day."

Though they won't admit it, women were much happier when all they had to do was bake shit and pump out kids.

Were You Aware?

The "ballot" stage is the final stage in the metamorphosis of the butterfly.

Discussion Questions

1. What the hell does it mean to "rock" a vote? Can a vote be R&B'd? Singer-songwritered?

2. Seriously, how come at 18 we're like, old enough to vote, but we can't have beer?

3. Which of the following is the best combination of reasons to vote for a candidate?
- A) Issues and eyes
- B) Party affiliation and hair
- C) Background and teeth
- D) Religious zealotry and tits

4. Can we put a sign in your yard?

5. Has your mother been seeing that guy Phil? Has he stayed over? Stop crying. It's *very important* that you tell me.

6. Minorities like African-Americans, Asians and Hispanics make up an increasingly large percentage of the American population, yet are underrepresented in public office. In fact, there is not a single black elected Republican in Congress. Do minorities think they are too good for Republicans or something?

J.C. Watts (R-OK) is a member of the Black Republican Hall of Fame. Actually, he is the member.

Classroom Activities

1. Make the Electoral College come alive! Divide your entire school into 50 groups of varying sizes. Then assign a point value to each group roughly based on its size. Have each individual student then vote on an issue – say, "chocolate or vanilla." Tally the votes but tell them the side with the most votes isn't necessarily the winner. Instead, calculate the winner within each of the 50 groups, then give the previously assigned point value to the respective flavor. Add up the point values and see who has more. Isn't this a better way to figure out a winner?

2. Disenfranchise a black student.

3. Have the students choose an official song for their imaginary run for president. Make sure it isn't that rap-metal crap they listen to.

4. Connect the dots for an Election Day surprise!

REFERENDUM 12: Would you accept a .071% tax increase to fund city schools through 2014?

yes

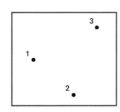

no

5. Hold a mock election. If you can't do this, mock a real election.

6. Match the candidate to the scandal that sunk his political ambitions.

 A. Gary Hart

 C. Edmund Muskie

 B. Joe Biden

 D. Richard Ramirez, a/k/a "The Night Stalker"

1. Plagiarized British Labour leader Neil Kinnock's stump speech
2. Cried in public
3. Went on murderous rampage in greater Los Angeles area
4. Extramarital affair captured on film on boat named *Monkey Business*

Answer Key: A-4, B-1, C-2, D-3,

Write a campaign speech incorporating as many of the words below as you can.

- Freedom
- Liberty
- Future
- Children
- America
- Americans
- United States
- Brave
- Heroes
- This Great Nation
- Great State of (State Name)
- Strong
- Founding Fathers
- Heartland
- Homeland
- Farmer
- Family
- Small Businessman
- Education
- Environment
- Strengthen
- Pursuit of Happiness
- Victory
- Good people
- Regular folks
- Hard-working
- Moms and Dads
- Charity
- Churches, Synagogues and Mosques

Extra credit:

- Wetlands
- Carpal Tunnel Syndrome
- Ching-chong Chinamen
- Hieronymous Bosch
- Pneumonoultramicroscopicsilicovolcanoconiosis
- Fagatini

Chapter 7

The Media: Democracy's Guardian Angel

A free and independent press is essential to the health of a functioning democracy. It serves to inform the voting public on matters relevant to its well-being. Why they've stopped doing that is a mystery. I mean, 300 camera crews outside a courthouse to see what Kobe Bryant is wearing when the judge sets his hearing date, while false information used to send our country to war goes unchecked? What the fuck happened? These spineless cowards in the press have finally gone too far. They have violated a trust. "Was the president successful in convincing the country?" Who gives a shit? Why not tell us if what he said was *true?* And the excuses. My God, the excuses! "Hey, we just give the people what they want." "What can we do, this administration is secretive." "But the last season of *Friends* really is news." The unmitigated gall of these weak-willed…You're supposed to be helping us, you indecent piles of shit! I…fuck it. Just fuck it…

>>Fig. 7.1

Johannes Gutenberg (c. 1400-1468). Gutenberg's development of the printing press allowed for the widespread dissemination of information or "mass media." Later, his invention would be used to publicly identify rape victims.

"We look forward to an endless future of taking it."

NBC

CNN

M S NBC

FOX NEWS channel

CBS ◉

abc

Chapter 7

The Media: Democracy's Valiant Vulgarians

[*Editor's note: We sincerely apologize for the false start on the chapter concerning the press. The authors have assured us it was a momentary lapse in restraint caused by a deadline-induced Red Bull binge. In no way was it meant to portray any sense of anger and/or disappointment in the behavior and standards of the modern media.[1]*]

What is the role of a free and independent press in a democratic society? Is it to be a passive conduit responsible only for the delivery of information between a government and its people? Is it to aggressively print allegation and rumor independent of accuracy or fairness? Is it to show boobies?

No.[2]

The role of a free press is to be the people's eyes and ears, providing not just information but access, insight, and most importantly context. It must devote its time and resources to monitoring the government, permeating the halls of power to determine who is doing the people's work, who is corrupting the process, and who will promise to be a mole in the State Department if their homosexuality is kept secret.[3] Only after that – and only with time permitting – should it move on to high-speed freeway chases. (For an exciting example of one such chase, check out the flipbook at the bottom right of this chapter.)

>>Fig. 7.1

Johannes Gutenberg (c. 1400-1468). Gutenberg's development of the printing press allowed for the widespread dissemination of information or "mass media." Had he foreseen this, he probably would have put more time into his other invention, the edible hat.

---

[1] "Modern media" is a wholly owned subsidiary of Warner Books, a wholly owned subsidiary of Time Warner, Inc.
[2] Well, not really.
[3] Guess!! It rhymes with "Missinger."

A Century of News Milestones

was foreshadowed last Friday, is a son of Vice Admiral Polo, who formerly represented Spain in this country. Señor Bernabe is now engaged in a special department of the Foreign Ministry at Madrid dealing with commercial matters and Consulates.

ALL AT SEA ABOUT SPAIN.

President McKinley Hopes for a Disavowal of the Assertions of Minister de Lome.

WASHINGTON, Feb. 14.—Assistant Secretary Day continues to be uncommunicative about the nature of the messages he has received from Minister Woodford, but is not unaware of the increasing interest in the evident dissatisfaction of the Administration with the nature of the response.

Rival New York publishers use accidental sinking of U.S. warship as call to arms. America goes on hunt for non-existent Spaniards of Mass Destruction.

| **1898** |
| **Remember the *Maine*!** |

Want to know how your meat is packed? No, you don't.

| **1906** |
| **Ewwwww!** |

Orson Welles's radio broadcast terrifies nation. Realizing they've been fooled, Americans shake their radios furiously to punish the little men inside.

| **1938** |
| **War of the Worlds!** |

Television debuts at World's Fair. People momentarily fascinated, then complain nothing's on.

| **1939** |
| **TV!** |

Chicago Tribune prints famously wrong headline. Pride causes newspaper to stick to story, and for next four years create an elaborate fictional universe in which Thomas Dewey is President of the United States.

| **1948** |
| **Dewey defeats Truman!** |

| **1912** |
| **Iceberg!** |

| **1927** |
| **Lindbergh!** |

| **1937** |
| **Hindenburg!** |

| **1952** |
| **Rosenberg!** |

Execution of alleged Russian spies Julius and Ethel Rosenberg finally brings end to "Berg" era of American history.

Magazine Milestones

| **1927** |
| **The Beginning of *TIME*** |

Time magazine launched. Mission: To build reputation for seven decades, then squander it by making O.J. blacker.

TIME

World watches in awe as Neil Armstrong takes historic first step on moon.

1969
The *Eagle* Has Landed!

World watches *Dick Van Patten Christmas Special* instead.

1973
***Apollo 17* Lands on Moon**

Geraldo Rivera is an incredible asshole. One example of that is when he opened Al Capone's vault in a much-publicized TV special, but there was nothing inside. There are many, many other examples.

1986
Al Capone's Vault!

Major news networks prematurely "call" Florida for Al Gore, then prematurely "call" Florida for George W. Bush, then sit quietly waiting for America to fall asleep. Media officially jumps the shark.

2000
Too Close To Call!

1963
Cronkite Cries!

Assassination of President John F. Kennedy makes Walter Cronkite cry like little girl. "What's the matter, Walter? Can't handle a little loss of national innocence?"

1974
Watergate!

President brought down by investigative journalists. Investigative journalists declare "nice work," take rest of millennium off.

1980
This Is *CNN!*

Ted Turner launches 24-hour news network. People doubt there will be enough news to fill 24 hours. People are right.

1996
Fox Populi

Fox News debuts, finally giving voice to white American males.

1975
Up With *PEOPLE*

Time begets *People*, turning full power of investigative journalism into search for sexiest man alive.

1977
Look At *US*

People begets *Us*, a magazine covering all the questions left unanswered by *People*.

1994
Reading *INSTYLE*

Us begets *InStyle*, a magazine for people who would like to know where the people in *Us* and *People* got their shirt.

InStyle

1999
Get *LUCKY*

InStyle begets *Lucky*, a magazine for retards about shopping.

Lucky.

Were You Aware?

While there is no "i" in "team," there is both a "me" and an "i" in "media."

>>Fig. 7.2

The town crier's call of "Hear ye! Hear ye!" was the colonial equivalent of today's "Fox News Alert," only without a shrieking metallic sound effect akin to fingernails scratching a chalkboard in hell.

(Continued from page 133)

For government to truly be "for the people," its inner workings must be exposed for the public to see. This lofty goal is known as **transparency**, and while it could be accomplished by sheathing all elected officials and public buildings in Saran Wrap, this has been deemed unwieldy, expensive and creepy. Instead, transparency is achieved via a **free press**, something so vital to democracy it has historically been given equal stature to the three branches of government—hence its nickname, "The Fourth Estate."[4] No less an authority than Thomas Jefferson wrote, "If it were left to me to decide whether we should have a government without a free press or a free press without a government, I would prefer the latter." He then added, "Now, if you'll excuse me, I have a lunchtime appointment with a fine slice of brown sugar. That last part's off the record."

So, has the American press lived up to the lofty status envisioned by the Founding Fathers? No. It has surpassed them. And the story of how the media transformed itself from a mere public necessity into an entertaining profit center for ever-expanding corporate empires is an inspirational one—one that will hopefully be optioned by our parent company's film arm and turned into a movie of the same name.[5]

The Media in American History: From New∫ to News

Perhaps at no other time in our history has the media played a more vital role than in the American Revolution. Yet back then only two forms of media existed: the **town crier** and the **pamphlet**. The town crier focused mainly on local news and had a circulation of whoever was walking by.[6] In contrast, the pamphlet was more meditative, analyzing and offering perspective on the day's events. It also included the occasional personal. Imagine the tiny booklet for sale by the Barnes and Noble cash register. Now imagine that instead of offering you *365 Reasons Why Golf Is Better Than Tantric Sex*, it urged you to cast off your oppressor and don the mantle of dignity that is every man's birthright. *That's* a pamphlet.

---

[4] The term also derives from the land holdings of its most successful members, i.e., "I hear Brokaw just closed escrow on his 'Fourth Estate,' a 9-bedroom chateau in Provence."

[5] We're not married to the name.

[6] And who wasn't deaf.

>>Fig. 7.3

Colonial-era personal

Thomas Paine was the most famous pamphleteer of his day and his manifesto *Common Sense* is widely credited with inspiring the young colonies to revolution. Not bad for a tract composed primarily of observations such as "Though it look a bit like a comb, a fork is not a comb, and woe be to any maid who confuse 'em," and the hilarious litany of insults entitled "You Might Be a Redcoat If…" Pamphleteers looked down on town criers, considering them glorified parchment readers blurring the line between information and yelling.[7] Pamphlets took time to print however, and criers would have their revenge with the major breaking news story "the British are coming." Paul Revere's midnight broadcast would be remembered as an essential piece of American lore. Less remembered was the following week's pamphlet headline, "The British Came."

The Founding Fathers were so grateful to the media for their role in the revolution that the foremost inalienable right codified in the Constitution's Bill of Rights was the **First Amendment** which guaranteed freedom of speech and freedom of the press. This right was revoked in 1798 by the Alien and Sedition Acts, but still, it had been a fun nine years. So when the Acts expired in 1801, the government pledged to never again use legislation to censor the media, vowing to only use intimidation and coercion from that day forward.

(Continue on page 140)

---

[7] An amalgam known at the time as "infoyelling."

America the Book Insta-Poll

How much do you support our troops?

- ◯ Lots
- ◯ Plenty
- ◯ Totally
- ◯ 110%

24-Hour News Networks: A Schedule Without Rest

On an average day 7 minutes of news happens. Yet there are currently 3 full-time, 24-hour news networks. So how did the creators of the 24 hour news channels solve that riddle? Below the actual blueprint from which it all sprang.

7 minutes ———▷ ACTUAL NEWS

3 minutes ———▷ BREAKING NEWS

25 minutes ———▷ Breaking NEWSGRAPHICS

22 minutes ———▷ TEMPERATURE HIGHS AND
LOWS IN PLACES YOU Don't live

1 HOUR ——▷ FORCED, LIGHT-~~HANDED~~ HEARTED BANTER

6 HOURS —▷ COMMERCIALS

• 2 HRS : ads ending in the phrase "may cause diarrhea"

• 30 MIN: guy with briefcase hustling someplace

• 30 MIN. creepy, over-chiseled exercise guy no one's heard of.

• 30 MIN : Lindsay Wagner talks about her dream mattress

• 20 min : scandal-plagued corporation touting one
thing they do that doesn't give you cancer

1 HOUR ~~~ CONTEXT AND PERSPECTIVE

1 HOUR ——▷ cross-promotion for on-network or parent-
company affiliated news or entertainment

10 minutes (could parent company's movie premise happen
for real?; others)

40 minutes ——▷ FOR YOUR HEALTH !

2 HOURS ———▷ NATURAL DISASTER !!

1 hour people huddling in a gym.
45 minutes correspondent being blown laterally.
15 min. suggestions from anchor to correspondent
regarding correspondent's maintenance of warmth

[36 minutes: b-roll of fat people from neck down]

20 min ——▷ "POP CULTURE MINUTE"

1 hour • HUMAN INTEREST
• footage of moose in suburban swimming pool
• water-skiing squirrel
• cheese-eating contest?

(Not per question! Cumulative)

15 minutes → satellite delays between anchor and foreign correspondent

15 minutes → dead air. Foreign correspondent feigning satellite delay while trying to think of answers to questions.

30 minutes → Jennifer Aniston did WHAT?!!?

20 minutes → a grumbling curmudgeon reads your e-mail

40 minutes → STOCK REPORT (NOTE: Hot chick?)

- ~~Cash Cash~~
- ~~Wall Streetwallet~~
- Money Honey ✓

GREAT, BUT NOT TOO HOT - MUST BE BELIEVABLE

1 HOUR → ROUNDTABLE DISCUSSIONS of relevant political issues

Possible Titles: Shut your Cakehole!

Douchebag V. Douchebag

1 HOUR → COMING UPS, UP NEXTS + STILL-TO-COMES
   30 minutes: infotainment
   30 minutes: propaganda
   30 minutes: infoganda
   30 ~~minutes~~ minutes: ~~Rivapainta~~ propa·tainment ~~✗✗✗✗✗~~   ⟵ TIME PERMITTING

1 HOUR → unconventionally attractive correspondent of indeterminate ethnicity talks about countries you don't care about

4 HOURS → RE·RUN CRAP FROM EARLIER IN THE DAY

23 hours, 57 minutes
+   3 minutes - praying for celebrity to commit crime
‾‾‾‾‾‾‾‾‾‾‾‾‾
!! (24 HOURS)

ALL 24 HOURS- a "crawl" at bottom of screen summarizing every possible story available to us.
Note: No celebrity is too insignificant for viewers to know it's their birthday.

Broadsheets (left) and tabloids (right) remain the two forms of newspaper most commonly printed. If you want to be treated as someone who doesn't know what they are talking about, call them "broads" and "bloids."

The Newspaper: Pulp Faction

The 19th century[8] saw the invention of ink that rubbed off on your hands, paving the way for the rise of the **newspaper** – a little bundle of democracy and coupons delivered right to your door. Dedicated to congressional debates and political arguments ranging from slavery to universal suffrage, newspapers sucked. The public wanted stories of tragedy, crime and entertainment, preferably all three at once.[9] So savvy publishers began gathering titillating gossip, experimenting with gigantic typefaces, and invented a unique way to "cross words" in puzzle form. In so doing, they created a new kind of newspaper called a **tabloid**. By the end of the century, tabloids would have their greatest triumph – plunging our nation into an unnecessary war.

1898. As tension grew between America and Spain over the Spanish colony of Cuba, newspaper magnates William Randolph Hearst and William Pulitzer engaged in a far more significant battle over circulation numbers. Each paper fought to outdo the other with salacious, or "made up," stories of Spanish atrocities, fanning the flames of a newfound American nationalism. Just as the war between Hearst and Pulitzer was about to get violent, relief came in the form of a ship, the *U.S.S. Maine*, accidentally blowing up in Havana harbor, killing more than 200 Americans. The papers blamed the Spanish and presto! The resulting war raised circulation for both men, and the pair's blend of fiction, bigotry and jingoism became known as **yellow journalism.**

Later, the phrase was shortened to "journalism."

>>Fig. 7.5

William Randolph Hearst was immortalized in the film Citizen Kane. *Those who have seen it know it ends with the newspaper titan lamenting "Rosebud," a beloved sled from his lost youth. Those who haven't seen it…um, don't worry, it's not that big of a plot point.*

(Continue on page 145)

---

8 That's the one with the 1800s.

9 For example, the 1848 saga of the adultering heiress killed alongside her piano-playing saloon keeper lover by a jealous earthquake.

We Have a Media in Canada Too, You Know!

By Samantha Bee

Sorry to bother you again. I just wanted to pop in here for a jif and let you know we have media in Canada too! In fact, we have *all* the media – TV, radio, newspapers, and I think even the internet now. They're just like yours, only ours tend to focus less on blowing things up and more on courtesy.

The biggest difference between our media and yours is the dominance of the Canadian Broadcasting Corporation. The CBC is fully funded by the government to produce public-interest programming and provide the kind of high-quality television you'd expect from a cash-strapped federal bureaucracy. My grandmother in Chesley loves it! (That's near the Bruce. It's a peninsula in Ontario. Ontario? That's a province. A province? You know what? It's our fault for not calling them states.)

Did you know Shania Twain is from Canada? She is one Canadian who is *definitely* in the media game!

Sorry.

The other strange thing about our media is we have "Canadian content" laws which mandate a certain percentage of our programming be home-grown. I hope that doesn't sound snobby. We know how hard it is for you to find markets for your culture outside your borders – but you might not always be around to make our TV for us. We just want to ensure we protect our essential "Canadian-ness," which we usually define by listing the ways we aren't like Americans. Canadian content laws also ensure Bryan Adams is paid the royalties he needs to keep his summer home on Mayne Island.[1]

Other than that, our media is kind of like yours. Honestly, looking back, I don't think the differences were substantial enough to justify this essay.

I'm sorry if my abrupt conclusion has created any layout problems for this chapter.

---

[1] Mayne Island is in British Columbia.

Sorry about the footnote.

America the Book Insta-Poll

What is the margin of error?

- ○ The thing that makes you think a poll has some kind of scientific grounding
- ○ The amount of people who hung up on the pollster divided by 100
- ○ A mid-80s new wave band
- ○ The only time the symbol +/- is ever used

Stephen Colbert's Guide to Dressing and Expressing Like a TV Journalist

Though fancy journalism schools will tell you otherwise, all you need to be successful in the world of television news is a rudimentary understanding of fashion and six different facial expressions. Oh, and a crippling need to be liked.

The Wardrobe

The Knot - Double Windsor... in a pinch a 1.5 Windsor will do, but never, ever less.

The Hair - Anchorman hair is something that can't be taught. You either have it or you don't. It's what gives the best newsmen their strength – Jennings, Brokaw, Rather – the lions of the field have manes to match.

The Vest - Pockets! Pockets! Pockets! The amount of experience you have in the field is measured by the number of pockets on your vest. Each successful assignment brings with it the awarding of a new pocket. By the time he retired, Edward R. Murrow's vest had 2,843 pockets.

The Bandanna - Necksweat — the gravitas killer.

The Suit - One word: Very expensive. That four-button crap is for CNN. I like Italian and the finer English couturiers if I have to buy off the rack, which I don't. I remember wearing a beautiful Hickey Freeman blue pinstripe three-button for the initial bombing of Baghdad. It felt right.

Rolled-up Sleeves - Nothing says you're hard at work on the story like rolled-up sleeves. And the best part? It takes very little work to roll them up.

The Truss - A good truss allows an anchor who's long since gone flabby and soft...wait... can you tell I'm wearing a truss?

The Pen & Notepad - Not that you're taking any notes—that's what your producer and cameraman are for. But as my acting teacher once taught me, it's nice to have a "bit of business" to do with your hands.

The Pants - Not technically necessary if you're sitting behind a desk, but it helps me stay focused on the task at hand.

The Shoes - A minor detail? Wrong! Expensive shoes for a job where your feet are never seen are what separate a weekend fill-in from network primetime. Mine have custom orthotics to accommodate my feet, which are both flat and arched at the same time. Also, I have hammer toe.

The Anchorman

The Crouch - Do your squats. This is the ready position for reporting the latest developments from the field - even though you are stationed comfortably inside the Press Center.

The Foreign Correspondent

The Outfit - Make sure you wear at least two pieces of khaki. Not only does it blend well with the uniforms of those with whom you're embedded, it also "pops" nicely when seen through a night-vision scope.

The Undercover Reporter

A word of explanation. You don't always get to choose where the job takes you. Over the years I've uncovered hundreds of scandals, and it just so happens a surprising number have required me to enter the shadowy underground world of the sado-masochistic homosexual community. Whether it's a meth ring run out of the back of a gay biker bar, a politician's forays into an S&M dungeon with his underage male "protégé," or an insurance scam involving a high-level CEO whose commute to work happens to pass by the aforementioned gay biker bar – this outfit is your ticket "in."

The Expressions

The most important skill a news interviewer must master is the "reporter reaction shot cutaway." You've got half a second—tops—to overshadow your subject. Make it count.

1. *"Your comments evoke a skepticism in me that I choose to convey smugly."*

2. *"You worked with Owen Wilson on this film—I understand he's a bit of a prankster."*

3. *"You discovered the gene that causes MS, and yet, I make more than you."*

4. *"I want the truth. How the hell did Charlie Rose get on the guest list and not me?!?"*

5. *"I asked you where you were wounded. I didn't ask to see it!"*

6. *"Tell me where he touched you." (Note: Never follow this question with face #2.)*

America the Book Insta-Poll

Do news organizations actually care about your responses to polls?

- ○ No
- ○ No, and they mock you for your participation
- ○ No, but they don't think you know that
- ○ No, in fact, they would prefer to reach through the TV screen and thrash you

Were You Aware?

In reality, Jews only control 82% of the media.

Control of the Media

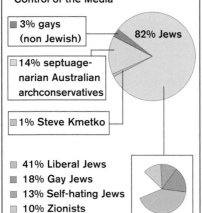

- ■ 3% gays (non Jewish)
- □ 14% septuagenarian Australian archconservatives
- ■ 1% Steve Kmetko
- 82% Jews

- ■ 41% Liberal Jews
- ■ 18% Gay Jews
- ■ 13% Self-hating Jews
- ■ 10% Zionists

What Will You Call Yourself?

Now that you've mastered expressions and outfits, it's time to turn your focus to the most important credential you'll need in TV journalism: A name. The one you currently have simply won't do. Trust us, the phrase "For all of us here at Channel 7, I'm Fred Zizniak," will ne'er be uttered on a television newscast.

Use one of the formulas below to create for yourself a new TV-approved name.

Examples:

Anchorman
Recommended formula:
One-syllable type of construction material + breed of horse

}
- • Brick Shetland
- • Chip Clydesdale
- • Stone Winchester
- • Wood Lippizaner

Sportscaster/weatherman
Recommended formula:
One-syllable kitchen-related verb + nonsensical two-syllable compound

}
- • Flip Greencat
- • Dash Sledboat
- • Slice Carhat
- • Squirt Mudbottom

Women
Recommended formula:
Regular first name with pretentious misspelling + alliterative surname that sounds like a first name

}
- • Daran Davids
- • Mikhaela Michaels
- • Larra Leslees
- • Jennn Jonnnson

Minorities

Hispanic
Recommended formula:
Name of Saint + Spanish curse word

- • Ignacio Cabrón
- • Maria Pendejo
- • Francisco Tu Madre Es Una Puta Fea

Asian
Recommended formula:
Name of child from *The Waltons* + sound you make when struck in solar plexus

- • Mary Ellen Huk
- • Ben Puh
- • John Boy Oh

Radio: With Great Frequency Comes Great Responsibility

Mass production of cheap newspapers helped unite and inform the populace of a growing nation. But at what price? Keeping abreast of the public discourse through newspapers took a great physical toll on the citizenry: The journey to purchase the paper, the turning of its many pages, to say nothing of the looking…the incessant looking. Left to right. Up and down. The nation's eyes were strained at the very time she needed them to see if the coolies had finished building the railroads. And what of the illiterate? Shouldn't the people least capable of making informed decisions have equal say?

Something had to give, and that something was **radio**. Through the magic of radio, people could stay informed without having to read. They could listen while remaining sedentary, with their eyes closed, perhaps gnawing on a delicious shank of lamb. Few could have imagined radio's influence based on the inanity of the first voice radio transmission: "One, two, three, four. Is it snowing where you are?"[10] But the message broadcast in response, "Typical weak-kneed liberal whining about the weather while decent Americans are out there shoveling," pointed the way to what was to come.

Radio transformed democracy. Not only was news and information now available 24 hours a day, seven days a week, but the birth of nationwide networks meant people in San Francisco were listening to the exact same broadcasts as people in Baltimore (though of course they gayed it up for San Francisco). The new medium offered not only such wildly popular radio shows as *The Shadow*, *Fibber McGee*, and *Uncle Petey's Old-Tyme Sound-Effects Hour*, but also high-quality broadcast journalism from such noted correspondents as Edward R. Murrow and Crazy *Hindenburg* Guy.

But perhaps the biggest change ushered in by radio was the expanded role of **corporate sponsorship**. Large companies not only paid for advertising time, but often sponsored entire shows, demanding "input" over con-

>>Fig. 7.6

Broadcast during the height of the Great Depression, President Roosevelt's famed "Fireside Chats" mocked a cold and hungry nation by offering vivid descriptions of how warm his fire was.

---

[10] Broadcast December 23, 1906, by Reginald Fessendon. (Note: This is the book's only factual footnote.)

tent along the way. More than one analyst of the day lamented how the influence of Chesterfield Cigarettes besmirched the creative integrity of the hilarious minstrel show *Amos 'n' Andy*. An important precedent was being set: Corporations would henceforward have a hand in disseminating information to the public.[11] Would those hands be used to gently push information along, "massage" it a little, or throttle it to within an inch of its life?

That would be left to a new medium to decide.

>>Fig. 7.7

The popularity of the radio show Amos 'n' Andy marked a more tolerant time, when two white men could portray demeaning racist stereotypes without being made to feel "guilty."

TV: Shiny, Pretty TV

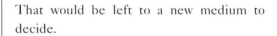
Mass production of cheap radios had helped unite and inform the populace of a growing nation. But at what price? The radio's over-reliance on words had forced Americans to connect mental images to a narrative. The country's imagination was dangerously well-developed at the very moment we needed not to think about what dropping an atomic bomb on someone might look like. Couldn't anyone create a device that would numb not just one, but *all* our senses, so information concerning our government could be absorbed by osmosis in the course of gathering the family to watch a funny man in a dress?[12]

Finally came the breakthrough mankind had been waiting for: **Television.** Hypnotic, absorbing, "Shut the hell up, kids, can't you see I'm watching *Sullivan*" television. Exactly where television originated is a mystery, though most scholars believe Prometheus stole it from the gods and gave it to the RCA Victor Company. In any case, TV quickly asserted

---

[11] It should be noted that National Public Radio remains largely "listener-sponsored" and relatively free of corporate oversight. (This message courtesy of latte-drinking, Volvo-driving, Seattle-living white people who are unbearable.)

[12] Uncle Miltie, not J. Edgar Hoover.

itself as the dominant medium of the 20th century, overtaking newspapers, radio and the film industry while simultaneously barring ugly people from ever participating in civic life again.[13]

Never was this last fact more apparent than in 1960, when America watched Richard Nixon (ugly) and John Kennedy (purr!) square off in the nation's first televised presidential debate. Nixon refused any but the crudest make-up and unwisely chose to wear his own nose. By contrast,

The transition from black-and-white to color television was eased by the 1962 invention of "sepia TV."

>>Fig. 7.8

TV viewers found Richard Nixon's appearance disturbing and untrustworthy. History would prove their superficial judgment 100% correct.

Kennedy arrived at the studio deeply tanned from a swing through California and flush with youthful confidence, having just been rimmed out by Jayne Mansfield. A majority of TV viewers said Kennedy had won the debate, while a majority of radio listeners said Nixon had come out on top. The conclusion was obvious: Radio was dead.

But television did have its downside: visceral immediacy. The country rushed headlong into the television age just in time to catch President Kennedy's assassination[14] and 58,000 Americans die in Vietnam. The nightly barrage of gruesome combat images, followed by the equally gruesome *Laugh-In*, helped turn the tide of public opinion against the war, and brought a premature end to the careers of Lyndon B. Johnson and Ruth Buzzi.

In just two decades, TV established itself as the dominant form of media in America. By the early 1970s the three major networks had been established and a new breed of celebrity, the "anchorman," had donned his moussed mantle atop the news kingdom. Though the '60s had seen its share of tumult, most Americans still maintained a fundamental faith in our government institutions. Shit, we put a man on the moon in '69.

(Continue on page 150)

---

[13] In your face, Lincoln!

[14] That show was so successful it was later spun off for Malcolm, Martin and Robert.

The Brain of the Pundit

Inside most talking heads on television, there's a brain. But in the case of the partisan political pundit, that brain has evolved over time into a specialized organ unique to our species.

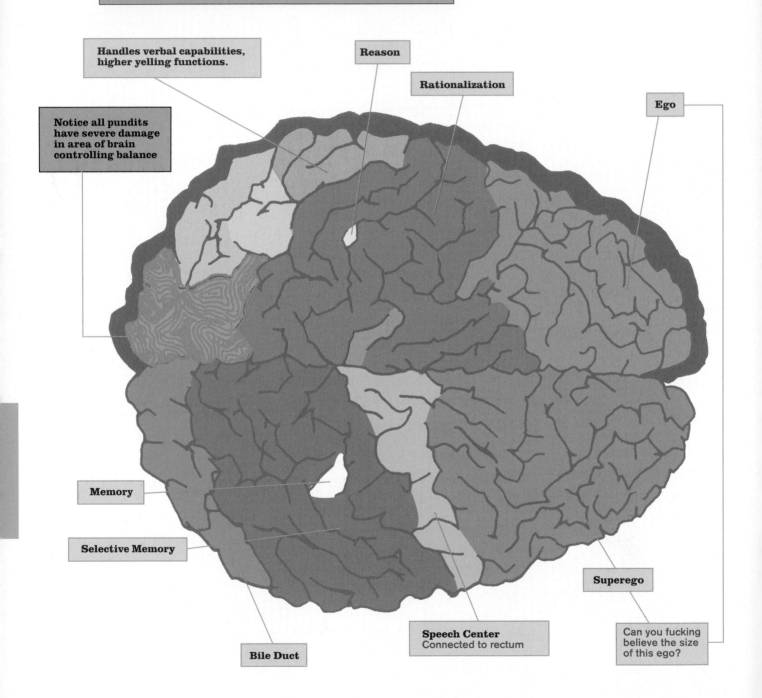

Handles verbal capabilities, higher yelling functions.

Reason

Rationalization

Ego

Notice all pundits have severe damage in area of brain controlling balance

Memory

Selective Memory

Superego

Bile Duct

Speech Center Connected to rectum

Can you fucking believe the size of this ego?

Partisan Brain: Left

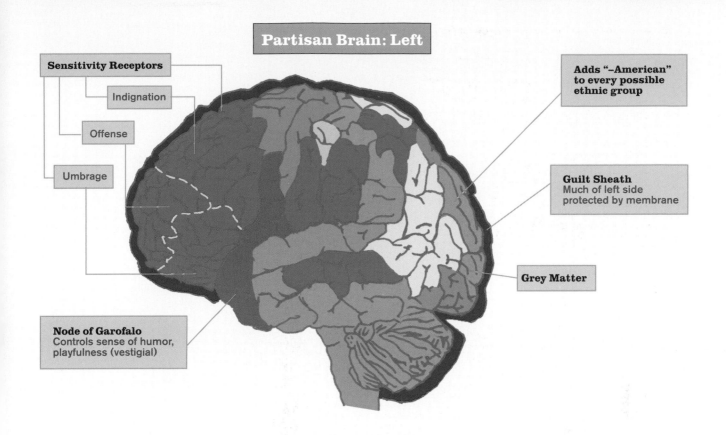

Sensitivity Receptors

Indignation

Offense

Umbrage

Adds "–American" to every possible ethnic group

Guilt Sheath
Much of left side protected by membrane

Grey Matter

Node of Garofalo
Controls sense of humor, playfulness (vestigial)

Partisan Brain: Right

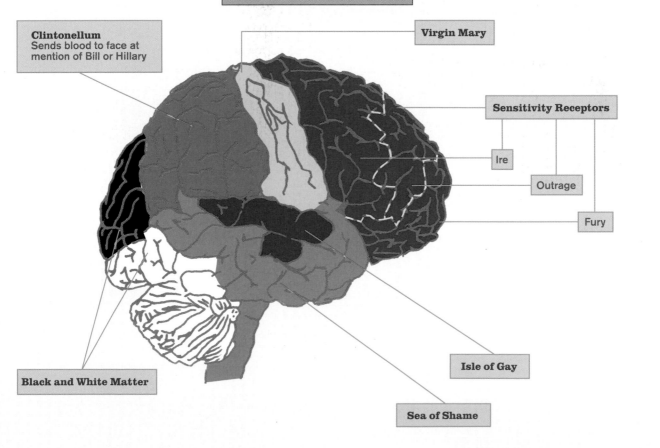

Clintonellum
Sends blood to face at mention of Bill or Hillary

Virgin Mary

Sensitivity Receptors

Ire

Outrage

Fury

Black and White Matter

Isle of Gay

Sea of Shame

>>Fig. 7.9

The Watergate Hotel. Among its amenities: 24-hour room service, complimentary continental breakfast, a fitness center, and the capital's most tappable phone lines.

(Continued from page 147)

That's what you call ending a decade on a high note.[15]

Then the newspaper, long left for dead, reached its icy hand up from the grave, grabbed hold of a president and brought him tumbling down.[16]

Watergate: Shame of a Press Corps

June 17, 1972. Five gentlemen are arrested breaking into the Democratic National Committee offices at the Watergate Hotel. The men are not loud or abusive, and are there only at the behest of the Nixon administration to adjust bugging devices installed in a previous break-in. It was a simple case of the executive branch having a little good-natured fun with a respected political opponent...that is, until two reporters for the *Washington Post*, drunk on curiosity, decided to blow the whole thing into proportion.

For months Bob Woodward and Carl Bernstein terrorized Washington by calling people and asking questions, oftentimes *not* during normal business hours. Ultimately their bullying tactics intimidated the Senate into stopping everything it was doing to look into it. That's when TV, recognizing Vietnam was winding down and needing a new hit, decided to get in the game. Its broadcast of the **Senate Watergate Committee** hearings gave the public an unprecedented behind-the-scenes look at our government. This made people very, very sad.

On August 8, 1974, Richard M. Nixon, a good man brought down by a press corps run amok, resigned. His final speech to the nation, containing the immortal line "I would prefer you hadn't known I was a crook," was a not-so-subtle jab at the out-of-control media. The entire affair cast a stain on the profession of journalism and has become known as the media's "Watergate." Thankfully, Woodward and Bernstein got their comeuppance by having the insufferable Dustin Hoffman and Robert Redford satirize them in a movie.

---

[15] 1969 was also the year of "Woodstock," which was like Bonaroo, only with shittier sound.
[16] Metaphorically.

The Modern Mediascape: Original Synergy

Today's media has recovered from its mid-70s bout of temporary insanity. Newspapers abound, and though they have endured decades of decline in readership and influence, they can still form impressive piles if no one takes them out to the trash. The radio star, allegedly killed by video in 1981, staged a comeback in the 1980s as the medium's abandoned husk was recolonized as an outpost for the paranoid and partisan. It now exists as a pacifier, reassuring the aggrieved that the government's recognition of Kwanzaa really is the reason their lives suck. It also helps cab drivers learn English...very angry English.

>>Fig. 7.10

The Internet is today's rawest, most unfiltered source of news, information, and a staggering array of human sexual fetish.

Television continues to thrive. One fifteen-minute nightly newscast, barely visible through the smoky haze of its cigarette company benefactor, has evolved into a multi-channel, twenty-four hour a day infotastic clusterfuck of factish-like material. The 1990s brought the advent of a dynamic new medium for news, the **Internet**, a magnificent new technology combining the credibility of anonymous hearsay with the excitement of typing.

But the most important factor in the rehabilitation of our national media came not from the editorial room but a more unlikely source: the board room.

The Media and Washington: Pas de Duh

Enter the media's white knight: **corporate ownership**. During the 1980s, corporations began to bail out our democracy by purchasing as many guerrilla newspaper, radio and television stations as they could. These mega-corporations became known as "parent companies" because of their patient, nurturing tendencies and for the way they sat the media down and told it, "Hey, you're over two hundred years old now...isn't it about time you settled down and made some money?" Thousands of uncontrollable, perilously independent media voices were finally organized into a more manageable five. And while it may be illegal for one company to own every newspaper, TV and radio station in a particular town, Rupert Murdoch's not dead yet.

>>Fig. 7.11

Ronald Reagan knew that unnecessary federal regulation was preventing the media from reaching its full potential. He also wanted to build lasers to shoot missiles out of the sky from outer space.

(Continue on page 154)

Holdings include:
CBS, UPN, MTV, Showtime, Nickelodeon, Paramount Pictures, Blockbuster VIdeo, BET, Simon and Schuster publishing, Comedy Central (and by extension, half the authors of this book)

What they can offer you:
TV
- Up to 20 minutes on *60 Minutes*
- Up to 90 minutes on *60 Minutes 2*
- All *48 Hours*

- Up to six friends Punk'd
- Up to nine rides pimped
- Kids out of control? Nickelodeon will raise them until they are 14
- Are you black? We have six letters for you – UPN and BET. Reorganize them and add as many "izzles" as you see fit.

Print
- Simon and Schuster called. Paramount can't make the movie until you write the book.

Bonus
- We own King World Productions. Ever felt like punching Alex Trebek? It can be arranged!

What can synergy do for you?

Newsmaker

"get"

TIME WARNER

Holdings include:
CNN, AOL, HBO, Cinemax, The WB, Warner Bros. Pictures, Court TV, Warner Brothers, *Time, Life, People*, Warner Books (and by extension, the other half of the authors of this book)

What they can offer you:
TV
- An hour with Larry King. He will go easy on you. (OK, easi*er*.)
- Want to swim naked with eight flabby suburbanites and a dolphin? HBO's *Real Sex* can hook that up!
- Want to go undercover at a strip club full of lesbian nymphomaniacs to investigate a series of erotic murders? Cinemax has you covered! (Pending Shannon Tweed's script approval.)

- Want to kill someone? *Court TV*'s sympathetic coverage will ensure your acquittal!

Print
- A book deal with Warner Books. They'll publish anything.

Internet
- Ever wonder who has "[Your First Name]@aol.com"? We know. Want it?

Bonus
- Imagine how impressed your friends will be when they see you have finally captured and killed The Road Runner. Meep-meep indeed!

Holdings include:
Walt Disney Pictures, The Disney Channel, Disneyworld, Disneyland, Eurodisney, Disney's California Adventure, the entire town of Celebration, Florida, ABC television networks, ESPN, A&E, Lifetime, E!, Disney Radio Network, Disney Cruise Line, Miramax Pictures, Touchstone Pictures

What they can offer you:
TV
- Diane Sawyer on Wednesday night and *GMA*'s Charles Gibson on Thursday morning. No other network lobs softer balls.
- Say the word and we stop production on *According to Jim.*

Film
- A three-way with Snow White and the Little Mermaid (Oh, they exist).

Theme Parks
- EPCOT. Take it.
- It doesn't matter *how* tall you are, you are getting on that ride!

Are you a "get"? Has your story become a national obsession? Did you kill your wife in such an abhorrent fashion that major news personalities are clamoring for your "digits"? Were you voted off something (an island? a house? a talent show?) in a dramatic and/or heartwarming fashion? Did you blow the president? If so, the competition for the extra two-share your public humiliation will bring a television news show can be parlayed into an exciting prize package worth millions of dollars through the miracle of synergy. And while nattering nabobs have been negative about the effects of this new corporate reality, few talk about the incredible benefits it can bring to those who have earned it.

News Corporation

Holdings include:
Fox, Fox News, FX, 20th Century Fox, HarperCollins, *The New York Post*, *TV Guide*, Fox Searchlight Pictures

What they can offer you: TV
- The full power of Fox News. All personal indiscretions past, present and future couched as irrelevant obsession of liberal media
- The full power of the Fox Network. Tell us *who* you would like the animals to attack
- This week's theme on *American Idol*: "All of them fucking you"
- Poke Alan Colmes in the eye

Print
- We own *TV Guide*. It could "Pick" you...or it could "Pan" you. The choice is yours.
- You've been sighted "canoodling" with a hot young star of *The O.C.*....How'd *that* get on Page Six of *The Post*?

Film
- *Star Wars Episode 7: The Revenge of* [Insert Your Name Here]

Holdings include:
NBC, CNBC, MSNBC, USA, Bravo, Independent Film Channel (IFC), American Movie Classics (AMC), Telemundo, Universal Pictures, Universal Studios, Universal Theme Parks

Bonus
- Ever wish upon a star? We own 3,459 actual stars. Have one. No, have two.
- Would you like to touch Walt Disney's frozen head?
- Why won't that girl/boy go out with you? Perhaps a little visit from Harvey Weinstein would convince them otherwise.

What they can offer you: TV
- Interview with NBC correspondent of your choice on any of our 27 fine *Dateline* programs
- Guest spot as corpse on *Law & Order*
- Guest spot as molested corpse on *Law & Order: Special Victims Unit*
- Gay man will come to your house and scold you for not using Lemon Verbena exfoliant (straight guys only)
- Know any Spanish? No? How about a guest spot as a corpse on *Mujeres Apasionadas?*
- While we're at it, we will make your success in the world's most popular sport one of our top goooooooooaa-aaaaaaaaaaals!
- We don't think you'll want to miss a personalized tour of Siberia's largest hydroelectric dam. Especially the way *Will and Grace's* Megan Mullally gives it.

Film
- *Law and Order: Special Victims Unit: Molested Corpse: The Movie* (Fall release, Jonathan Mostow [*Breakdown, U-571*] slated to helm)

Bonus
- How many fawning executives does it take to change your lifetime supply of free lightbulbs? As many as you desire.
- Always wanted your very own aircraft engine? You're in luck! We make aircraft engines!!!
- Personalized MRI machine more to your taste? Guess what – we make those too!
- We don't normally let people do this, but press this button. You just smartbombed a target of opportunity.
- One gift certificate to bring three (3) good things to life.

(Continued from page 151)

Now, more secure in their relationship, government and the media are entering a golden age of harmony, aiding each other whenever possible. Lawmakers recognize that counterbalancing their excesses is a lot of work. So today's government officials, aware of the intense deadline pressure of the 24-hour news cycle, are kind enough to send their media colleagues hard news, known as "press releases" or "leaks," to be read verbatim on air. The benefits of this are twofold: The public remains informed of the good things the government is up to, and the media is freed up to use its entire arsenal for the next photogenic child's disappearance.[17]

When disputes on policy do arise, the two political parties provide the media with analysts that can argue the issue from the only two valid points of view, "right" and "left." These disputes are settled graciously in media forums such as *Crossfire*, *Hardball*, and *Fuck You with Pat Buchanan and Bill Press*. In return for help killing time, the media agrees not to analyze the truthfulness of the debate, only which team seems to be winning. Without the input of concerned politicians and the briny think tanks they float in, today's journalists would be hamstrung by research demands and unable to provide the speculation we've come to rely on.

Yes, our press has never been freer, its status never quo-er. By removing the investigative aspect of investigative journalism, today's modern media finally has the time to pursue the ultimate goal the Founding Fathers envisioned for newsgathering organizations: To raise the stock price of the media empire that owns them. ◐

Were You Aware?

Barbara Walters is not even trying. She is estimated to have given up in 1983.

>>Fig. 7.12

Reasoned debate and deliberative examination of relevant social and political issues are a hallmark of Fuck You with Pat Buchanan and Bill Press.

---

[17] White child. All other videotapes will be returned unopened.

Determining Newsworthiness

These simple equations will help you determine where to place news for your broadcast or newspaper.

 ### Kidnapping

y = Family Income $\times$ (Abductee Cuteness $\div$ Skin Color)^2 + Length of Abduction $\times$ Media Savvy of Grieving Parents^3

(where y = minutes of coverage)

 ### Relative Story Values

Renegade moose in yard < septuplets! < renegade truck on fire < conjoined babies < new disease outbreak (Africa < rest of the world) < war! < disgruntled man with gun < baby briefly imperiled by celebrity

 ### Body Count Conversion Rate

2,000 Massacred Congolese = **500** Drowned Bangladeshis = **45** Fire-bombed Iraqis = **12** Car-bombed Europeans = **1** Snipered American

 If p then q, where p = "it bleeds" and q = "it leads"

 104.3 = The Frequency*

*Source: Kenneth

 ### The "Jacko" Formula

1 Michael Jackson allegation = **2** Tito Jackson convictions + $\left(\dfrac{\textbf{5}\, \text{LaToya Jackson nude pictorials}}{\text{Marlon Jackson}} \right)$

 ## Trials

Defendant	Points
	(measured in Buttafuocos)
A-List celebrity	100
B-List celebrity	60
Z-List celebrity	75
Athlete	80
Ex-athlete	75
Clergy	50
Crazed / disgruntled loner	25
Crazed / disgruntled loner (cannibal)	45
Journalist	-20
Non-famous person	1

Nature of Crime

Sexual (unspeakable acts)	100
Sexual (speakable acts)	60
Sexual (clergy-related)	80
Murder	75
Assault / biting	50
Kidnapping	65
Kidnapping (involving son of famed aviator)	95
Shoplifting	35
Shoplifting (clergy-related)	36
Drugs / alcohol	15
White collar	3

Scoring

 10 - 50 Buttafuocos = Trial Force One (Moderate Coverage)
(Local camera crew; regularly scheduled updates)

 51 - 115 Buttafuocos = Trial Force Two (Heavy Coverage)
(Send a crew; live break-ins and updates; get Jeffrey Toobin on line 3)

 116 or more Buttafuocos = Trial Force Three (Obscene Coverage)
(Get sleeping bag and hunting knife; you are now living outside of a courthouse)

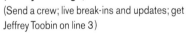

Speculation Caveats

With 24 hours to fill, the majority of your screen time will be idle speculation. Use these handy disclosures to avoid charges of irresponsibility.

?
"I hate to speculate, but…"
"I certainly don't have anything to back this up, but…"
"I know what I'm about to say is irresponsible and goes against everything I've been taught as a journalist, but…"
"Just for shits and giggles, let's say…"

Hyperbole Bank

85% of all news events fall into one of three categories: tragedy, scandal and disaster. Modifiers are your only chance to separate yourself from the pack. Apply as needed:

P
Appalling, dumbfounding, heartbreaking, lachrymose (*The New Yorker* only), mother-of-all, OJ-esque, sad (*USA Today* only), shocking, staggering, unimaginable, unspeakable, unthinkable, un-(anything)-able, eye-opening, jaw-dropping, scrotum-clenching

Transitions (anchors only)

As an anchor you have the difficult task of moving between stories of varying tones relying on nothing more than your own humanity. Lacking that, try these:

Upbeat → Tragic
"In more somber news…"
"Let's move from the Northeast to the Middle East…"
"Sadly, not every child can be as lucky as Little Miss Texas…"

Tragic → Upbeat
"In lighter news…"
"Thankfully, there were plenty of survivors at last night's Key Club Fun Fair!…"
"Anyway, that's ethnic cleansing for you. Now ARE YOU READY FOR SOME FOOTBALL?…"

Source Terminology

The days of access and people speaking on the record are over. Here's what to call your dubious sources:

OR — **Sources close to the story** = other reporters

Hi — **Highly placed source** = Google

WH — **A White House spokesperson** = overheard on line for White House tour

AS — **Anonymous source** = midnight phone call from Bob Novak

UR — **Unconfirmed report** = something remembered from dream

GB — **Source vaguely familiar with story** = direct quote from President Bush

Appearance Decoder

IR — **investigative reporter** = TV reporter + leather jacket

ME — **military expert** = loud, older gentleman + medals (if medals >5)

SA/SU — **weekend anchor** = news anchor - charisma

TP — **TV pundit** = fired advisor + 2 years + mounting debt

-P — **network news magazine anchor** = network anchor - penis

Get to Know Your News Sources

	Newspapers	Television	Radio	Internet	Company Newsletter
How they get their stories	Grit, moxie, pluck and spunk (great gams a plus)	Roving van	Combining meth-amphetamine with part of the brain that hates	Girlfriend's roommate; fellow bloggers' girlfriends' roommates	Beth in HR
Reporter's qualifications	Two years at *The Podunk Weekly Shitrag*	Hotness	Will you work the overnight? You're qualified.	Social Anxiety Disorder	Willingness to do company newsletter
News cycle	Daily (cities); weekly (towns); monthly (hamlets and/or burgs)	Constant, relentless. You've got to fill the maw, man. Feed the beast. "Has the lady with the waterskiing squirrel called back? No? Fuck it. Somebody get the Columbine survivor to makeup!"	"On the Twos"	Please wait . . . buffering . . . 9% . . .	As soon as you get your submissions in. Come on, people! It's *your* newsletter.
Goes well with	Coffee	The couch	Driving	Work	The other things in your garbage
Corrections policy	See page D-12, square inch between lingerie ads	" . . . I'm sorry, I'm just receiving word that photo is not the serial killer, but rather a beloved pediatrician. In other news . . . "	None. That is a sign of weakness.	The what's this now?	Uncomfortable apology delivered at water cooler
Top feature	The Jumble	"It's Kojo time!"	Someone else is saying the terrible, terrible things you think	Mpeg of piss-drinking monkey	*Comings & Goings* section, to find out who's been shitcanned without you noticing
Placement of celebrity rape trial	Section A, page 17, National News	Everywhere. "Let's go out to Dave for an update."	What is the political affiliation of said rapist?	Dude, *I started* that story!	Awkward segue into reminder about office Sexual Harassment Policy
Alternate use	Kindling	Babysitter	Monster truck event information center	Debt reduction, penile enhancement	7-minute distraction from interminable soul-crushing job you swore you'd never end up in

The Political Cartoon

If there's one thing Americans love, it's satire.[18] We also love drawings. So it's no surprise that political cartoons have been part of the American media landscape since long before the invention of the refrigerator magnet. The cartoonist must be able to boil down a complex political issue into one simple panel. It's a concise and powerful way to preach to the choir.

The Colonial Era
Ben Franklin invented the American cartoon with his famous "Join, or Die" engraving. Although many at the time thought it was merely the worst map of the colonies ever drawn.

May 9, 1754

A Nation Divided
With cartoons, Americans were able to laugh at the horrors of the Civil War, as long as they weren't a slave or soldier. At right is one of the many variations on the theme of Abraham Lincoln "fixing" a broken nation.

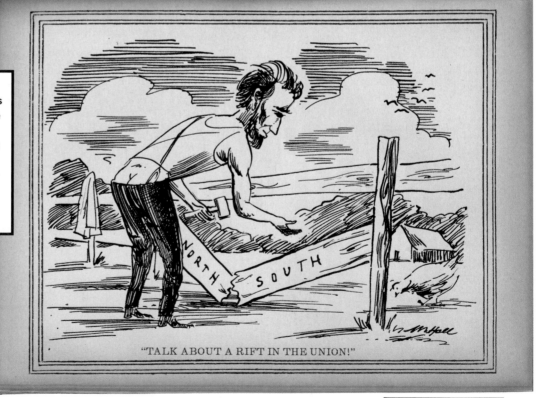

"TALK ABOUT A RIFT IN THE UNION!"

April 27, 1863

---

[18] For an example of satire, re-read this sentence.

— "BEHOLD THE TAMMANY TIGER, A SYMBOL OF THE RAMPANT GRAFT AND CORRUPTION IN OUR FAIRE CITY. THE TWEED RING CONTROLS PATRONAGE, BRIBES JUDGES, BUYS VOTES…"

— "WAIT A MINNIT, CHESTER…"

"THAT'S A REAL TIGER!"

August 5, 1877

PEANUTS

November 28, 1953

DOONESBURY

The first comic strip to ever win a Pulitzer, Gary Trudeau's *Doonesbury* was known for its sometimes excessively dry humor.

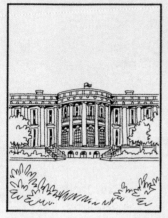

March 3, 1982

Now

Some of today's cartoons celebrate the current administration rather than poke fun at it. At the forefront is reporter-duck Mallard Fillmore, who is the White House's best friend among cartoon waterfowl.

MALLARD FILLMORE

October 1, 1998

WHICH "TRICKY" WHITE HOUSE OCCUPANT HAS SEEN HIS POLITICAL CLOUT RISING?

A→

HERE WE GO WITH ANOTHER RIDICULOUS

FOLDING PAGE

The nation has re-elected our chief executive, spurning his challenger — a Democrat who made voters say "Bleeechh!" It seems like nothing could possibly stop this Quaker mover and shaker now. Veeblesnortz!

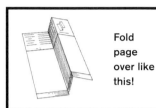

Fold page over like this!

←B

RICHARD   NIXON HAS WORKED QUITE HARD
NIXING   HIS   SIZABLE   OPPOSITION

A→ |

| ←B

February 5, 1973

A Who's Who of Political Interviewers

There is no shortage of venues where politicians can go to take their message directly to the people. Choosing the right one can be the difference between a comfortable re-election and shameful exile to a think tank or, God forbid, academia. Below, a menu of television options for today's skilled politician.

Credibility:

The pundits say your insistence that Russia is a continent makes you a foreign-policy lightweight, but a respectable showing on either of the following two shows instantly lowers your retardation quotient.

Ted Koppel
Nightline, ABC

Inside that gigantic head lurks one of the most agile minds in TV journalism. His high standards and unquestioned professionalism are the reasons he is only allowed on television very late at night. Do not dissemble, for he can cloud your mind and haunt your dreams. Also, he is a shapeshifter.

Tim Russert
Meet the Press, NBC

Holding your own against Russert is a political rite of passage akin to the Masai teenage-warrior circumcision ritual and only slightly easier on your penis. But tread carefully: It's early Sunday morning, and he fact checks.

Practice:

Not quite ready to get in the ring with Tyson? Why not pad your record with Gerry Cooney! Hone your skills on a palooka and lower your risk of being Quayled.

George Stephanopoulos
This Week, ABC

The nine inch tall ex-politico is the perfect host to get you all your sparring and street work. Go ahead…try out that new talking point or stumble through a just-hatched damage control strategy. George will put up just enough resistance to help you build strength but not enough to embarrass. You'll learn which facial expressions best convey earnestness and which body language tics give away your utter contempt for the truth. Don't be afraid to make mistakes because *This Week* doesn't count in the official standings.

Redemption:

Why did you have to take that money…or drug…or person's life? Political career flatlining due to an inherent character flaw? Don't worry, Washington has two defibrillators charged up. Just add tears and…CLEAR!!!

Larry King
Larry King Live, CNN

If the word that most often precedes your office title is either "disgraced" or "indicted," it's time for an audience with the King. Larry knows you are a decent person. He'll give you the chance to make up your side of the story. And it's easy to cry on the show because Larry King smells like onions.

Barbara Walters
20/20, ABC

Do you need to save your career but are afraid one of the people you have mercilessly screwed over may get through the phone screener? Then Barbara is the one for you. The only things softer than the focus are the questions, because her relentless pursuit of the interview has created a bond she could never betray. Friends don't do that to friends. For extra coddle pretend you are still considering giving the exclusive to Connie Chung.

Bill O'Reilly
The O'Reilly Factor, Fox News

This is the venue for those who could use an immediate and certain judgment concerning their value as human beings. Are you a man amongst men whose moral clarity and vision stand unsurpassed or a maggot feeding upon the flesh of the dying? You will be told within the first minute of the program. Do not question the judgment. Accept it, and make the necessary changes.

Chris Matthews
Hardball, MSNBC

Talk, talk, talk. Everywhere you go they expect you to talk. Not on *Hardball*. Matthews will deliver the sound waves; all you need to do is take a page from the guy sitting in the Maxell ad and hang on. As long as you grunt or nod enough to uphold the minimum body language requirement of the social contract you just bought yourself a half hour of free television time. (Caution to asthmatics and those with heart conditions: Carbon dioxide levels around Matthews can become dangerously high. In the event of a diatribe, oxygen masks will drop from the ceiling. Help yourself, then help the children.)

America the Book Insta-Poll

How many poll responses do you usually read before they start to get annoying?

- ○ One does the trick.
- ○ I don't mind if there are two.
- ○ Three is a perfectly appropriate number.
- ○ Around four, they start to get a bit grating.
- ○ Five, I would say, is probably pushing it.
- ○ Six responses is definitely too many.
- ○ At seven, I really get angry.
- ○ I will destroy you.

America the Book Insta-Poll

Do you think all these poll questions were added to the manuscript just before the deadline as a way to fill up gaping holes in the page layout?

○ Yes   ○ No

Diane Sawyer
Primetime Live, ABC

There is no valid reason to appear with Diane Sawyer.

Were You Aware?

Stone Phillips creates his own nourishment from a process known as photosynthesis.

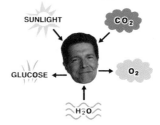

Which classic example of photojournalism most gnaws at your soul?

Viet Cong Execution

Iraqi Prisoner Torture

Child Coal Workers

Scientists Astounded by Amazing Batboy!

Discussion Questions

1. What are the top 100 TV shows you would rather watch instead of the nightly news?

2. The Pulitzer Prize is awarded for journalistic excellence. Why is it named for a late 19th century media baron who loathed journalistic excellence?

If you're at the right exhumation of the right mass grave at the right time with the right camera and capture just the right combination of anguish and loss, one of these babies is all yours!

3. Given human fallibility, is objective reporting ever possible? Phrase your answer without indicating a bias toward one point of view or the other.

4. Digital television recorders like TiVo have made it easier for viewers to skip past commercials. How can exciting, groundbreaking companies like **verizon** reach customers?

5. Baby, did you ever wonder...wonder whatever became of me? (Hint: I'm living on the air in a medium-sized city in southern Ohio.)

Hint #2: I work with him.

Classroom Activities

1. Meet the press. Failing that, face the nation.

2. Write the word "Reuters" on 25 different slips of paper. Pass one out to each student. The one who pronounces it correctly is too smart for your class. Send him or her to private school.

3. Train your pooch to be a media watchdog! Set him in front of a TV and in a firm, commanding voice say, "Are Democratic candidates getting more air-time than Republicans? Are they, boy?" He should bark if they are.

4. Using a marker, randomly select a sample for your opinion poll. But remember — pick a black person! Also, you're gonna want Hispanics in there. Asians you can take or leave.

Opinion poll samples:

5. Match the hair to the anchor head!

1.

2.

a.

b.

3.

4.

c.

d.

5.

6.

e.

f.

7.

8.

g.

h.

Answer key: 1-e, 2-h, 3-f, 4-g, 5-b, 6-a, 7-c, 8-d

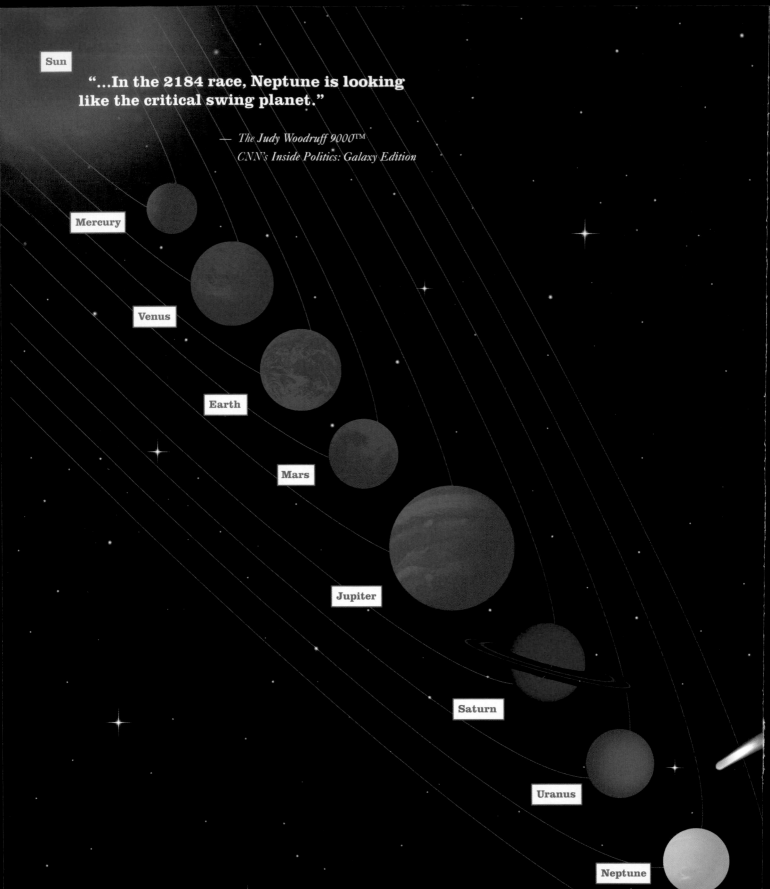

Classroom Activities

1. Meet the press. Failing that, face the nation.

2. Write the word "Reuters" on 25 different slips of paper. Pass one out to each student. The one who pronounces it correctly is too smart for your class. Send him or her to private school.

3. Train your pooch to be a media watchdog! Set him in front of a TV and in a firm, commanding voice say, "Are Democratic candidates getting more airtime than Republicans? Are they, boy?" He should bark if they are.

4. Using a marker, randomly select a sample for your opinion poll. But remember — pick a black person! Also, you're gonna want Hispanics in there. Asians you can take or leave.

Opinion poll samples:

5. Match the hair to the anchor head!

1.

2.

a.

b.

3.

4.

c.

d.

5.

6.

e.

f.

7.

8.

g.

h.

Answer key: 1-e, 2-h, 3-f, 4-g, 5-b, 6-a, 7-c, 8-d

Sun

"...In the 2184 race, Neptune is looking like the critical swing planet."

— *The Judy Woodruff 9000™*
CNN's Inside Politics: Galaxy Edition

Mercury

Venus

Earth

Mars

Jupiter

Saturn

Uranus

Neptune

Pluto

Chapter 8

The Future of Democracy: Four Score and Seven Years from Now

The great experiment that is the United States of America has succeeded beyond the Founding Fathers' wildest expectations. Even the young nation's most optimistic thinkers estimated the Union would last no more than 30 to 50 years before being torn asunder by internal divisions (i.e., slavery) or external forces. After all, the British, French, Spanish and the rest of the European continent couldn't go more than 12 years without a good war.[1] But no. Thanks to blessedly isolated geography, a can-do spirit and an indigenous population with primitive weapons and surprisingly weak immune systems, the United States has experienced consistent growth and expansion over its entire history.

>>Fig. 8.1

Tomahawks? They thought they could slow us down with tomahawks?

Will You Be Aware?

Before he entered politics, President Schwarzenegger used to be a successful star of action movies and high-concept comedies.

But what of the future? Will this growth continue unabated? Or will a new power arise and take America's place as heir to the throne of this island Earth? And if a new power does arise, will it make us drive smaller cars? 'Cause right now a lot of SUV owners are in long-term leases and it's kind of difficult to get out of those without paying some killer fees. Just putting that out there.

(Continue on page 170)

---

[1] Remember, these were the people who brought you something called the "100 Years War," which actually lasted 229 years.

Emerging Issues

Predicting what specific issues will challenge future generations is an exercise in idle speculation. Here are those issues.

Population

Managing the earth's rapidly growing population will be a dominant issue for years to come, and with improved medicine we can no longer count on a new killer virus to conveniently "thin the herd." Perhaps future scientists will somehow develop a miraculous method of birth regulation or "control"… one that isn't a sin against Our Lord.

The United Nations has fixed July 15, 2027 as the day the world's growing population will need to be connected by a "seventh" degree of separation.

Global Warming

Non-issue. Red herring. Not happening.

The current average temperature for the planet is 59 degrees. There will be perfectly good explanations for why global temperature will continue to rise 1.2 degrees every 10 years. Here they are.

59.0-60.2	El Niño
60.3-61.4	La Niña
61.5-62.6	Angry sun
62.7-63.8	It's just you
63.9-65.0	Cold shortage
65.1-66.2	Great Barbecue Craze of 2065
66.3-67.4	Cow flatulence/equine irritable bowel syndrome
67.5-68.6	Dude, you're wearing a sweater!
68.7-69.8	Hmmm … this *is* odd. Let us study this for 30 years and get back to you.

New Global Trouble Spots

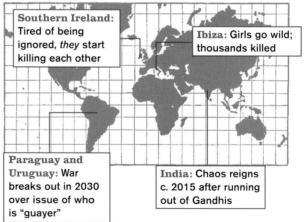

Southern Ireland: Tired of being ignored, *they* start killing each other

Ibiza: Girls go wild; thousands killed

Paraguay and Uruguay: War breaks out in 2030 over issue of who is "guayer"

India: Chaos reigns c. 2015 after running out of Gandhis

Distribution of Wealth

Computer models project a future in which the rich get richer and the poor poorer. By 2050, it is believed the meek shall inherit, at best, a shit sandwich.

Take a good look, meek. You ain't inheriting this anytime soon.

Demographics

In the 1990s, the Hispanic population of the U.S. rose 38%, comprising 12% of the populace by 2000. If these growth rates remain constant, 124% of all Americans will be Hispanic by 2060.

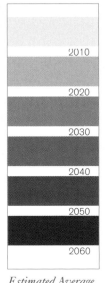

2010

2020

2030

2040

2050

2060

Estimated Average Color of Americans

Obeausity

Around 2015, Americans will realize it would be much easier to change their standard of beauty than to lose weight. From that point on, we will embrace our indulgent lifestyles. Gyms will close, fad binge books will rule the best-seller lists, and singles ads will end with the phrase "Yes fatties."

In the future, you will want to "tap" this.

Water

When alien races visit our planet thousands of years from now, their Earth Rover probes will discover this barren, windswept dust bowl was at one time "wet" and capable of supporting life. Reserves of fresh water will slowly dissipate over the next few decades, but many fluidish substances will arise to fill the void.

28%	Hydrestra™ water-flavored drink beverage liquid gel
24%	The squeezing of wet things
15%	Closed-car condensation window-lickings
14%	H_2O
9%	Urine (own)
5%	Harvested air-conditioner drippings
3%	Urine (others')
2%	Fanta

Estimated sources of fluid, 2100.

Energy

Policy analysts see no alternative to America's continued dependence on foreign oil, barring some unforeseen development like slightly modifying our lifestyles. Fortunately, the finite supply of fossil fuel is no match for the bottomless well of American optimism.

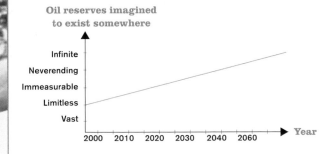

Oil reserves imagined to exist somewhere

Infinite
Neverending
Immeasurable
Limitless
Vast

2000 2010 2020 2030 2040 2060 → Year

Contrary to scientists' dire predictions, the size of the oil reserves the average American believes must exist somewhere are expected to increase through 2050, even after reserves actually run out in 2043.

Will You Be Aware?

The widely held perception that "Congress is made up of blood-thirsty cannibals" replaced the earlier, more genial perception, "Congress is inefficient."

Rep. Tom Kiper, D-WI. Back before The Sickness, congressmen like Kiper were notorious for engaging in lengthy fili-busters and committee hearings, not feasting on the flesh of their constituents.

(Continued from page 167)

Speculating about the future is a tricky business. Scientists, sociologists and religious leaders all have their theories. They are all wrong. But in the interest of fairness we will briefly present those theories to you now. Then, after you've read those, we will present to you the **absolute truth** about what will happen in the future. Be warned however: If you skip ahead now and just read that part, it won't come true. And it's really great.

So unless you want the whole world – especially your children – to be mad at you, read on.

Democracy's Future v.1.0 – Robots ... Robots Everywhere

In this version of the future, our worst fears about America's increased reliance on technology at the expense of our fundamental humanity are realized.

Our democracy will prove ill-equipped to combat the very tools we've created to sustain it. Power will inevitably become centralized in the hands of the very few – those who control the technology and their disproportionately attractive wives. And don't think we'll be able to send a robot back from the future to fix our problems or unplug from some vast computer grid to which we've been enslaved. Our overlords will have seen those movies too, and the dystopia of their creation will be far more original and horrible than anything concocted by Messrs. Cameron and Wachowski.

In the technofuture a typical election day will proceed as follows:

After learning about political candidates via neurally inserted infochips, the Voter of Tomorrow will pull on his armless shearling vest, strap on his jet-pack[2] and zip on down to the crumbling middle school gymnasium where they still gamely set up polling stations. (Some traditions die harder than others.) After consulting the 300-year-old poll worker, he will get in line with his fellow citizens, cyber-citizens, and "enhanced" children –

---

[2] They're coming, we swear! But they'll be made by Honda and they won't be as cool as you think they'll be.

a sub-race of genetically perfect identical blonde toddlers who are only allowed to vote because they can kill with their minds. (Thanks for nothing, ChildTec!)

>>Fig. 8.2

This sample indicates opposition to Stadium Referendum Bill #48.

Since "voter intention" became an issue during the 2000 Florida election, high-tech methods of withdrawing opinion will be used. Sedation will be necessary. Fluids, drawn from the spinal column and from beneath the brain's dura mater, will reveal the true intentions of the voter after automated biodemocratic analysis. If you survive the procedure,[3] you'll then verify your vote by punching out holes in a card with a stylus.

By the way, with an increasingly diverse population and an evolutionary process creating larger, hairless *Homo sapiens* with gigantic craniums, the above mentioned Voter of Tomorrow will look like this:

>>Fig. 8.3

So much for the mechanics of voting. What of the health of our democracy itself? We are, after all, social creatures. But once technology supplants God and the institution of family, the idea of "community" will no longer

(Continue on page 173)

---

[3] One in four do!

>>Fig. 8.4

Genetically "enhanced" children will talk at a younger age, be born toilet-trained and never get sick. They will also lack the capacity to love.

Will You Be Aware?

There was a time when it was not only legal to talk about urning-bay the ag-flay, but even to do so.

The TV News Screen of the Future

Grabber Crawl

LOOK! NEWS! UP HERE! HEY! LOOK! NEWS!

11:45 **Time**

Dow
10,025.34

Nasdaq
1942.85

Naodex
87,004,56
2,934.4

118°C **Temperature**

57%

Terror Alert Purple: Heads Up!

Real-time Presidential Approval Rating

Remote-controlled inter-active Anchor-Wheel (your choice of black, white, Hispanic, alien or Asian)

Icecaps A look back

Time you personally have left to live

Years	15
days	214
hours	15
minutes	57

Click here for pro-American slant

Subtle

Jingoistic

Somi

ThalmYdrac

VIOXX

Fagajiz®

Cialis®

Instant Feedback Box

○ ○ ○ Instant message with Newshound 2037

Newshound 2037: his story blowz!

Mukraker12: "rotflmao"

(Mukraker is typing a message...)

GO!

Celebrity Trial Webcam

YOU ARE OUT OF MILK. SHOWBIZ NEWS: TONIGHT, YOU WILL WATCH "REAL WORLD 68

MINOR EVENT HAVING NOTHING TO DO WITH WHAT ANCHOR IS TALKING ABOUT !

News Crawl

Personalized Crawl

SCREEN OF THE FUTURE

(Continued from page 171)

bind us. We will be isolated in ways we could never have imagined – which isn't as bad as it sounds, since we will also no longer have the ability to imagine. While scattered pockets of religious folk and proud "Bostonians" will still exist here and there,[4] America will exist only as a name on a much swampier map. The Era of the Superpower will end. Our national greatness will cease to be.

On the bright side, Cialis wants you to know rock-hard, 5-hour erections are only the beginning.

Democracy's Future v.2.0 – ¡Viven de largo los Estados Unidos!

In this version of the future, our worst fears about America's rapidly shifting demographic landscape overwhelming our federal infrastructure are realized.

First up, the Latinos. Like the Kool-Aid man, no wall can contain them. Their numbers will continue to grow until this nation only speaks English as a cute homage.[5] Schools will be bilingual – that is, if our Spanish-speaking conquistadors mercifully allow SSL (Spanish as a Second Language) to be taught in our *escuelas públicas*.

Desperate and angry anglos will fight back the only way they know how: white flight. After that fails, they will fight back the other only way they know how: exploiting the law to their advantage. Redrawing congressional districts will fail as a stopgap measure, forcing the wholesale creation of new states. Among those joining the Union: Orange County, Texas II, and an amalgam known as Manhattachester. North Dakota will split into North North Dakota and Mid North Dakota, while South Dakota will divide itself into Dakota and the Commonwealth of Greater Mount Rushmore-Wall Drug. There will be 17 Carolinas.

(Continue on page 176)

---

[4] In the latter case, predominantly in and around Boston.
[5] Like the French-speaking Canadians. We'll be that lame.

Will You Be Aware?

Canada used to be a separate country, with its own government and laws and everything!

Old Canadian flag (c. 2004)   *New Canadian flag (c. 2019)*

>>Fig. 8.5

The liberal denizens of New York City and Westchester County will finally do what they've been grumbling about for decades: form their own state. It will be horribly run.

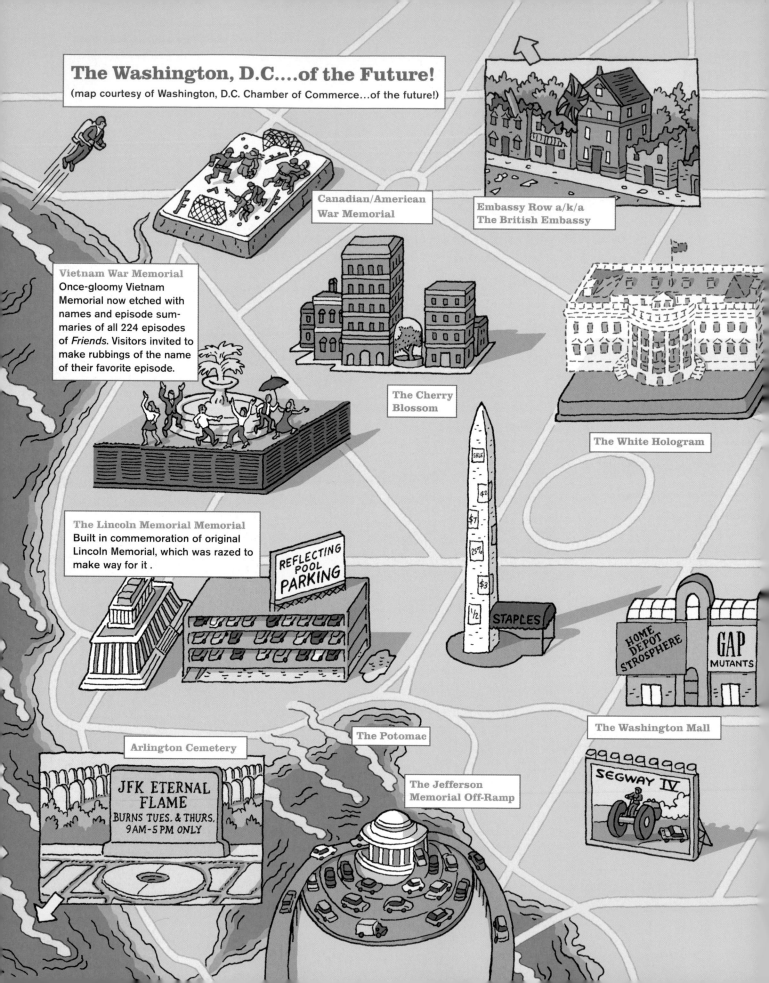

The Washington, D.C....of the Future!
(map courtesy of Washington, D.C. Chamber of Commerce...of the future!)

Canadian/American War Memorial

Embassy Row a/k/a The British Embassy

Vietnam War Memorial
Once-gloomy Vietnam Memorial now etched with names and episode summaries of all 224 episodes of *Friends*. Visitors invited to make rubbings of the name of their favorite episode.

The Cherry Blossom

The White Hologram

The Lincoln Memorial Memorial
Built in commemoration of original Lincoln Memorial, which was razed to make way for it .

REFLECTING POOL PARKING

SALE
$2
$7
25%
$3
1/2
STAPLES

HOME DEPOT STROSPHERE

GAP MUTANTS

The Washington Mall

Arlington Cemetery

The Potomac

JFK ETERNAL FLAME
BURNS TUES. & THURS. 9AM-5PM ONLY

The Jefferson Memorial Off-Ramp

SEGWAY IV

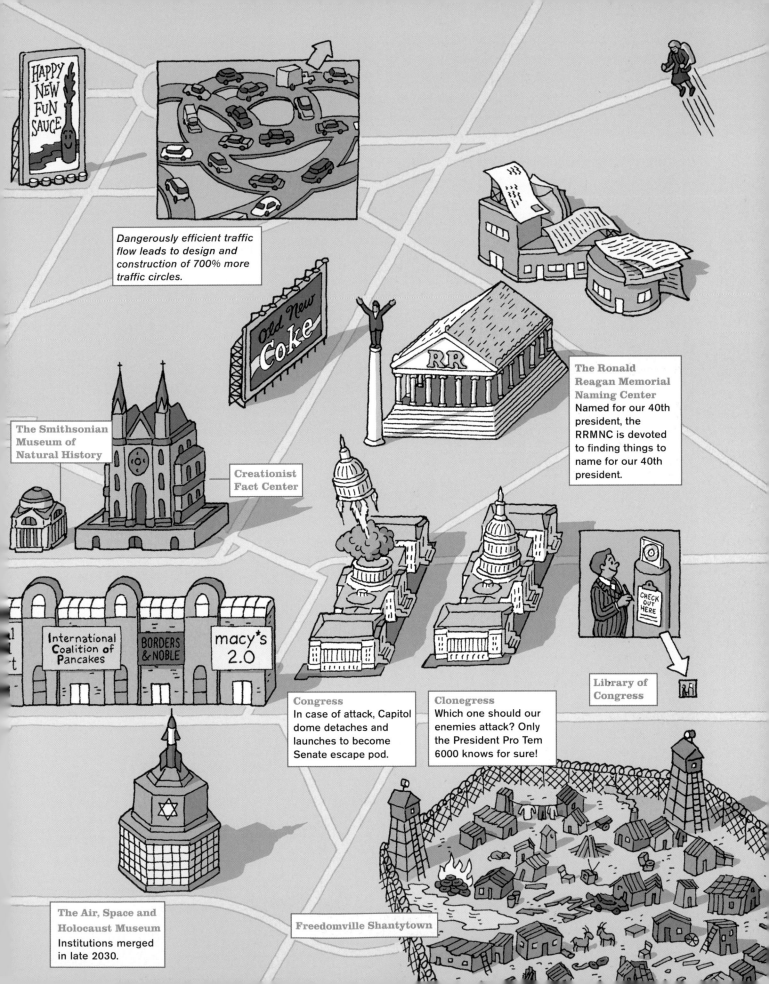

HAPPY NEW FUN SAUCE

Dangerously efficient traffic flow leads to design and construction of 700% more traffic circles.

Old New Coke

The Ronald Reagan Memorial Naming Center Named for our 40th president, the RRMNC is devoted to finding things to name for our 40th president.

RR

The Smithsonian Museum of Natural History

Creationist Fact Center

CHECK OUT HERE

Library of Congress

International Coalition of Pancakes

BORDERS & NOBLE

macy's 2.0

Congress In case of attack, Capitol dome detaches and launches to become Senate escape pod.

Clonegress Which one should our enemies attack? Only the President Pro Tem 6000 knows for sure!

The Air, Space and Holocaust Museum Institutions merged in late 2030.

Freedomville Shantytown

(Continued from page 173)

But it will be to no avail. The bloated federal bureaucracy, unable to provide for the growing underclass in all 81 of our states, will collapse. Social services will exist only in pockets of extreme wealth. Tortillas, however, will reach new heights of deliciousness. Meanwhile, outnumbered, outvoted and outcast, America's Caucasian population will be reduced to a disempowered army of day laborers wandering the dusty southwest looking for menial jobs. In perhaps the greatest irony of all, they will fail to see the irony of all this.

Will You Be Aware?

The Social Security Administration once granted retirees a monthly check, instead of just a coupon good for a free side salad at Denny's.

Democracy's Future v.3.0 – Christ v. Antichrist: Whose Side Are YOU On?

>>Fig. 8.6

Have you heard the Good News?

In this version of the future, our best hopes and dreams about Jesus Christ returning and separating out the worthy from the damned are realized.

Though the *Book of Revelation* covers this in more detail, the essentials bear mentioning: After the shout of the Archangel is heard, the living and the dead in Christ (i.e., those who have not worshipped the beast and are free of his mark upon their foreheads) shall reign with God in Heaven for one thousand years. Then, once the Rapture has occurred and the saved are off the planet, the Democrats will regain both the House and the Senate.

Democracy's Future v.4.0 – The Absolute Truth

You read ahead, didn't you? Or if you didn't, know that someone else did and ruined the future for you. For all of us, really. You know, like when Lot and his wife were told not to look back on Sodom and Gomorrah? You know what happened. She was turned into … something. Perhaps candy.

Point is, let that be a lesson to you about disobeying the third-person omniscient voice.

Alas, the future of democracy is not difficult to imagine at all, for human beings, though the amount of hair on their bodies and slope of their foreheads may change, are a predictable lot. Democracy will continue to exist in that delicate balance between lofty ideals and human fallibility. The United States will not remain the globe's lone superpower because we simply aren't fucking at a rate commensurate with the world's emerging nations. Sooner or later, someone's going to be richer and more powerful. China's a good bet – though don't rule out India. They're scrappy, they already have nukes and according to one recent study, every single Indian citizen is a computer genius who has already taken your job in programming.

How did that feel? Get used to it. ◔

>>Fig. 8.7

Rajiv. He replaced you.

Will You Be Aware?

The human mind didn't always operate on the Windows OS.

Windows 6703.2 is unnecessary if you have Windows 6703.1.

Capture Time in a Capsule!

A time capsule is a great way to send a message to the future. That message: We didn't need any of this stuff. One tightly sealed canister made of copper, aluminum or stainless steel can hold the secrets of who we were, the lives we led, and the *tchotchkes* we wanted to clear off our desks.

Here are a few suggestions for what to include in a time caspsule to help introduce the people of 2004 to the cannibalistic humanoid underground dwellers (C.H.U.D.) of 2104.

Finally, label the time capsule *Peanut Brittle* and spring-load its contents with amusing cloth-covered snakes. Dear people of the future: Zing!

To give future man understanding of our religious beliefs.

Not so much to understand the comedy of our time, but more to get rid of her.

It allowed Apple Computer to survive for five more years before being crushed by Microsoft.

Lest the people of the future think for a second we were unpatriotic.

An unopened time capsule from a previous generation to show how little we cared about time capsules in 2004.

A newspaper is a good place to start, and *USA Today* offers a good general overview of American life. Nothing will help future scholars reconstruct the essence of our time like a three-color infographic of "What We're Barbecuing."

The person of the future's face will break into a cracked and leathery smile at this low, low number.

Man of the future will marvel at how few bees we could fit in our mouths.

To show our ability to bravely merchandise even in the face of tragedy.

POR FAVOR, NO ABRA HASTA QUE 2104
PLEASE DO NOT OPEN UNTIL 2104

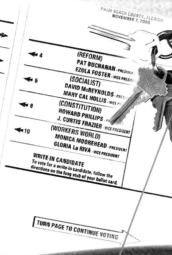

So future generations can continue the hunt.

What better way to explain to future humans why they live in a blasted, remorseless hellscape?

Our keys. Fuck!

To show the people 100 years from now what people 36 years ago thought the world would be like 3 years ago.
(Note: A copy of *1984* will do in a pinch – either the Orwell novel or Van Halen album.)

Classroom Activities

[Note to readers: In this chapter, Classroom Activities come before Discussion Questions … because in the future, everything will be upside down!]

1. Lose hope.

2. Robots vs. Humans.
Divide the class into "robots" and "humans" engaged in an epic battle of survival. To simulate postapocalyptic combat, chart each side's academic achievement over the course of the semester. Highest grades win … but at what cost?

3. The year is 2571. You have been convicted of thought crimes against Overlord Zargax and sentenced to life imprisonment on the toxic desert penal colony planet of Trucyyln-9. Prove your innocence.

>>Fig. 8.8

Overlord Zargax

4. Time Machine.
Turn your classroom into a time machine by making the students perform tedious busy-work for the entire morning while you read a John Grisham novel. When they're done, close your book, point to the clock, and announce, "See? We're three hours into the future!"

5. Construct a well-ventilated, insulated underground shelter capable of withstanding a nuclear attack. Make sure it has ample room to stock non-perishable foods and is hooked up to a fresh water supply. You'll probably want to have it completed before April of next year. What do you mean, "why?" Don't worry about it. Just do it.

6. In the future, all of life's major milestones will come in pill form. Match the event with the appropriate pill.

1.   2.   3.

4.    5.    6.

A. Your high-school graduation
B. The birth of your twins
C. Your first kiss
D. Your birth
E. Your retirement
F. Your death by choking on a giant pill

Answer key: 1-D, 2-C, 3-A, 4-B, 5-E, 6-F

Discussion Questions

1. How will changing demographic trends, specifically the increased prevalence of minorities, alter the socio-political landscape blah blah blah?

2. How will electronic or "e-voting" change our democracy? Will it become an "e-democracy"? In your answer, put the letter "e" before as many words as possible.

3. Where do you see democracy 500 years from now? How about 502 years?

4. What form of government would you like to see after our democracy finally eats itself, then shits itself out, and then re-eats its own self-shit in 2007? Express your answer in tears.

5. Name three things about contemporary politics that seem like they're as bad as they could possibly be, but which we'll look back at in 10 years with nostalgia for how simple a time it was.

6. According to Nostradamus:

> In the Castle of Figueras on a misty day
> A sovereign prince will be born of an infamous woman:
> Surname of breeches on the ground will make him posthumous,
> Never was there a King so very bad in his provenance.

How did he know?

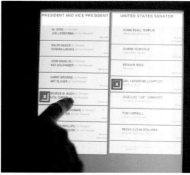
>>Fig. 8.10

Electronic voting machines are a bold first step toward fulfilling Lincoln's prophetic vision of government "by the machines, of the machines, for the machines."

>>Fig. 8.9

Nearly half a millennium ago, Nostradamus (1503-1566) eerily predicted his picture would appear in this book. Coincidence … or meta-joke?

Will You Be Aware?

Spam was once seen as an annoyance rather than the last vestige of emotional contact between human beings.

"Do...you...speak...English?"

Chapter 9

The Rest of the World:
International House of Horrors

As you can tell by the large number of pages in your left hand and the dwindling handful in your right, we are nearing the end of our brief guided tour of the past, present, and future of American democracy. But before you start exchanging goodbyes and e-mail addresses with your fellow readers while tearfully reflecting on your fond memories of, say, chapter 4 (Fig. 9.1), one important order of business remains.

>> Fig. 9.1

Has it really been that long since we made it through Chapter 4 together? Man, time flies.

Some of our book's more astute readers[1] may have noticed that in detailing the complex and bewildering institutions that comprise our government, we inadvertently called your attention to some slight imperfections in our otherwise perfect Union — inefficiencies, inequities, injustices, absurdities, hypocrisies, and an overall failure to live up to the lofty ideals expressed in our nation's founding documents. Those type of things. Some of these readers may even feel so angry, they may be tempted to consider living some place other than America, some place freer, safer, less bomb-happy, less hated by the rest of the world. Some place like, oh, the rest of the world.

And to these readers we say…*have you seen the rest of the world lately?*

Chances are, the answer to that question is no. With recent travel bans, a slumping economy, and our nation's love affair with xenophobia, your exposure to other systems of government is limited at best. In fact, odds are you could name five fictional U.S. presidents more readily than one foreign prime minister. Quick, try it. See?

So, in the interest of presenting the complete picture and reasserting America's superiority, the rest of the world, its peoples, systems of government, cultures and histories have been encapsulated on the following pages. Bon voyage!

---

[1] I.e., those with GEDs.

Africa

Population: 700 Million

The story of Africa in the modern age is one of war, disease, corruption, repression and poverty. On the upside, there are tons of monkeys and you never need a jacket.

Africa was not always so dreadful. It was, after all, the birthplace of our species; ancient Egypt was once the most advanced civilization on earth; rich tribal cultures flourished on the Western shore for untold centuries; Meryl Streep even stopped by to grow coffee and bang Robert Redford. Still, critics note ancient Egypt was rife with slavery, Meryl Streep is overrated, and while early man may have originated in Africa, he migrated to other continents as soon as he could stand upright.

Blame for Africa's modern-day ills can be laid squarely at the feet of two oppressors: white people and black people. Europeans' systematic rape of sub-Saharan Africa's resources, territory, and slaves cast the continent into centuries of misery. But when colonialism collapsed in the mid-20th century, many local black leaders thought, "Hmmm… if the white man got rich and powerful by turning my homeland into an unrecognizable husk of sewage and mass graves, maybe I can, too!"

So, is there hope for a truly democratic Africa? Long answer: Only if continent-wide improvements in educaton, human rights and public health are coupled with an aggressive and far-sighted debt-relief program that breaks the cycle of subsistence farming and urban squalor. Short answer: No.

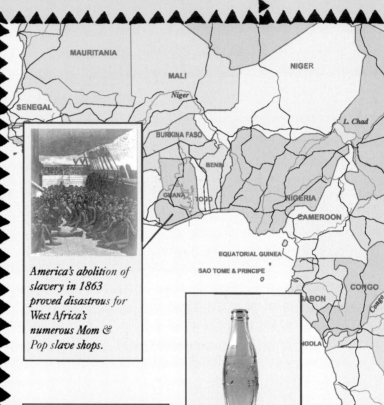

America's abolition of slavery in 1863 proved disastrous for West Africa's numerous Mom & Pop slave shops.

End Apartheid

South Africa
Must Be Free
Divest Now

For decades, South Africa's racist policy of "apartheid" effectively barred Miami Steve Van Zandt from entering the country.

The discovery that led Masai scientists to a shocking conclusion about their deities' mental health.

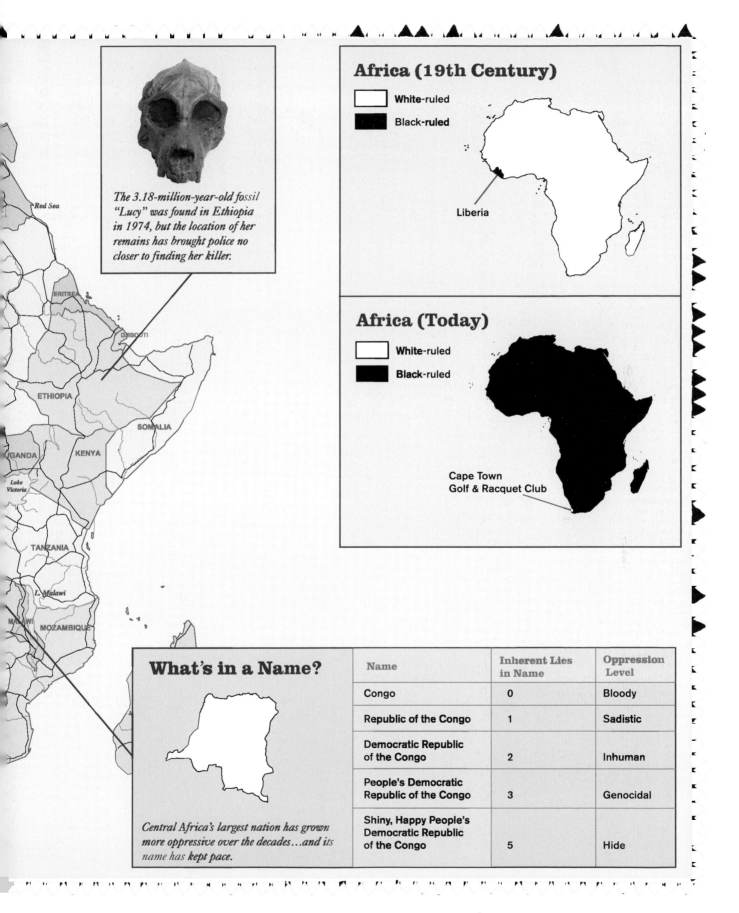

The 3.18-million-year-old fossil "Lucy" was found in Ethiopia in 1974, but the location of her remains has brought police no closer to finding her killer.

Africa (19th Century)

☐ White-ruled
■ Black-ruled

Liberia

Africa (Today)

☐ White-ruled
■ Black-ruled

Cape Town
Golf & Racquet Club

What's in a Name?

Central Africa's largest nation has grown more oppressive over the decades…and its name has kept pace.

Name	Inherent Lies in Name	Oppression Level
Congo	0	Bloody
Republic of the Congo	1	Sadistic
Democratic Republic of the Congo	2	Inhuman
People's Democratic Republic of the Congo	3	Genocidal
Shiny, Happy People's Democratic Republic of the Congo	5	Hide

Australia

Population: 19,731,000

Imagine if American politics were a boomerang, and you threw that boomerang and it came back to you exactly like it was... except now it had a dark, leathery suntan and was wearing corduroy shorts and an orange Ocean Pacific tank top. This gives you an idea of the surprising similarities between Australia and the United States. Other similarities: language (sort of), wholesale slaughter of indigenous population and geography. Like America, Australia has two or three important cities on the opposite coasts and a whole lot of nothing in between. What we call "Flyover Country," they call "The Outback." Oh, one other thing: most of the white inhabitants are descended from hardened criminals whom Mother England deliberately sent as far away as geographically possible to avoid contamination by their putrid gene pool.

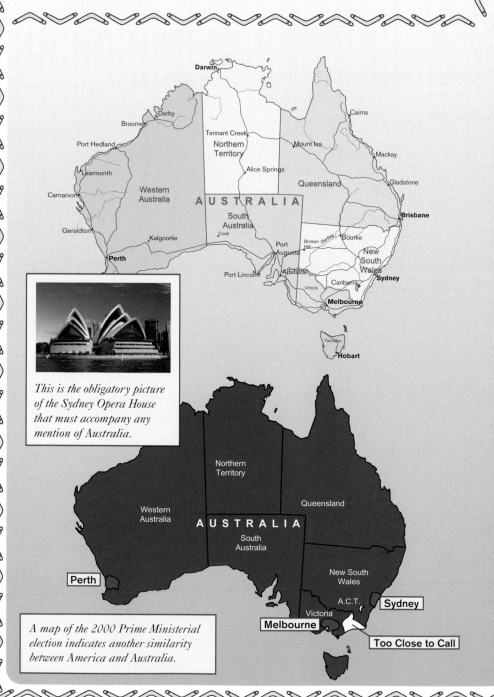

This is the obligatory picture of the Sydney Opera House that must accompany any mention of Australia.

A map of the 2000 Prime Ministerial election indicates another similarity between America and Australia.

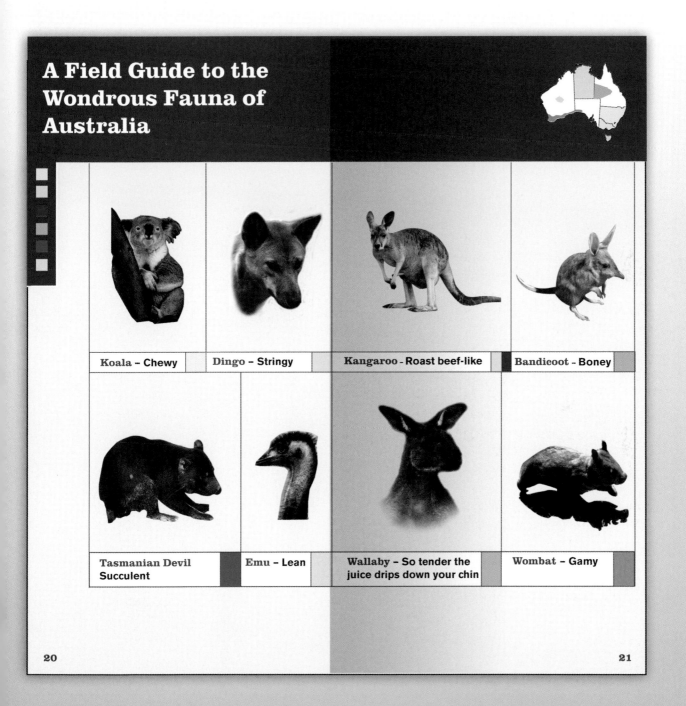

A Field Guide to the Wondrous Fauna of Australia

Koala – Chewy

Dingo – Stringy

Kangaroo - Roast beef-like

Bandicoot – Boney

Tasmanian Devil Succulent

Emu – Lean

Wallaby – So tender the juice drips down your chin

Wombat – Gamy

20

21

Australian Weaponry: A Primer

That's not a knife.

This is a knife.

Much of the Australian national character can only be explained as a byproduct of their perpetual drunkenness.

Kylie Minogue looks like Britney Spears.

You can begin to understand what Geoffrey Rush is saying.

Didgeridoo music pleasant.

Australia's unofficial national anthem is *Waltzing Matilda*.

Below, the first 8 lines of this beloved song with annotation to help with their quaint colloquialisms:

Once a jolly swagman[1] camped by a billabong[2]

Under the shade of a coolibah[3] tree

And he sang as he watched and waited
till his billy[4] boiled

"Who'll come a-waltzing Matilda with me?"[5]

Down come a jumbuck[6] to drink at
the water hole

Up jumped a swagman and grabbed him in glee

And he sang as he stowed him away in his
tucker bag[7]

"You'll come a-waltzing Matilda with me."

---

[1] **swagman:** tramp
[2] **billabong:** dry river bed
[3] **coolibah:** apparently some kind of tree
[4] **billy:** ummm…a smaller dry river bed?
[5] This line seems to indicate some kind of dancing, probably a waltz, possibly with someone named Matilda
[6] **jumbuck:** Come on! That can't possibly be a word!
[7] **tucker bag:** Fuck this. "English-speaking" country, my ass.

Midnight Oil guy looks like Britney Spears.

Russell Crowe seems like a "decent bloke."

Vegemite palatable.

NEW ZEALAND

Australia's Canada

Population: 3,875,000

New Zealand is pretty much the same thing as Australia, except it has Maoris instead of Aborigines and they shot *Lord of the Rings* there.

Auckland
Hamilton
Rotorua
New Plymouth
NEW ZEALAND
Westport
Greymouth
Wellington
Christchurch
Timaru
Invercargill
Dunedin

Once every 50 years, New Zealand's North and South Island ram each other in a primitive battle for supremacy.

New Zealand boasts a remarkable 50 sheep for every Orc.

SOUTH PACIFIC ISLANDS

The lure of breadfruit brought early European sailors, who fell in love with these islands and their loose sexual morals, perfect weather and easy lifestyle. Fifty syphilitic years later, the canoes no longer came out to meet the boats, the natives were obese and ugly and the merchants realized too late that breadfruit was, in fact, a starch.

Yes, yes, yes, very nice…but do you have an elaborate system of checks and balances?

Chinese People Familiar to Average American

Mao Zedong[1]   Jackie Chan   Yao Ming   Chow Yun Fat (maybe)   Guy Who Almost Got Run Over by Tank in Tiananmen Square

CHINA

★

Crouching Tiger, Hidden Oil Reserves

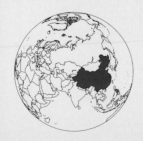

Population: 1.3 Billion

By the time you finish reading this sentence, three million more Chinese people will have been born.[2] That's life in the world's most populous country. Though its economy still lags behind that of many punier industrialized nations, rapacious First World capitalists are correct in their designation of China as a "sleeping giant." Here's the rub: *They're all a bunch of Communists! Filthy, filthy Communists!* Okay, that smear doesn't have the zing it once had, but China is still a police state. That means things Americans take for granted – freedom to practice Scientology no matter how transparent a ruse it is; freedom to publish a picture of President Bush with a Hitler moustache on your lame blog; even the freedom to listen to Paul McCartney's horrible song "Freedom" – are against the law in China. The forces of globalization may yet change all this, but until that day comes you are better off adopting one of their readily available babies[3] and taking her to see Richard Gere stand side by side with the Dalai Lama as they make yet another plea for a Free Tibet. If you are lucky, Bjork will do a set.

★

[1] A name that can and has been spelled 94 different ways.

[2] This footnote adds another million.

[3] Females only! (For you see, they are a burden.)

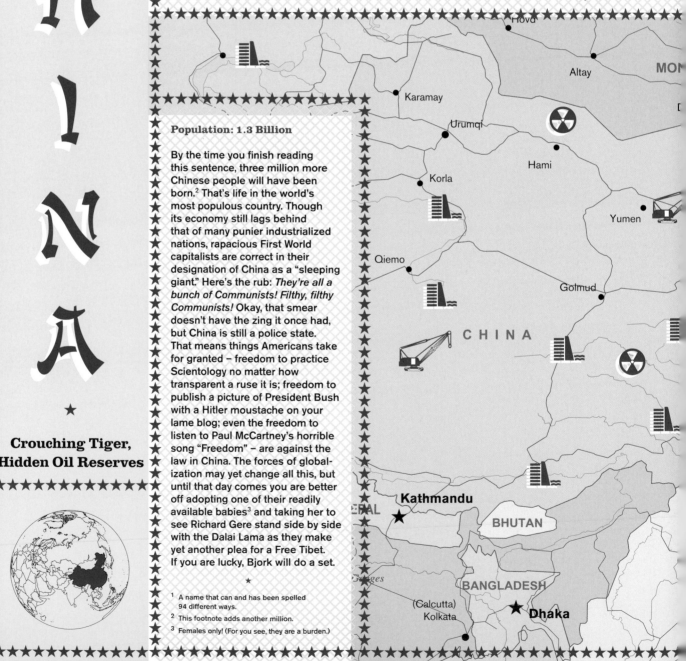

Hova

Altay

MON

Karamay

Urumqi

Hami

Korla

Qiemo

Yumen

Golmud

CHINA

Kathmandu

NEPAL

BHUTAN

Ganges

BANGLADESH

(Calcutta) Kolkata

Dhaka

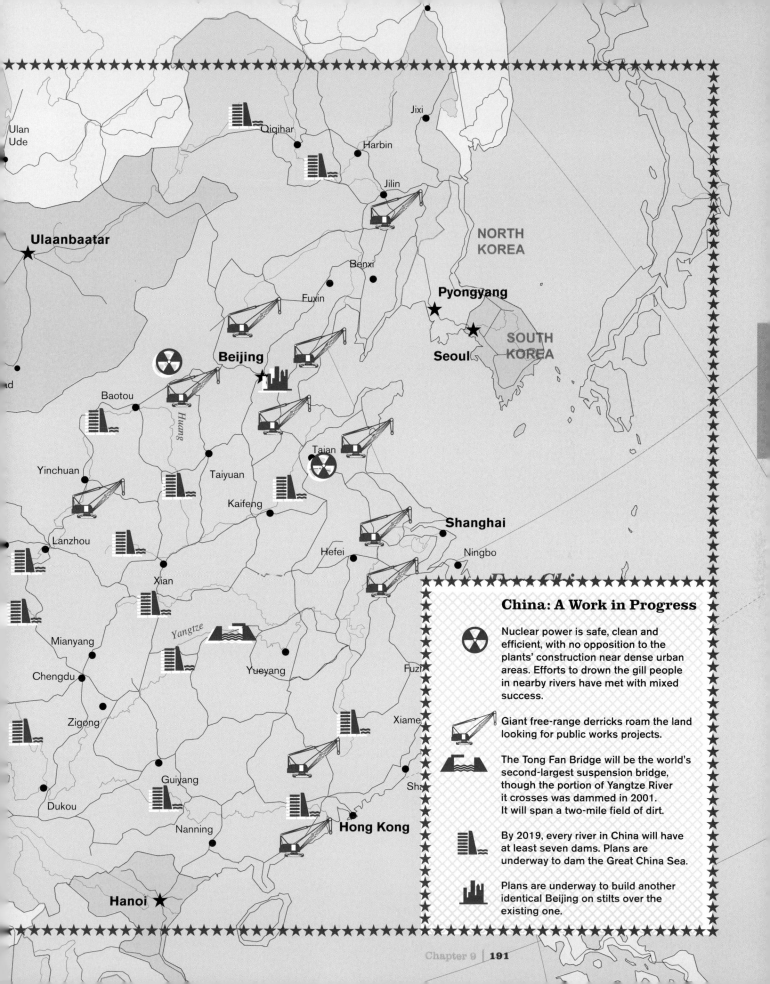

China: A Work in Progress

Nuclear power is safe, clean and efficient, with no opposition to the plants' construction near dense urban areas. Efforts to drown the gill people in nearby rivers have met with mixed success.

Giant free-range derricks roam the land looking for public works projects.

The Tong Fan Bridge will be the world's second-largest suspension bridge, though the portion of Yangtze River it crosses was dammed in 2001. It will span a two-mile field of dirt.

By 2019, every river in China will have at least seven dams. Plans are underway to dam the Great China Sea.

Plans are underway to build another identical Beijing on stilts over the existing one.

Chinese History in Words

Though widely perceived as an historic act of civil disobedience, the famed Tiananmen Square protester was actually an OCD sufferer who only felt comfortable standing in front of large objects.

The popular "Chinatown" section of Shanghai.

Marco Polo discovered China by repeatedly shouting his own first name, then waiting for China to respond with his last.

and Phrases (and Pictures)

Dynasties

Match the priceless vase with the appropriate Dynasty.

A. Ming
B. Han
C. Tang
D. Qing
E. Bong

1.
2.
3.
4.
5.

Answers: A-2, B-5, C-4, D-1, E-3

Fill in the missing words in these vaguely familiar phrases:

1. The Great Leap _____

2. The _____ Revolution

3. The _____ Wall of China

4. Chinese _____ Drill

5. Honey, my parents are coming over; can you take out the good _____.

6. That guy's got more chins than a _____ phonebook.

(Choose from: fire, great, the, leprosy, cultural, China, forward, Sondheim, maxillofacial, Chinese, kippered)

Old Europe

Total population 350,000,000
Total royals 87,000
Journalists devoted
to "watching" them 564,000
Famous Europeans . . . . Ernest Hemingway
                                  Gertrude Stein
                                    Johnny Depp
                                    Jim Morrison

No region's stature has plummeted more over the past 100 years than Old Europe, a once-dominant region now reduced to sucking at the geopolitical teat of the American hegemon. To be fair, they are very tired. When they weren't fighting each other, they spent the better part of the last millennium conquering the world and taking the good stuff home with them. *You* spend one thousand years plundering and see if that doesn't slow you down a step. And what do they get for their troubles? Ungrateful colonies demanding their independence. And after they taught them how to play cricket!

Well, the loose collection of social democracies making up western Europe are not going to take it anymore. They've banded together to form a powerful coalition – the European Union – that will once again propel Europe to its rightful place amongst the world's most powerful…just as soon as they all adopt the same currency…and sign their constitution…and ratify their trade agreements. Wait, where's Belgium going?… We wanted to show you the new logo…

France

Paris is considered the world's most romantic and seizable city.

Spain

Spain is the world's leading exporter of naps.

Italy

Given the stability of Italy's government, this young Neapolitan boy has a 56% chance of serving as Prime Minister at some point in his life.

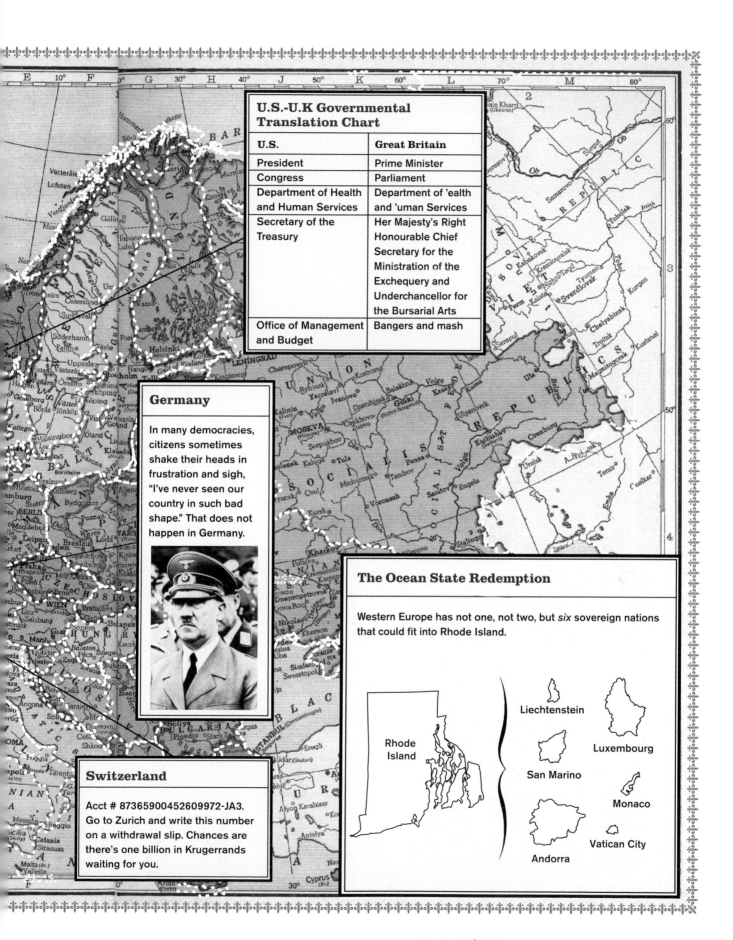

U.S.-U.K Governmental Translation Chart

U.S.	Great Britain
President	Prime Minister
Congress	Parliament
Department of Health and Human Services	Department of 'ealth and 'uman Services
Secretary of the Treasury	Her Majesty's Right Honourable Chief Secretary for the Ministration of the Exchequery and Underchancellor for the Bursarial Arts
Office of Management and Budget	Bangers and mash

Germany

In many democracies, citizens sometimes shake their heads in frustration and sigh, "I've never seen our country in such bad shape." That does not happen in Germany.

The Ocean State Redemption

Western Europe has not one, not two, but *six* sovereign nations that could fit into Rhode Island.

Rhode Island

Liechtenstein

San Marino

Andorra

Luxembourg

Monaco

Vatican City

Switzerland

Acct # 87365900452609972-JA3. Go to Zurich and write this number on a withdrawal slip. Chances are there's one billion in Krugerrands waiting for you.

European War Records

Country	W	L	Pct.	Notes
England	351	23	.938	Not including soccer riots
France	17	9	.654	Pre-Napoleon 16-1, post-Napoleon 1-8
Portugal	16	9	.640	16-8 on water, 0-1 on land
Spain	22	14	.611	Olé
Austria	(n/a)	(n/a)	(n/a)	(see Germany)
Holland	10	10	.500	Did you not expect the Dutch to split evenly?
Germany	3	3	.500	Quick out of the gate, but fades in the stretch
Greece	2	20	.100	Have fared poorly since loss of Odysseus
Italy	0	9	.000	When in war don't do as the Romans do
Switzerland	0	0	.000	Pussies

European Culinary Quiz

Match the country with the local specialty as ordered by an American tourist.

1. England

2. France

3. Italy

4. Netherlands

5. Switzerland

a. "Them fancy chocolates what got all the Kahlua inside."

b. "Pizza. What, no crazy bread?"

c. "Excuse me, I asked for fish and chips, but I think you gave me French fries."

d. "Le Croissandwich."

e. "Hey, this really is *Gouda* cheese! Get it? D'ya hear what I said about this bein' *Gouda* cheese?"

Is Europe in Decline?

The Mona Lisa
Warping

Michelangelo's David
Cracking, with
significant shrinkage

Notre Dame
4-7 last year

**The Leaning
Tower of Pisa**
Straightening

Finnegans Wake
More unreadable by the hour

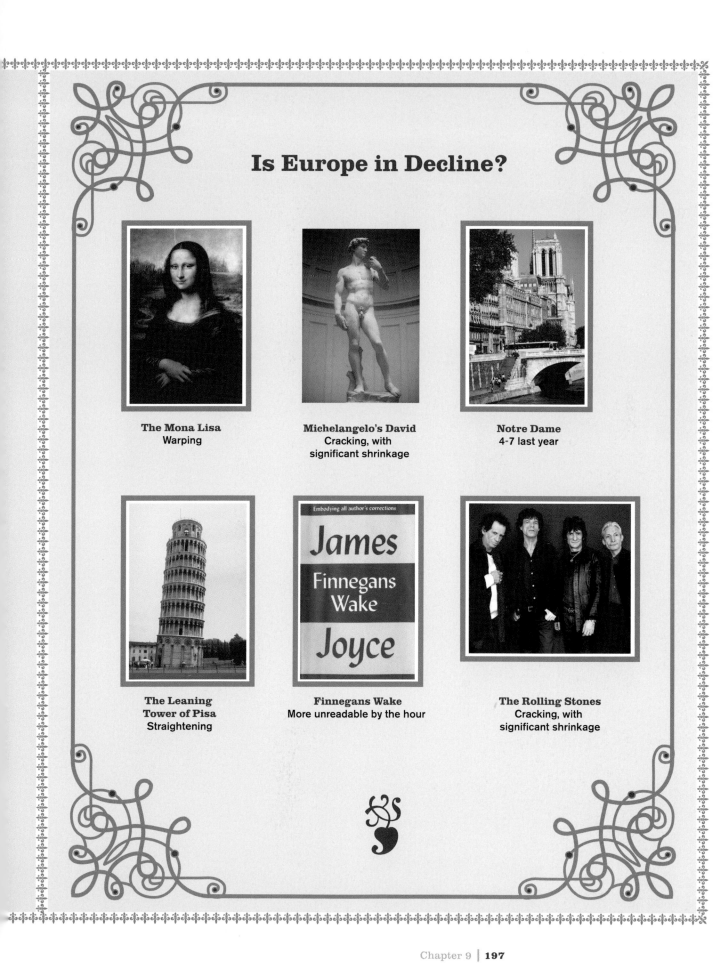

The Rolling Stones
Cracking, with
significant shrinkage

JAPAN

POPULATION: 127,654,000

Konnichiwa. My name is Mineko. I will be your submissive geisha servant during your stay on this page. While I draw a hot bath, please enjoy a few humble facts about our country. Not only will they make you happy, I expect you will find them fun and super as well. You are most welcome to visit Japan. Do you have an American Express Card? It will be most useful, for you see, even your big American wallets will not be able to contain the amount of cash needed to enjoy our beautiful island nation. May I see how much you have? No. That will not be nearly enough. (*giggles, covers face*)

PUBLIC TRANSPORTATION

BULLET TRAIN

PRIVATE TRANSPORTATION

BULLET RICKSHAW

MATCH THESE THINGS YOU'LL
FIND IN JAPAN TO THEIR NAMES

1. Chutoro
2. Pachinko
3. Tamako, the robot game show host
4. Commando

A.

B.

C.

D.

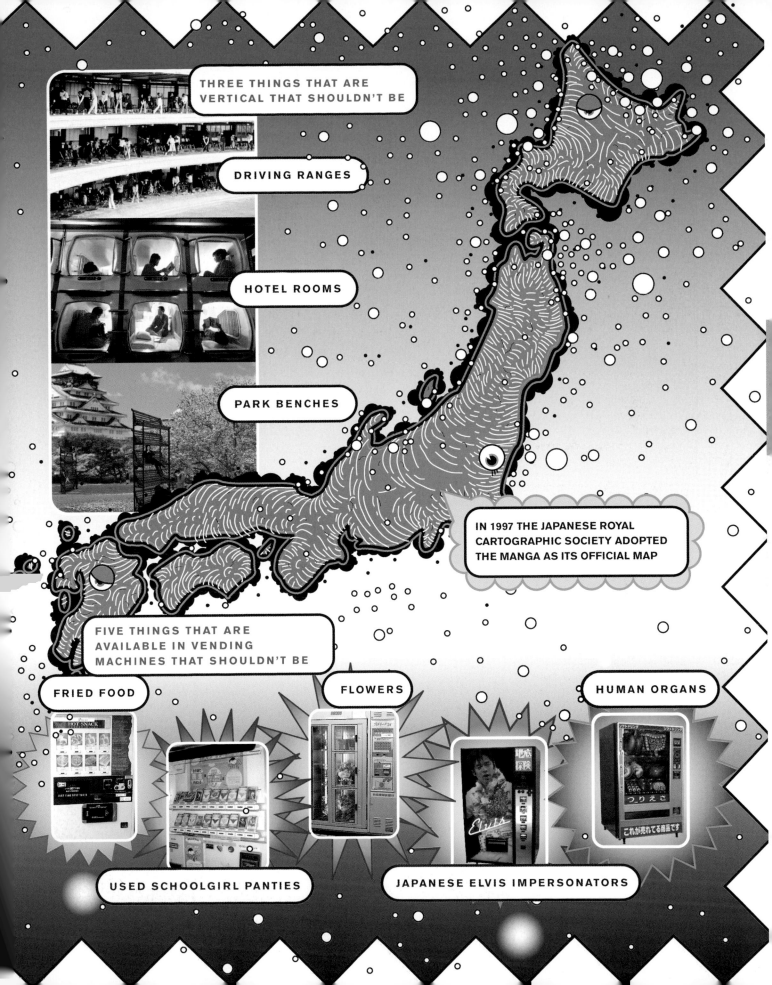

THREE THINGS THAT ARE VERTICAL THAT SHOULDN'T BE

DRIVING RANGES

HOTEL ROOMS

PARK BENCHES

IN 1997 THE JAPANESE ROYAL CARTOGRAPHIC SOCIETY ADOPTED THE MANGA AS ITS OFFICIAL MAP

FIVE THINGS THAT ARE AVAILABLE IN VENDING MACHINES THAT SHOULDN'T BE

FRIED FOOD

FLOWERS

HUMAN ORGANS

USED SCHOOLGIRL PANTIES

JAPANESE ELVIS IMPERSONATORS

Latin America

Population: 500,000,000

Number of Churches: 723,000,000

Guy you shouldn't bring up: Cortez

Whether you are a Marxist with camping skills or an ex-Nazi looking for a fresh start, no place says "hola!" like Latin America. Mexico, Central America and South America make up this region of five hundred million peop...wait...it looks like 20 of 'em are making a run for it. Anyway, known for its diverse agricultural products, distinct rhythms and massive foreign debt, Latin America is a wonderful destination for those dissatisfied with our government, but willing to try one our government has propped up. But be warned: You might have to head for the hills at a moment's notice, so pack light. When the coup happens, they don't take too kindly to foreigners and intellectuals...and it's a long, lonely drop from the C-130 to the South Atlantic below.[1]

[1] Especially when you're blindfolded

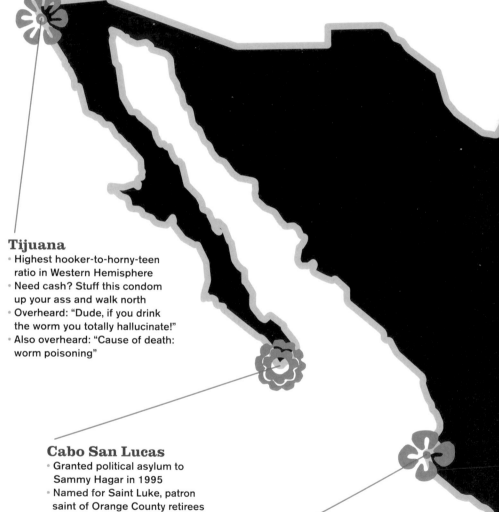

Tijuana
- Highest hooker-to-horny-teen ratio in Western Hemisphere
- Need cash? Stuff this condom up your ass and walk north
- Overheard: "Dude, if you drink the worm you totally hallucinate!"
- Also overheard: "Cause of death: worm poisoning"

Cabo San Lucas
- Granted political asylum to Sammy Hagar in 1995
- Named for Saint Luke, patron saint of Orange County retirees

Puerto Vallarta
- The *Love Boat* stopped here once in 1977
- Ideal honeymoon spot for even-numbered wives

Understanding Latin America

The national pastimes of Latin America are fútbol and irrational emotion.

Although the Mayan, Incan and Aztec cultures were incredibly advanced, the Spanish found them surprisingly killable.

Mexico's Major Cities, As Far As You're Concerned

Cancun
- Birthplace of the Wet T-Shirt Contest
- Ancestral home of Señor Frog
- Last parasailer to slam into side of high-rise hotel: 1997

Acapulco
- Cliff diving + smallest bathing suits imaginable = awkward episode of *Wide World of Sports*
- Ideal honeymoon spot for odd-numbered wives

Mexico:

Pro:
You can walk there.

Con:
The immigrant influx you are fleeing...guess where it's coming from.

Central America

"Banana Republic" originally described oppressive dictatorships run at the behest of U.S.-owned fruit companies. Now it describes a place you can buy a T-shirt for $39.

Belize

Honduras

Guatemala

El Salvador

Nicaragua

Panama

Costa Rica

One of these countries had something to do with Iran/Contra.

The construction of the Panama Canal led to the world's most famous palindrome: "A man, a plan, an American effort to control shipping lanes in the Western Hemisphere, Panama!"

Are You a "Strong" Man?

If you are thinking about running any of the Central American countries it helps if you are a strongman.

- Do you wear a military uniform of indeterminate rank and sunglasses at all times, including bathing?
- Do you find that many of your problems are solved through "jungle dumping"?
- Are you most comfortable standing and smiling in the back seat of an open Jeep?
- Does the word "junta" come up regularly in conversation?
- Look around. Are you the only one in the room not holding a machine gun?
- When people make disparaging remarks about strongmen, do they look at you and say... "no offense"?

If you answered yes to any of these questions, congratulations, the CIA would like to open up a checking account for you.

South American Economic Cycle

Brazil is the largest exporter of jiggling buttcheeks in the entire hemisphere.

A native delicacy of the Chilean Andes is *jugador congelado del rugbi* ("frozen rugby player").

In 1982 England went to war with Argentina over the Falkland Islands...because some barren, windswept expanses of strategically insignificant nothingness are worth fighting for.

A trip to South America is always a balance between fun and danger.

Each country below is rated for "funness" on a scale of one monkey to a barrel

"Danger" is measured on a scale of youth gang to death squad

Country	Funness	Danger	Don't Miss...
Argentina	🐒🐒🐒	⚔⚔	The Ghost Penguins of Tierra del Fuego
Brazil	🍺	⚔⚔⚔⚔	The Amazon rainforest. You have about 5 years
Bolivia	🐒🐒	💂💂💂	Butch Cassidy and/or Sundance Kid
Chile	🐒🐒	💂	Pinochet's imminent death
Colombia	🐒🐒🐒🐒	💂💂💂💂	Juan Valdez Museum of Decaffeination
Ecuador	🐒	💂💂💂	Large black line running through country
Paraguay	🐒	⚔⚔⚔	The former third-in-command at Buchenwald
Peru	🐒🐒🐒🐒	💂💂💂	Machu Picchu/Lake Titicaca/Mount Zoinks
Uruguay	🐒	⚔⚔	Okay, miss it
Venezuela	🐒🐒🐒	💂💂💂💂	$1=4,000,000,000 peso exchange rate

The Middle East

Population: 200,000,000

Number of Kosher meal orders: 6,400,000

The rich history of the Middle East is well-documented, so there is little the authors need to add by way of discouraging you from visiting there. From the fertile crescent of the Tigris and Euphrates Rivers to the olive and pomegranate strewn streets of Jerusalem, the story of man began in this magnificent region. And clearly, this region is where the story will end. From the day God chose one of the three different religions who claim this land as their own, the shit has been hitting the palm fronds. Perhaps God himself best explained the almost non-stop violence that has plagued the area:

"Who amongst thee are my favored people: Jews, Christians or Muslims? I don't know. I guess we will just have to see who wants it more."
- Luke 1:11:04

With the ongoing violence in the region, journalists must be creative with their descriptions of the political climate.

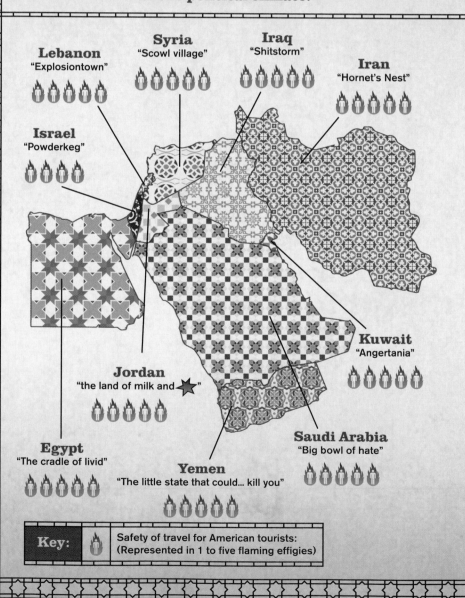

Lebanon
"Explosiontown"

Syria
"Scowl village"

Iraq
"Shitstorm"

Iran
"Hornet's Nest"

Israel
"Powderkeg"

Jordan
"the land of milk and ⭐"

Kuwait
"Angertania"

Egypt
"The cradle of livid"

Yemen
"The little state that could... kill you"

Saudi Arabia
"Big bowl of hate"

Key: 🔥 Safety of travel for American tourists: (Represented in 1 to five flaming effigies)

Middle East or Middle of the Road?

It is critical during the "War on Terror" that Americans are able to distinguish between polarizing Mideast figures and comforting icons of Middle America. Can you tell the difference?

1. Al Jazeera
2. Al Jarreau
3. Al Roker
4. Al Qaeda
5. Ben Gurion
6. Ben Gazzara

Key: ME (Middle East)
MA (Middle America)

1. ME 2. MA 3. MA 4. ME
5. ME 6. MA

The logo for an inflammatory regional news outlet

A lite jazz singer

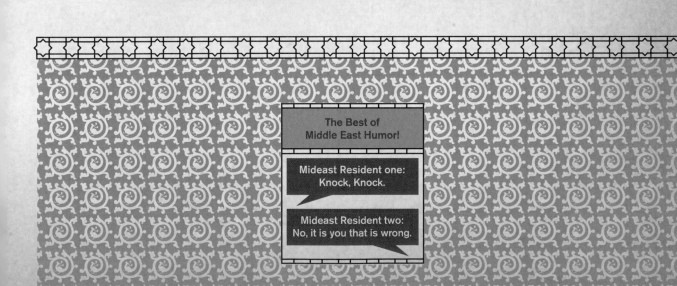

The Best of Middle East Humor!

Mideast Resident one: Knock, Knock.

Mideast Resident two: No, it is you that is wrong.

☼ **Fun Task** ☼

What do you think the borders of the Middle East should be?
Don't be afraid to group people with no regard for history and ethnicity.
It worked for the British and French! Invent new countries and
create interesting and fresh conflicts!

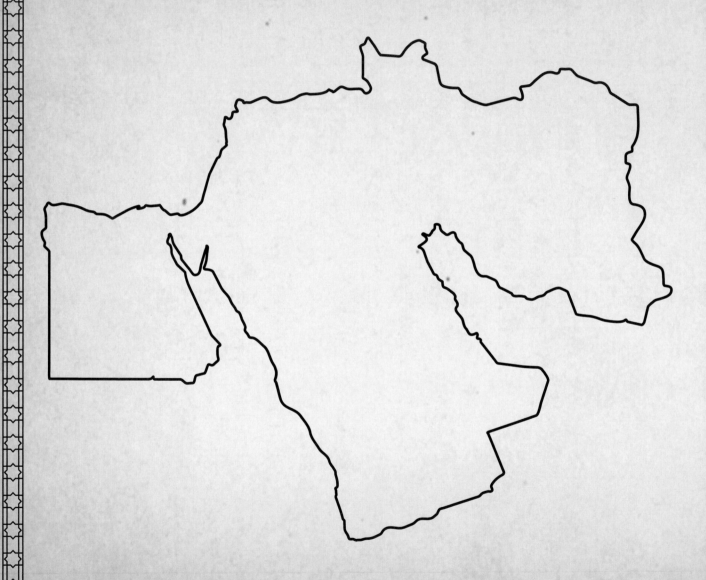

Match the Country to Its Sworn Enemy

A. Bahrain   1. Israel

B. Lebanon

C. Qatar

D. United Arab Emirates

E. Egypt

F. Syria

G. Jordan

H. Iran

I. Iraq

J. Saudi Arabia

K. Algeria

L. Morocco

M. Yemen

N. Oman

O. Kuwait

Answers: A. 1, (etc.)

The Best of
Middle East Humor!

A Priest, a Rabbi and an Imam walk into a bar.

All are offended by what they see.

A Middle East Jumble

LEGBA

EDFLINI

ROPWE

NEVCOILE

Answer: " ⃝⃝ ⃝⃝⃝⃝ ⃝⃝⃝ "

Jumbles: Bagel, Infidel, Power, Violence
Answer: We Love Oil

WHAT THE FUCK
AM I DOING
HERE?

RUSSIA &

Soviet Union, c. 1988
Civil Wars: 0
Olympic Gold Medals: 395 (Summer Only)
Representative Cultural Icon: Solzhenitsyn

SWEDEN
FINLAND
RUSSIA
POLAND
SLOVAKIA
HUNGARY ROMANIA
YUGOSLAVIA BULGARIA
MACEDONIA
ALBANIA GEORGIA
GREECE ARMENIA AZERBAIJAN
TURKEY
NORTH CYPRUS TAJIKISTAN
CYPRUS SYRIA
LEBANON
ISRAEL IRAQ AFGHANISTAN
JORDAN IRAN
MONGOLIA
CHINA
NORTH KOREA
SOUTH KOREA
JAPAN

Population: 300,000,000

Remember the CCCP? What about the USSR? No? Hmmm. How about *Rocky IV*? Yeah, well that's all over now. With the fall of the Berlin Wall in 1989, the Communist nations of the Soviet Union threw off the yoke of a failed political system and rushed to embrace Western-style capitalism. But like Lennie in *Of Mice and Men*, these retarded man-children did not know their own strength. Lacking infrastructure, experience, and

understanding of market controls, Russia has been tossed into swirling chaos. Yes, Western goods and services are now available, but chances are those Levis must first pass through the grubby hands of a bulbous-nosed mobster in a shiny tracksuit and $800 Bruno Magli loafers. He will kill you if you look at him funny. But first you will be tortured. And your disappearance will not be investigated. So that's Russia.

As for Eastern Europe, particularly the Balkan region, it remains a powder-keg of ethnic tension where the Croats hate the Serbs, the Serbs hate the Kosovars, the Poles hate the Ukrainians, and everyone hates those goddamned Albanians. By all accounts, Estonia is lovely.

EASTERN EUROPE

Russia & Eastern Europe, 2004
Civil Wars: 47
Olympic Gold Medals: Melted down and converted to petrodollars
Representative Cultural Icon: TaTu

Yugoslavia

1980

1992

1997

2004

No country better exemplifies the complexities of Eastern Europe than what was once known as "Yugoslavia." Over the past 25 years Yugoslavia has split into more and more ethnic enclaves. Today, each resident lives in the Independent Republic of Himself.

In the 15 years since *perestroika* took hold, Russia has
plunged headfirst into its new economic system by way of fire sale.
But hurry, supplies have a very definite half-life.

Russian Mail Order Direct

 # 2743

Chemical Plant

Hello. I am Svetlana Petrochemical, Inc. Am being born from Russian investors. Desire strong gentle American venture capitalist for to introduce me to Western customs and currency. Must get along with child laborers.

 # 3765

Country

Breakaway Republic could be yours! 500,000 acres of almost usable land. Don't drink the groundwater! Needs TLC and new supply of natural resources. Fully armed.

 # 7240

Nuclear Missile

Decommissioned Burya AS-4 (La-350 ICCM) back on market and ready to move! Fundamentalist? Separatist? Angry teen? We don't discriminate! (Cash only, buyer responsible for shipping.)

 # 3948

Oil Derrick

Abandoned Kazakh oil field with circa 1977 Soviet-era drilling equipment seeks American energy conglomerate oil-services concern for brief retrofitting, possible take-over.

RUSSIAN WOMEN: A PRIMER

Russian women are known for three qualities: their beauty, their heartiness, and the speed with which one becomes the other.

Miss Vladivostok

Miss Vladivostok, two weeks later

THE VODKAS OF RUSSIA: AN APPRECIATION

Potato Vodka	Beet Vodka	Whiskey Vodka	Furniture Vodka	Grief Vodka

SCANDINAVIA

Population: 24,270,000

Non-blondes: 4

A Highly Efficient Guide to Scandinavia

Americans consider life in Scandinavia to be as sweet and white as a vanilla snow cone from the fjords of Bjordensen. Norway, Sweden, Denmark, Iceland and Finland have blended cold, hard Teutonic efficiency with European social liberalism to create five of the cleanest nations on the planet. You can literally eat off the sidewalk in Copenhagen. Scandinavians enjoy the lowest levels of pollution, homelessness and illiteracy in the world. And yet most of them will commit suicide. Why? Because six months of glorious sunlight must cede to six months of spirit-crushing darkness. It is the yin and yang of Scandinavia – full employment but a minimum 50% income tax rate. This dilemma is perhaps most thoroughly manifested in Scandinavia's bikini teams, which consistently rank among the world's hottest, even though the region's beaches suck.

Great Leaders of Scandinavia

Denmark
Christian II
1481-1559

Finland
P.M. Pehr Evind Svinhufvud
1850-1934

The Scandinavian Paradox

Sweden
P.M. Bjorg Samuelsson
1911-1992

Norway
P.M. Thorvald Jacobsen
1942-

Scandalnavia!

Scandinavia's Juiciest Political Scandals

1906

Women granted suffrage in Finland. High-ranking official jokes, "As long as my dear wife returns from the polls in time to boil potatoes for our family, it is fine with me." Insensitive remark results in immediate censure and dismissal.

1939

Sweden declares WWII neutrality. Yet contingent of renegade Parliamentarians hint they are "leaning towards Allies."

1967

Norwegian Størting votes 136 to 13 in favor of joining EEC. Thirteen "nay" voters are mildly upset, but feel better after going home and having sex with their physically perfect spouse.

1993

Investigative journalists uncover Norwegian who once paid for something out of his own pocket. Størting votes to reimburse the man and subsidize "something nice" for his kids.

In the first millennium A.D., Norse Vikings raped, pillaged and conquered their way across large swathes of Europe. They got it all out of their systems, setting the stage for a thousand complacent years of dried fish consumption and occasional whale watching.

Hagar the Horrible

Hagar the Minister for Hydroelectric Energy Research

On November 22nd, 1998, Norway became the first Scandinavian country to draft a constitution in accordance with Dogma 95.

Winter 1995: Norway's constitution ratified using only available light, as per Dogma 95

A Capital Quiz

Match the capital city to the word that made it famous:

A. Oslo
B. Stockholm
C. Helsinki
D. Copenhagen
E. Reykjavik

---

1. Chewing Tobacco
2. Homicidal Glacier
3. Accords
4. Syndrome
5. Rindinki

southern asia

**Population: Guess!...
higher...higher...higher.**

With its incredible natural beauty and crushing social problems, Southern Asia offers a unique mix of paradise and hell. In more ways than one, Southern Asia is where the action is. Obviously, the astonishing breadth and creativity of this region's sex trade is beyond this book's scope. However, we can still marvel at how far these former sex-slave based economies have come. Today, some of the world's most dynamic economies and political cultures can be found here. The so-called "Asian Tiger" economies have embraced a no-holds-barred brand of capitalism that, among other things, has given birth to a poaching industry so profitable, actual Asian Tigers have been driven to extinction. With their 29-hour workdays and salaries in the high peanuts, Southern Asia is slowly destroying us.

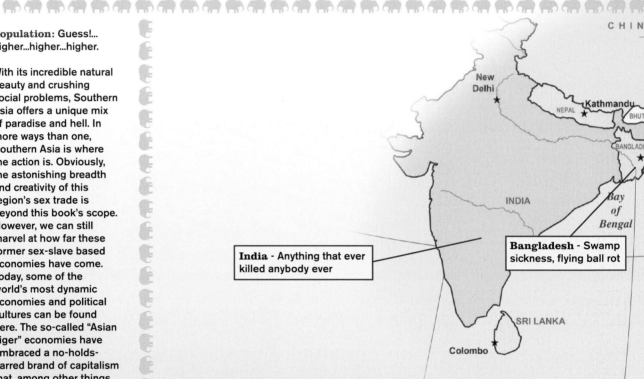

India - Anything that ever killed anybody ever

Bangladesh - Swamp sickness, flying ball rot

Asian Democracy: Highlights

Country	Democracy since	Propped up by	Dynastic political families/ *De facto* one-party rule/ Major election fraud?
Thailand	1932	Devotion to the King, fierce chilis	
India	1947	Nukes	√
Singapore	1957	The worldwide capitalist conspiracy	√
Malaysia	1963	Rubber industry, Allah	√
Philippines	1986	U.S. Navy divisions	√
South Korea	1987	U.S. Army divisions	
Bangladesh	1991	Makeshift network of earthen levees (until next monsoon)	
Indonesia	1999	Oil, gold, anti-terrorism dollars, oil	√

Not participating: Brunei, Cambodia, Laos, Myanmar, Pakistan, Vietnam
Really not at all even remotely participating: North Korea

Southern Asian countries and the diseases you can get there you thought had been eradicated

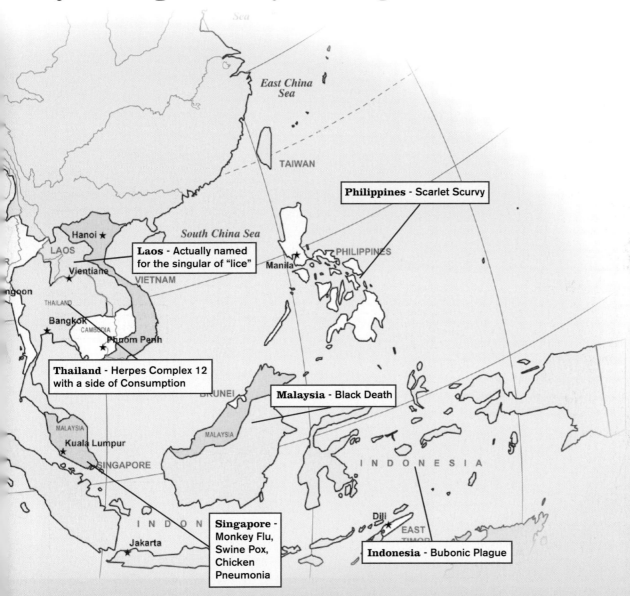

Philippines - Scarlet Scurvy

Laos - Actually named for the singular of "lice"

Thailand - Herpes Complex 12 with a side of Consumption

Malaysia - Black Death

Singapore - Monkey Flu, Swine Pox, Chicken Pneumonia

Indonesia - Bubonic Plague

How Democracy Translates

Western values	become	Asian values
Individualism	------>	Group consensus
Multiparty debate	------>	Respectful silence
Free speech rights	------>	Respectful silence
Independent investigative media	------>	Respectful silence

Breakdown of Typical Weeklong Business Trip to the Region

August 2004	September 2004
S M T W T F S	S M T W T F S
1 2 3 4 5 6 7	1 2 3 4
8 9 10 11 12 13 14	5 6 7 8 9 10 11
15 16 17 18 19 20 21	12 13 14 15 16 17 18
22 23 24 25 26 27 28	19 20 21 22 23 24 25
29 30 31	26 27 28 29 30

13 Monday 257/109	**14** Tuesday 258/108	**15** Wednesday 259/107 — Rosh Hashanah begins at sundown — Declaration of Independence (M)
2 Hours	Making a deal to send all your company's jobs over to them	
10 Hours	Smoky hut, watching two sisters shoot ping pong balls into a fish tank with their vaginas	
36 Hours	The Madness. (Hallucinogenic fever caused by getting off the plane.)	
11 Hours	Up at night wondering if the blistering on your scrotum is humidity-based	
8 Hours	Blackout brought on by drinking liqueur made from rattlesnake semen.	
3 Hours	Paperwork on the outsourcing deal.	
14 Hours	Panic.	
9 Hours	Making arrangements for wiring money that will convince authorities the girls' death was accidental.	
1 Hour	Cab ride back to the airport where you reconcile who you believe you were as a person, with what you did on the trip.	

Is Outsourcing Worth It?

Many companies struggle with the decision to send their blue collar jobs overseas to Southern Asia. Run this simple cost-benefit analysis:

1. Would you rather pay your employees in
- A. Money
- B. Fruit rind

2. Would you rather your company have a
- A. Health plan
- B. Endless supply of workers to replace the fallen

3. Would you prefer your employees to have
- A. Self-esteem and adaptable skills
- B. Calluses and deformed knuckles

4. Would you rather employ
- A. One 60-year-old
- B. Ten 6-year-olds

If you answered **(A)** to any of these questions, congratulations! You've just been fired by the guy who answered **(B)**.

Malaysia's Petronas Towers are the world's tallest buildings. For leasing information, please contact Sy Hershberg Properties Mgmt.

Which product was not produced in Southern Asia?

A.

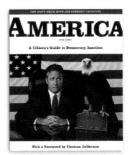

America (The Book)

B.

Sneaker

C.

Pad Thai

D.

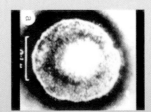

Gonorrhetic Syphillis

Answer: C.
The Pad Thai was actually made in a Greenwich Village restaurant by Mexicans. People from Thailand would find it bland and unfamiliar.

Afterword

Well, that's all the time we have here in *America (The Book)*. By completing this book, you are now qualified to found your own democracy. Congratulations!

The bad news is, there are no new lands upon which to do your founding—no new oceans to cross or jungles to clear. We know exactly what is out there beyond them thar hills. In fact, we've GPS'ed it.

The good news is, many of the existing lands out there are fixer-uppers, filled with willing, desperate, broken and hopeless people. You might even be one yourself. And if you are, representative democracy, for all its flaws, still offers you and your fellow cold and huddled masses the best chance of improving your lot in life. Hell, even if there isn't a Jefferson or Hamilton among you, if you just smash together the basic ideas of this book you're bound to wind up with something better than North Korea.

Now go out there and make your Fathers proud.

Trieste-Zürich-Paris, 1914—1921

VOX : POPULI : SEMPER : FIDELIS : 2004

★ AMERICA ★
(THE BOOK)

Certificate of Completion

_____

has hereby completed *America (The Book)* and is thus fully
qualified to practice, participate in, or found a democracy.

Awarded this 221st page of *America (The Book)*

_____
America (The Book)

Other Books by *The Daily Show*

PARDON ME, BUT COULD
I INTEREST YOU IN A
BOOK ABOUT CANADA?
by Samantha Bee

THE DAILY SHOW WITH JON
STEWART PRESENTS
GET READY FOR THE METRIC
SYSTEM

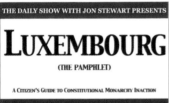

THE DAILY SHOW WITH
JON STEWART PRESENTS
LUXEMBOURG (THE
PAMPHLET)
A Citizen's Guide to
Constitutional Monarchy
Inaction

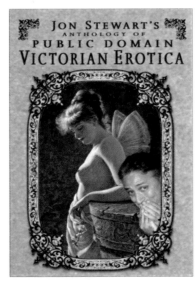

JON STEWART'S
ANTHOLOGY OF PUBLIC
DOMAIN VICTORIAN
EROTICA

THE GREAT GATSBY
by Jon Stewart and The
Daily Show Writers as
told to F. Scott Fitzgerald

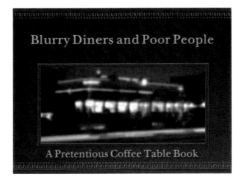

BLURRY DINERS
AND POOR PEOPLE
A Pretentious Coffee
Table Book

Acknowledgments

There are no jokes in these acknowledgments. Okay, there is one. But it comes later.

First of all, thanks to Jamie Raab and everyone at Warner Books for their patience, trust and exceedingly helpful guidance.

Second, this book would look like an impenetrable wall of meaningless text if it were not for the designers at Pentagram, led by Paula Scher. Julia Hoffmann worked comically long hours, delivering page after page of beautiful design on, let's face it, sometimes tedious material. And Jennifer Rittner calmly dealt with a million details, getting every single one of them right. In addition, thanks to Seymour Chwast/Pushpin, Keith Daigle, Derrick Lee, Joe Marianek, Adriana Deléo, Scott Buschkuhl, Moon Sun Kim, Jessica Park, Mickel Larrieux, and Dinah Fried.

Writing a book while doing a TV show is hard. Writing a book while doing a daily TV show is damn near impossible. These people made it possible:

Stewart Bailey, Kahane Corn, Georgia Pappas, Chuck O'Neill, Hillary Kun, Paul Pennolino, Beth Shorr, Alison Watson, Kira Klang, Erin Dougherty, Ari Fishman, Rory Albanese, Justin Melkman, Adam Lowitt, Rich Korson and everybody at *The Daily Show*.

Also, huge thanks to Dan Strone, James Dixon, Matt Labov, Ellen Beck, Bill Farren and all the fine people at Comedy Central.

To Dr. Maya Angelou, thanks for the dick joke on page 118.

The following people supported and endured in a way that makes all of us feel very lucky: The Blomquist family, The Flanz clan, Helen Green, Amy Havlan, John and Maureen Hay, The Jacobson family, Susannah Keagle, Tom Keeton, Manoj Kohli, Anne Martin, Loretta Martin, Bruce and Zac North, Kathy O'Connell, Lisa and Calvin Perrine, Kathy Profeta, Andy, Penny and Stephen Reich, Nicole Revere, and Sheryl Zohn.

Finally, thanks to Tracey, Paola and Debra.

Geraldo Rivera: **AP;** Paul Begala: **CNN, Andrew Eccles;** Tucker Carlson: **CNN, Andrew Eccles;** James Carville: **CNN, Andrew Eccles;** Robert Novak: **CNN, Andrew Eccles;** Aaron Brown: **CNN;** Chris Mathews: **MSNBC;** Barbara Walters: © **2004 ABC Photo Archives. 134:** Remember the Maine: **The New York Times;** Orson Welles: **AP;** Harry Truman: **AP;** TV: **Hemera;** Titanic headline: **The New York Times;** Lindbergh: **San Diego Aerospace Museum;** Hindenburg: **Navy Lakehurst Historical Society;** Rosenbergs: **AP. 135:** Space shots: **NASA;** Walter Cronkite: **CBS Photo Archive;** Woodward and Bernstein: **AP. 137:** Personal ad: **DS. 138-139: Dinah Fried and Mickel Larrieux. 140:** Daily Times: **Newspaper Archive: newspaperarchive.com; Daily News: Eric Fettmann Newspaper Collection (supplied by The Newsmuseum, Washington D.C.);** William Randolph Hearst: **AP. 142-143:** Stephen Colbert: **DS. 145:** Radio family: **LOC. 146:** TVs: **Hemera/DS;** Amos 'n' Andy: **AP. 147:** Nixon/Kennedy debate: **AP;** Walter Cronkite: **AP. 150:** Watergate: **Watergate Hotel. 151:** Spam screen: **Daily Show;** Ronald Reagan: **NARA. 154:** Buchanan and Preiss: **DS. 155:** Joey Buttafuoco: **AP;** Michael Jackson: **AP. 158:** Lincoln: **Marcellus Hall;** Thomas Nast: **Maria Schneider;** Peanuts: **R. Sikoryak. 160:** Doonesbury: **R. Sikoryak;** Mallard Fillmore: **R. Sikoryak. 161:** Nixon: **Al Jaffee. 162:** Ted Koppel: **ABC News;** George Stephanopoulos: **ABC News;** Larry King: **CNN;** Tim Russert: **NBC News;** Barbara Walters: **ABC**

News. **163:** Bill O'Reilly: **AP;** Diane Sawyer: **ABC News;** Stone Phillips: **NBC News. 164:** Vietnam: **AP;** Iraqi prisoners: **AP/Courtesy of The New Yorker;** Child labor: **LOC;** Batboy: **American Media, Inc. Reprinted with permission;** WKRP: **AP. 165:** Little head: **Ablestock;** Connie Chung: **AP;** Wolf Blitzer: **CNN, Andrew Eccles;** Dan Rather: **CBS News;** Tom Brokaw: **NBC News;** Peter Jennings: **ABC News.**

Chapter 8
166: Planets: **Jessica Park. 167:** Tomahawk: **Hemera. 168-169:** Globe: **Ablestock;** Seven degrees common folk: **Ablestock;** Kevin Bacon: **AP;** Large woman: **AP. 170:** Zombie: **DS. 171:** Needle: **Hemera/DS.** Vin Diesel: **AP;** Boy: **Ablestock. 172:** Collage: **Ablestock, Hemera, Pentagram, DS. 173:** Flags, map: **DS. 174-175:** Washington, D.C.: **R. Sikoryak. 176:** Crucifix: **Hemera. 177:** Computer guy: **Hemera. 178:** Whoopi Goldberg: **AP.** Timecapsule: **Joe Marianek 180:** Overlord: **DS;** Pills: **DS. 181:** E-voting: **AP;** Nostradamus: **Art Res; Réunion des Musées Nationaux/Art Resource, NY.**

Chapter 9
Title Page: Tourist: **Ablestock**

Africa: Slave Ship: **LOC** Skull: **Hemera**

Australia: Animals: **Hemera, Ablestock** Knives: **Hemera** Kylie Minogue: **AP** Geoffrey Rush: **AP** Didgeridoo: **Hemera** Midnight Oil: **Time Life Pictures/Getty Images** Russell Crowe: **AP**

New Zealand: Tahiti:

Ablestock. Sheep: **Ablestock**

China: Mao: **AP.** Jackie Chan: **AP;** Yao Ming: **AP;** Chow Yun Fat: **AP;** Tiananmen Square tank: **AP;** Chinese History in Words: **AP/DS;** Chinatown, Shanghai: **AP;** Marco Polo: **SEF / Art Resource, NY;** Vases: **Hemera;** Bong: **DS**

Europe: Eiffel Tower: **Ablestock;** Italian boy: **Hemera;** Hitler: **AP;** Notre Dame: **Ablestock;** Tower of Pisa: **Ablestock;** Rolling Stones: **AP**

Latin America: Soccer Player: **AP;** Aztec pyramid: **Ablestock**

Middle East: Al Jarreau: **AP** Jumble cartoon: **R. Sikoryak**

Russia: Solzhenitsyn: **AP** Tatu: **AP;** Chemical plant: **Ablestock;** Nuclear Missile: **AP;** Oil derrick: **Ablestock** Young Russian Woman: **Ablestock;** Old Russian Woman: **AP;** Vodka bottles: **DS**

Scandinavia: Swedish Bikini Team: **Getty Images;** Scandinavian Guy: **AP;** Seventh Seal: **Janus Films;** Hagar: **R. Sikoryak**

Southern Asia: Schedule: **Adriana Deléo;** Petronas Towers: **AP;** Southeast Asian Products: **DS, AP**

Japan: Geisha: **Getty Images;** Hello Kitty: **AP;** Sumo wrestler: **AP;** Cherry Blossom: **Hemera;** Pheasant: **Hemera;** Hot Dog Eater: **AP;** Bullet Train: **AP;** Rickshaw: **DS;** Soldier: **Department of Defense;** Sushi: **Hemera;** Robot: **AP;** Driving Range: **Getty Images/Paul Chesley;** Cubicle Hotel Rooms: **Getty Images/ Paul**

Chesley; Park Benches: **DS;** Flower machine: **Douglas Mann, www.photomann.com;** Underwear machine: **William Purness, www.photomann.com** Fried Food Machine: **Douglas Mann, www.photomann.com;** Elvis, Organ vending machines: **DS**

Shadow Government poster: Derrick Lee

Election Guide
Don King: **AP;** Kerry: **U.S. Senate;** Bush: **United States Government;** Wood: **Ablestock;** Bricks: **Ablestock;** Rob Reiner: **AP** Iraq Torture Picture: **AP/Courtesy of The New Yorker;** Blowing the Presidency: **AP/DS;** Bush/Helms: **AP;** Kerry/Corddry: **AP;** Thomas Hutchinson: **Ablestock** Hand-Marked Ballot: **AP** National Show of Hands: **DS;** Stopwatch: **Hemera** Shoebox: **DS;** Laura Bush: **United States Government** Jenna Bush: **AP;** Barbara Bush: **AP;** Neil Bush: **AP** Martin Bush: **AP;** Lauren Bush: **AP;** George P. Bush: **AP;** Noelle Bush: **AP;** Teresa Heinz Kerry: **AP** Alexandra Kerry: **AP** Vanessa Kerry: **AP** Christopher Heinz: **AP** Culture War Chess Set: **DS**

Key:
LOC= Library of Congress Prints and Photographs Division Washington, D.C. 20540 USA
DS= Daily Show
AP= Associated Press

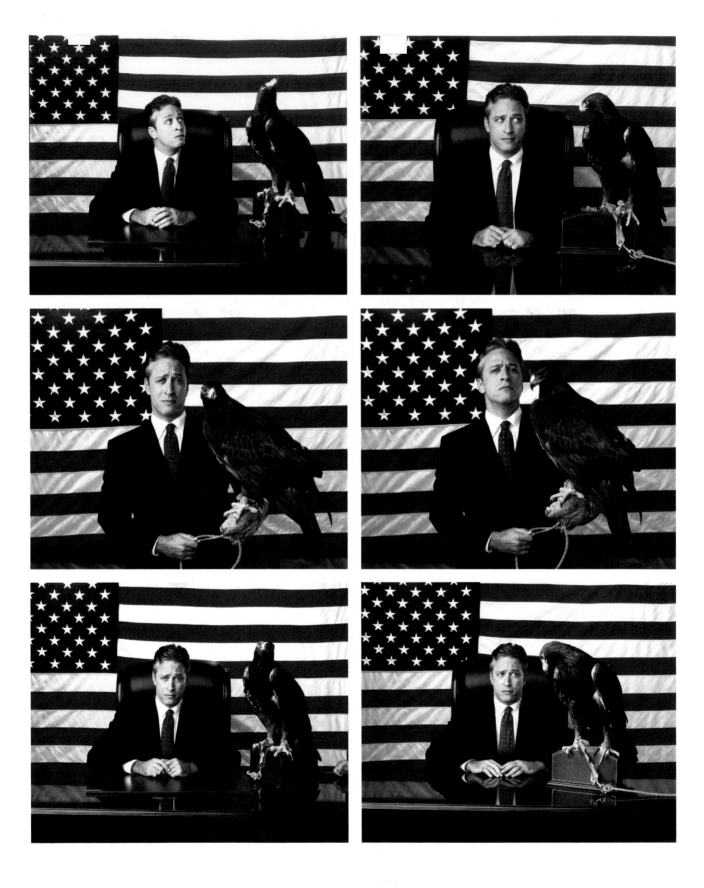

Election 2004

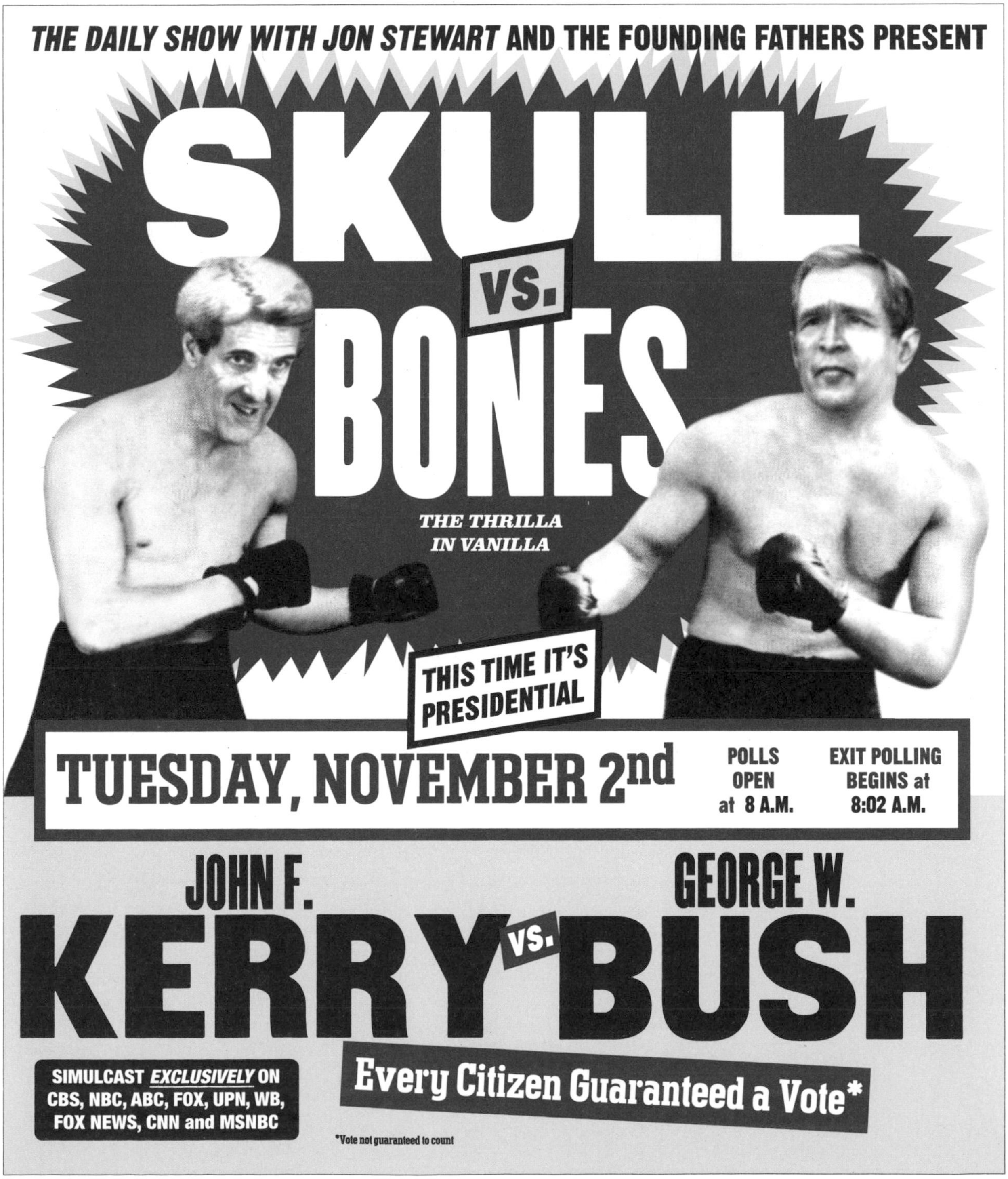

FROM THE PROMOTER

Salutations! Ladies and most gentle of men, it is my deep privilege to extend hospitable welcome to the American voter, that most perspicacious of all aggregations of constituent sagacity.

The confrontation that draws us together is no mere congressional conflict, no senatorial skirmish, nor even a gubernatorial gladiatoriolus. It is a battle royale between two political pugilists in peak pecuniary preparation.

In one corner: the defending Champion, his most pugnacious presidentatious purveyor of unilateralatiousness. The Texas Tax-Cutter! The Crawford Creationist! Look out world, he's re-makin' you! George Walker Bush, Jr.!

In the other corner: the Challenger. A lean, lankitudinous leopard of liberal legislative largesse. The King Kong of the Mekong! He ain't dull, he's just deliberatin'! John Forbes Kerry!

Each man has expended Croesus-levels of fiduciary millionitudes in his seeking of supreme Presidentiality and the handsome belt that goes with it. The outcome of this epic clash of electoral quadrenniousness will determine our future standing in the Community of Man and the fate of the world.

Now, the debates have been debated, the orations orated, the ads negated; the mud flung, labels hung, accusations slung and the swing states swung. Tonight, in association with the Founding Fathers and Don King Productions, we will bear splendiferous witness to a frenzied fracas of grandiloquemetudinous proportions as one of these two men earns himself the title of Commander-in-Chief and Leader of the Free World.

My cut is 40%.

Only in America!

Don King

THE TALE OF THE TAPE	KERRY	BUSH	Advantage

Vital Statistics

	KERRY	BUSH	Advantage
Height	6' 4"	5' 11"	Kerry
Weight	178	194	Bush
Chest	36" (normal), 37" (expanded)	35" (normal), 44" (when challenged by inquisitive reporter)	Bush
Crags Per Square Inch (CSI)	83	11	Bush
Words Per Sentence (WPS)	61	3	Bush

Biography/Personal

	KERRY	BUSH	Advantage
Military Service	Decorated Vietnam Veteran	How many times do we have to go over this? We have documents *clearly* showing he served.	Kerry
Military Commendations	Bronze Star Silver Star Purple Hearts	Dannelly Air National Guard Base "No New Cavities" Award	Kerry
Languages Spoken	French, English	English (some)	Kerry
Building material most compared to			Bush
Thinks this Rorschach blot looks like…	A wolf face, maybe clasped hands?	Terrorism	Bush
Viscous Substance Underpinning Personal Fortune			Bush

On the Trail

	KERRY	BUSH	Advantage
Photo-op Transportation of Choice	Harley-Davidson	Pickup truck	Even
Actually Drives	In Limo	Drunk	Kerry
Bearded Celebrity Endorsement			Bush

Issues

	KERRY	BUSH	Advantage
Abortion Rights	For	Agin'	Even
Education	No Child Left Awake	No Child Left Behind	Bush
Environment	Clear skies, healthy forests	"Clear Skies," "Healthy Forests"	Kerry
Bringing It On	For	For	Even
Gay Marriage	For (really); Against (publicly)	Agin'	Kerry
Defying International Community and Invading Another Country Based on Questionable Military Intelligence Without Practicable Exit Plan, Ultimately Invoking Wrath of Entire Arab World	No	Yes	Even

GEORGE WALKER BUSH: HURDLING THE LOWERED BAR

George Walker Bush, our 43rd president, has overcome an incredible lack of obstacles to attain his success.

BORN ON July 6, 1946, in New Haven, Connecticut, the young Bush had little time to enjoy his tony surroundings. When Bush was but a boy his father, fed up with the lack of oil in Connecticut, moved the family to Texas to fulfill his dream of being a magnate. The early years were rough as the young Bush watched his father, George Sr., struggle just to find enough decent servants to put food on the table.

BUSH WAS a realist. He knew that to have his way made for him in the world he would need the appearance of an excellent education. But from where?

What New England preparatory school worth its salt would take a chance on a mediocre student from a powerful family? Luckily, all of them. George W. Bush attended Phillips Academy, Andover, where he faired. Building on that momentum he put himself through Yale, though only after earning the coveted "Barbara Bush Scholarship."

AND THEN…war. After graduating Yale *summa cum C average,* George Bush suddenly found himself eligible for the draft. He was at a crossroads. Should he enlist and fight a war he supported, or was there perhaps a different, less dangerous route? There was, but it wouldn't be easy. The Texas Air National Guard selected only the elitest of the elite. George Bush would need a note. As fate would have it, his father knew the people who could make things like that happen. Five years later, with Vietnam winding down, it was clear George Bush had turned up for National Guard service most of the weekends he was required to.

STILL HAUNTED by flashbacks that it was the weekend and he would have to report to the base, Bush tried to leave Vietnam behind and somehow begin having the pieces of his life put back together for him. Armed only with a Harvard MBA, a Rolodex of powerful oil business connections, and "moxie," George Bush struck out. He was eager to start writing the story of his life. Chapter 1: Chapter 11. Bush proved uniquely adept at driving companies into the ground and was soon bankrupting larger and larger entities. It was a lesson in failing up he would not soon forget.

AND THEN a chance meeting with the vice president of the United States changed George Bush's life. The vice president saw something in the young man. That's when George Bush, Sr. offered George Bush, Jr. his support in a run for governor of Texas.

HAVING NEVER held any elected office, George Bush found governing fulfilling. While he wasn't able to bankrupt Texas, he did add many new and interesting particles to its air. Always a friend to the energy industry, Bush tripled the amount of electricity flowing through death row. Even the retarded took notice.

TEXAS TAMED, Bush turned his eyes to the Oval Office. The 2000 election was quintessential Bush: He lost the popular vote, thus winning the presidency. In just four years President Bush has streamlined our bloated job market, tossed over the unnecessary ballast of international allies and ensured that our military does not become bored and complacent.

HE IS widely expected to lose the election, serve a second term and then be named Emperor in 2008.

JOHN F. KERRY: MONOGRAMMED FOR GREATNESS

John Forbes Kerry entered the world on December 11, 1943, blessed with the same initials as John Fitzgerald Kennedy. Since that day, every moment of John Forbes Kerry's life has been orchestrated to prove that this fact is somehow significant.

THE QUEST started early. Upon being slapped at birth, Kerry applied for, and was awarded, the first of his 27 Purple Hearts.

AT THREE months old, already six-foot-four and craggy, Kerry faced the nursery with a stentorian manner and an inherited lack of humor. His father, Richard, had been a pilot in World War II, and his post-war recovery from tuberculosis was considered one of his lighter moments.

THE KERRY FAMILY was close-knit, with a patrician bearing and high expectations for success. Growing up, John and his siblings passed many an evening competing in jaw-squaring and blazer-wearing contests. On Christmas Eve the whole clan would gather around an old upright piano and stare silently at one another.

THE YOUNG Kerry was unlikable, but made up for it with drive and arrogance. His eye was always on the legislative prize. Determined to prove his precious initials were no fluke, Kerry spent countless childhood hours practicing ventriloquism on the chance that in student council elections he could nominate and second himself without detection.

THE ONE area Kerry was decidedly un-Kennedyesque was with the ladies. He lost his virginity his senior year only after an intense lobbying and letter-writing campaign aimed at persuading the school slut to "grant him franking privileges."

AFTER PREP SCHOOL, Kerry matriculated at Yale, where his classmates gave him the playful nickname "Senator Kerry." Upon graduation, inspired by his initial-sake, Kerry enlisted in the Navy. He served as a Swift Boat officer in the Mekong Delta and was constantly trying to get his boat sunk so he could rescue people. Upon completing an act of heroism, Kerry would receive a medal, which he would then hold up in front of the poster of JFK in his room and shout "I'm closing in, bitch."

BUT KERRY RETURNED from Vietnam to find the nation had changed. War heroes weren't writing *Profiles in Courage* and swimming in pools of hot and cold running poontang – they were reviled. Perplexed, Kerry consulted his WWJFKD bracelet and emerged an adamant anti-war activist, co-founding "Vietnam Veterans Against the War." In his televised testimony before the Senate Foreign Relations Committee in 1971, Kerry famously asked the panel, "How do you ask a man to be the last man to die for a mistake?" before adding "Huh? Pretty quotable, no?"

BUT KERRY'S eloquence failed to ignite the passion young Kennedy had stirred years earlier. His lifelong plan to succeed Kennedy had been missing two crucial elements: a corrupt ruthless billionaire father and charisma. Kerry was at a crossroads. Where could a terse, stentorian know-it-all succeed if not politics? The answer: law.

KERRY RECEIVED his law degree from Boston College and went to work as a prosecutor in Middlesex County. He remembers those days fondly as "great bio fodder."

ULTIMATELY Kerry realized that following in the path of John Fitzgerald Kennedy was a daunting task. The times and his early death had conspired to create a myth around the young Kennedy too great to match, even for one sharing his initials. John F. Kerry knew he could never be John F. Kennedy…but look at Teddy. He's a United States Senator and he's half-retarded. If Kerry could simply remain upright and pantsed it would be a snap.

TWENTY-FIVE years later, John F. Kerry is a successful four-term senator from Massachusetts.

DEBATE SCORECARD

After each presidential debate, a popular question for pundits and voters alike is "Who won?" But is there really a way to quantify results of something as amorphous as a modern political debate? Yes, there is. Below is a handy scorecard no debate watcher should be without.

The Debate Schedule

1st DEBATE: SEPTEMBER 30TH - UNIVERSITY OF MIAMI

2nd DEBATE: OCTOBER 8TH - WASHINGTON UNIVERSITY

3rd DEBATE: OCTOBER 13TH - ARIZONA STATE UNIVERSITY

Debates typically involve ten questions, or "innings." The candidate will be up ten times with a chance to answer the question he has been asked, or a question of his own choosing that he pretends is the question he has been asked.

	1	2	3	4	5	6	7	8	9	10
BUSH, G.W.										
KERRY, J.F.										

HOW TO KEEP SCORE

When each candidate speaks, record the technique(s) used and the point value in the appropriate box.

+1

RCS	Recycled Campaign Slogan
Stp	Smooth Segue to "Talking Point"
DRAA	Depressing "Real American" Anecdote
MOP	Misstatement of Opponent's Platform
ST	Use of Phrase "Straight Talk"

-1

Ftp	Forced Segue to "Talking Point"
DAS	Dismissive Audible Sighing
MOP	Misstatement of Own Platform
FIT	Food in Teeth

+2

PP	Podium Pound
AHZ	Ad Hominem Zinger
DUH	Positive Allusion to America
SSS	Swing State Shout-Out
Up	Unfulfillable Promise

-2

DRAA(f)	Depressing "Real American" Anecdote (fictional)
ZZZ	Statistics
DAM	Dismissive Audible "Motherfucker"
AST	Actual Straight Talk
HP	Post-debate Handshake "Psyche"

EXAMPLE

1. John Kerry is asked a question on his specific plan on how he will be able to create ten million jobs. Kerry dodges the specifics, awkwardly offering a story about Fred, an unemployed steelworker from Western Pennsylvania with half a lung.

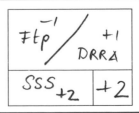

A NIGHT OUT WITH...

While you could pick a president based on voting records, stances on various issues, or foreign or domestic policies, pollsters have found most voters choose a candidate based on a more intangible criterion, namely, "likability." In modern media parlance this translates to: Which candidate would you rather have a beer with?

In 2000 it was widely accepted that Al Gore had a superior command of the issues as well as experience in government. George Bush, on the other hand, had the highest Bennigan's Happy Hour Q-Rating since U.S. Grant.

To settle the issue once and for all, we gave Rob Corddry and Ed Helms $30 in petty cash and sent them out for a night of drinks and discussion with the current presidential candidates.

ED HELMS: MY NIGHT WITH PRESIDENT GEORGE W. BUSH

The president ambled into the seldom-seen wood-paneled rumpus room located in the White House basement. I had wanted to go out to a jazz bar in nearby Georgetown, but was told it would be a logistical nightmare and that the president had deemed the idea "faggy."

The president flashed his trademark grin. "Hiya, Stretch!" ("Stretch" is the special nickname he reserves for me and every other member of the press corps over five-foot-nine.)

Bush then gave a quick wave to the seven Secret Service agents who surrounded me in a protective phalanx. "Evenin', Shorty, Grumbles, Buzz, Scar-Lip, Pottsy, Snagglepuss, Asian Guy." The Secret Service men all gave little waves back, except for the one nicknamed Buzz, whose hands were occupied by the rifle he happened to be pointing at my head.

"So," said a familiar voice behind me. "What'll you have? O'Doul's? Kaliber? We don't stock the strong stuff here."

I turned around to find Dick Cheney had quietly slipped into the bar. I asked for an O'Doul's and Cheney ordered three of them – one for each of us. We sat down

on barstools, Cheney carefully positioning himself between Bush and me.

We uncapped our non-beers and drank for a moment in silence.

I knew I was not allowed to discuss the current situation in Iraq, or anything pertaining to the Middle East. The economy was also off-limits, as were the first 40 years of Bush's life, the activities of his daughters, any legislation passed or signed during his term of office, his governorship in Texas and his relationship with his father.

As I searched for a question, the only sound in the room was Bush, opening and closing the tiny paper parasol he had demanded with his beer. He opened and closed it, opened and closed it, opened and closed it, until Cheney finally reached over, gently took the parasol from Bush's hands, and tucked it into his jacket pocket.

"So," I asked, leaning forward to see past Cheney, "how's Laura?"

"She's fine," said a voice behind me. I turned around to see Communications Director Karen Hughes. She sipped from a virgin daiquiri and took a seat to my right.

"She's perfectly fine. The president loves her very much." Bush vigorously nodded his agreement at this sentiment.

There was another long, awkward pause.

"How 'bout them Mets?" I asked.

White House Press Secretary Scott McClellan tapped me on the shoulder. I hadn't even heard him come in. "I don't think I should have to tell you that the president loves all baseball teams equally," he said. "He believes baseball embodies the freedom that God has given to all Americans."

The president reached for a second paper parasol, but Cheney smacked his hand before he could reach the bowl.

I decided to try one more time. "What do you—"

And with that, a finger fell gently to my lips, silencing me. It was Condoleezza Rice. "Please," she said. "It's been a long day. The president is very tired."

Cheney nudged Bush, who hopped off the stool to his feet. As the president strode confidently out of the room behind Dr. Rice, he turned, winked and shot me double guns. He pointed to the Addams Family pinball machine in the corner.

"Knock yourself out," he said with a devilish grin. "It's rigged so you can play free."

Our night out was over. It was 7:15 p.m. and I was alone with three O'Doul's bottles and a $10.50 tab. It was the greatest night of my life.

ROB CORDDRY: MY NIGHT WITH SENATOR JOHN KERRY

"Wanna see a picture of my hog?"

Before I could answer, the junior senator from Massachusetts whipped out a small wallet-size photo of a Harley-Davidson motorcycle. In so doing, he knocked over his can of Iron City beer onto my lap.

"Son of a fuck, shit…" he spat out, quickly wiping up the spill with an oil-stained bandanna. "My bad, man."

The senator signaled our bartender for another round. I thanked him for the brew.

"Don't thank me—thank St. Teresa!" That was his nickname for Mrs. Heinz-Kerry—a nickname he tossed off with greater frequency as cans of Iron City gave way to shots of Jack.

Kerry leaned into me. "Terry's fucking great," he snarled, before mentioning the actress Morgan Fairchild and that he had once "tapped that" when it still meant something.

John Kerry is a regular guy. Real salt of the earth. In fact, all regulars at Leon's Shamrock Pub and Grill in Boston's North End have been told precisely that each and every time Kerry pops in, usually with a camera crew or an intrepid reporter like myself. They've gotten used to his boozy ramblings and have learned to recognize his warning signs.

My heads-up came as a glancing blow to my temple, which knocked me off my barstool and onto the floor. As I came to, I could see interns restraining Kerry by the fringes of his "Born to Kill"

biker's vest. Red-faced and spitting, he yelled at me, "'Police action?' The two pieces of shrapnel still in my ass say it was a war!"

Truth be told, I hadn't actually called Vietnam a "police action," but instead had said "It's getting late, Senator, I should go."

Kerry's chief campaign strategist helped me to my feet. "Don't take it personally," he said. "The senator's just so strong on defense, his warrior's rage gets the best of him sometimes."

Another campaign aide clapped his hands twice, instantly summoning two large bearded veterans who went by the names "Dusty" and "T.J." They escorted me outside and told me to stay there until the senator cooled off.

As I hit the night air, I could taste blood in my mouth. Just then, the door of the pub swung open and Kerry bounded out. I braced myself for another stinging punch, but instead he swung a sober arm around me, pulled his face in close and whispered:

"Don't worry, it's cool. I'm not even drunk. Just be sure to write about the part where I hit you."

THE ELECTORAL MAP

Keeping track of the Electoral College is easier than you might imagine. Before a single vote is cast, upwards of 30-35 states have already been decided! Like California. It is the largest electoral prize and it is going to Kerry. See, we've already colored it in. Meanwhile, the South has united for George Bush. Isn't it comforting to see those states together again?

The truth is, only a handful of states really matter on Election Day. They are called **swing states** and they're where most of the campaigning and just about all the advertising dollars have been focused. Ohio, for example, has not aired a regularly scheduled commercial since June. And in Wisconsin it's difficult to get a hotel room. *Wisconsin,* for God's sake!

The states in white will determine the outcome of the 2004 race. Color them in on Election Day and be the first on your block to officially call the winner.

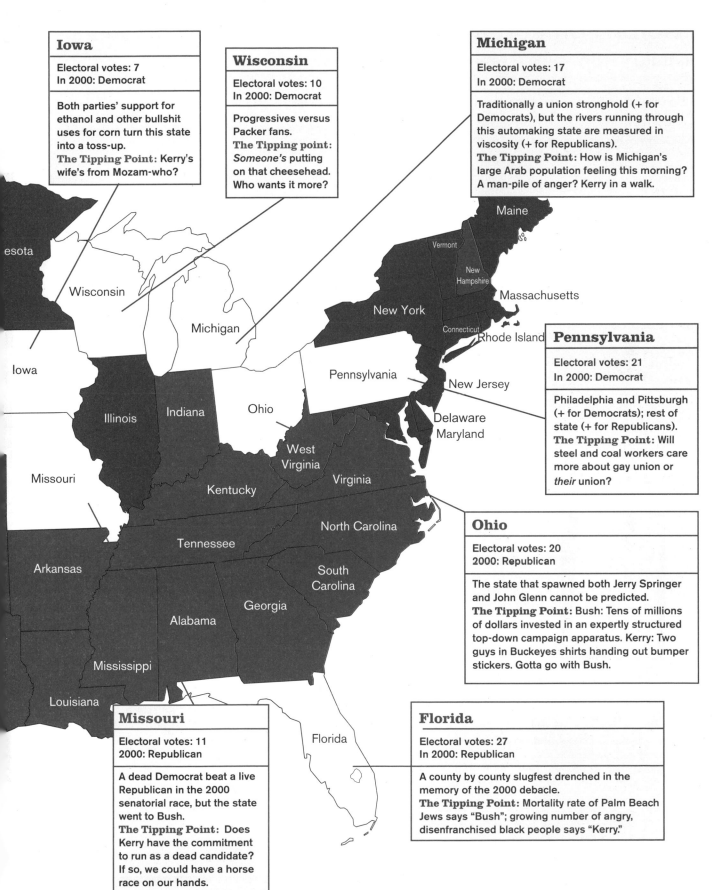

Iowa

Electoral votes: 7
In 2000: Democrat

Both parties' support for ethanol and other bullshit uses for corn turn this state into a toss-up.
The Tipping Point: Kerry's wife's from Mozam-who?

Wisconsin

Electoral votes: 10
In 2000: Democrat

Progressives versus Packer fans.
The Tipping point: *Someone's* putting on that cheesehead. Who wants it more?

Michigan

Electoral votes: 17
In 2000: Democrat

Traditionally a union stronghold (+ for Democrats), but the rivers running through this automaking state are measured in viscosity (+ for Republicans).
The Tipping Point: How is Michigan's large Arab population feeling this morning? A man-pile of anger? Kerry in a walk.

Pennsylvania

Electoral votes: 21
In 2000: Democrat

Philadelphia and Pittsburgh (+ for Democrats); rest of state (+ for Republicans).
The Tipping Point: Will steel and coal workers care more about gay union or *their* union?

Ohio

Electoral votes: 20
2000: Republican

The state that spawned both Jerry Springer and John Glenn cannot be predicted.
The Tipping Point: Bush: Tens of millions of dollars invested in an expertly structured top-down campaign apparatus. Kerry: Two guys in Buckeyes shirts handing out bumper stickers. Gotta go with Bush.

Missouri

Electoral votes: 11
2000: Republican

A dead Democrat beat a live Republican in the 2000 senatorial race, but the state went to Bush.
The Tipping Point: Does Kerry have the commitment to run as a dead candidate? If so, we could have a horse race on our hands.

Florida

Electoral votes: 27
In 2000: Republican

A county by county slugfest drenched in the memory of the 2000 debacle.
The Tipping Point: Mortality rate of Palm Beach Jews says "Bush"; growing number of angry, disenfranchised black people says "Kerry."

Map labels: Minnesota, Wisconsin, Michigan, Maine, Vermont, New Hampshire, Massachusetts, New York, Connecticut, Rhode Island, Iowa, Pennsylvania, New Jersey, Illinois, Indiana, Ohio, Delaware, Maryland, Missouri, West Virginia, Virginia, Kentucky, North Carolina, Tennessee, South Carolina, Arkansas, Georgia, Alabama, Mississippi, Louisiana, Florida

A GUIDE FOR VOTERS – UNDERSTANDING YOUR ELECTION TOOLS

The Ballot

Come November 2nd everyone in America will be voting for the same presidential candidates, yet no two ballots are exactly alike. Why? Because standardized ballots would make too much sense and where's the fun in that?

Below, some of the most common ballot formats.

The Butterfly (ret.)

It took five years and a team of 23 designers to devise a way for a vote for the second candidate listed to correspond with the third hole down. Now just add old Jews, and presto!

The Punch Card

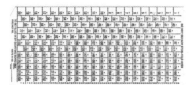

Poke a hole through your choice. The ballot is then run through the same machine that graded your PSATs. With only a 30% margin of error, you may not get "the" winner but you'll certainly get "a" winner.

The Ol' Fashioned Hand-Marked Fold-Up

It's really quite simple. Look for the box next to the candidate you'd like to vote for. Check it. Fold the paper and stick it in the box. The box will then be taken to a van, which is then driven into a river.

National Show of Hands

The same common sense approach used to answer the question "Who here is from out of town?" is easily applied to a national election. But remember, you must be outside when the plane passes over for your vote to count.

The Voting Booth

The only thing standing between us and dictatorship is a fetid, mildew-stained curtain. But be aware! Many places look like voting booths, but aren't. If you find yourself reciting your sins, typing in your PIN or inserting quarters and instructing strangers to "put 'em on the glass," you are NOT in a voting booth.

It is customary to exit the voting booth by flinging open the curtains and taking a deep bow. Encores, however, are discouraged.

Electronic Voting Machines

These machines run on the same rock-solid Windows platform that never crashes on your home computer.

MISCELLANEOUS TIPS

Make sure you choose a comfortable polling site. If your current site is not to your liking, move to a different neighborhood before Election Day.

Never vote on an empty stomach. The failed policies of former Arkansas governor John Deliciouschocolate could have easily been avoided had voters heeded this warning.

Coach says don't have sex the night before voting 'cause it saps your strength.

If the election happens to be on St. Patrick's Day, be sure to wear green or risk a pinch from the pollster! Also, double-check the date – the election really should be in November.

On ballot proposals, always vote "no." Things are fine the way they are. Why change them?

A GUIDE FOR NON-VOTERS

Though a great deal of media attention is focused on Election Day, it should be noted that a full 50% of eligible voters choose to sit out. Below some tips for the oft-ignored "swing non-voter."

WHAT TO DO ON ELECTION DAY

What will you do with the hour you didn't spend getting to the polling place, waiting on line, filling out the ballot and applying your "I Voted" sticker? A few suggestions:

○ Get a hot stone massage (60 min./$135 not including tip).

○ Set up an "alternative polling place" in your living room for voters fed up with "establishment" politics.

○ Count from 1 to 3600.

○ Drive around and around your nearest polling place, with the windows rolled down, screaming "Suckers!" and laughing maniacally.

Feeling conspicuous without an "I Voted!" sticker? Here's a great do-it-yourself project that hides your apathy. Cut out one of these and glue it to your shirt or jacket.

Helpful excuses for when you're asked "Did you vote today?"

In case the sticker doesn't throw nosey do-gooders off the trail, try one of these...

Did I vote? Yeah, I voted. Voted to not take my grandfather off life support at the hospital where I spent my whole morning.

Yes, actually I did. In fact, I left my voter's guide in the car. Let me just get it to show you. (Run to car, drive away quickly)

Twice!

Actually I can't vote. I'm a convicted felon.*

*If they're not convinced, you may have to show them your prison tat. If you don't have a prison tat, go get one.

Justify Your Apathy

There are many things you can do to counterbalance your lack of participation in the democratic process. Here are two easy ones...

1. Cure cancer. This is a good one, especially if you're a noted scientist on the verge of curing cancer.

2. Search for terrorists. Not voting is perfectly acceptable – if you're busy preventing another 9/11.

MEET THE FIRST FAMILY

Laura Welch Bush

America's Librarian General

BORN IN: Midland, Texas

COLLEGE: Southern Methodist University, bachelor's degree—education, minor—blank staring

GRADUATE SCHOOL: University of Texas - Austin, master's degree in library science. (It is too a science!)

CAREER AND PUBLIC SERVICE: Public school teacher and librarian in Houston, Dallas and Austin school systems; First Lady of Texas; First Lady of the United States; First Lady to be called "The Welchinator" by sitting President of the United States.

AS FIRST LADY SHE HAS... Returned the office to the insignificance it once enjoyed. "I mean honestly, it's one thing to wear pants, but it's another to think you can chair a committee meeting!"

MISC. Enjoys pretty things; has vice-like grip capable of killing hares, small coyotes.

Jenna and Barbara Bush

They've Settled Down

Barbara (top) and Jenna (bottom). The Bushes' twin daughters have graduated from college and are working on their father's campaign. After that, they will take their pick from any job they want in the whole world.

The "Other" Bushes

While father George, Sr. (a former president), mother Barbara (an imperious, scary matrician) and brother Jeb (a governor) are well-known, there are other notable family members who for some reason they don't talk too much about...

Neil Bush

The Baby Brother

Remember the S&L scandal? That was him! He pioneered a new breed of creative financial dealings as a board member of the Silverado Savings and Loan, whose collapse cost taxpayers $1 billion. Plus, his recent divorce featured paternity rumors, a defamation suit and an admission of sex with high-priced Asian escorts. He's like a Roger Clinton who can do real damage.

Marvin Bush

He's Shady Too

Marvin Bush was a principal in a company called Securacom that provided security for the World Trade Center, United Airlines, and Dulles International Airport. In addition, the company was backed by KuwAm, a Kuwaiti-American investment firm on whose board Marvin Bush also served. So you see, President Bush isn't the only Bush with a good 9/11 story!

Notable Bush Nephews and Nieces

Which species of Bush niece or nephew is most alien to the family?

A. Lauren Bush, fashion model

B. George P. Bush, charismatic Hispanic heartthrob

C. Noelle Bush, recovering crack addict

Answer: A. Addiction and Latino culture are familiar to most Bushes, but nothing stops a Bush family barbecue faster than the phrase, "Last week, Isaac Mizrahi and I..."

MEET THE CHALLENGER'S FAMILY

Teresa Heinz Kerry

BORN IN: Mozambique, which could make her the first African-American First Lady in history

EDUCATION: The Arianna Huffington Academy of Unplaceable Accents

NICKNAMES: The African Queen, Little Miss Fancy Scarf

SPEAKS: Five languages, giving her the ability to communicate with more Americans than any candidate's wife ever. Yet will be "gotten" by fewer Americans than any candidate's wife ever.

BEFORE KERRY THERE WAS... A marriage to the late Senator John Heinz resulting in the inheritance of $500 million, though to get at it, you have to turn her upside down and smack her on her feet.

MISC. Has most potential of any candidate's wife since Nancy Reagan to be gay camp icon.

The Kerry-Heinz Children
America Hates Overachievers

The marriage of John Kerry and Teresa Heinz brought together a level of talent, ambition and wealth that should not exist in one family.

Alexandra Kerry, 30: Filmmaker and sometimes actress (*State and Main, Spartan*). Wore see-through dress at 2004 Cannes Film Festival, can now be found on any one of 21,800 websites.

Vanessa Kerry, 27: Third-year medical student at Harvard; taking year off to work on Kerry campaign.

Christopher Heinz, 31: Harvard MBA. Quit job as investment banker to work on Kerry campaign. Enjoys spotlight, energetic speaker, dated Gwyneth Paltrow. He's like the VHS copy of the DVD of JFK, Jr.

Christopher Heinz is just like JFK, Jr, if you squint.

One Kerry daughter is a Harvard medical student, the other is a filmmaker/actress. Can you tell which is which?

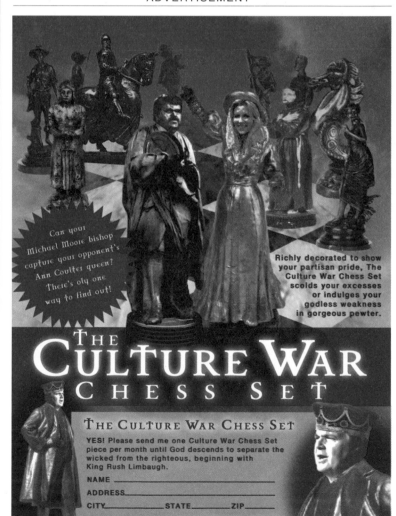

AMERICA
(THE BOOK)
★ ★ ★

MR SEAN PENN
c/o HOLLYWOOD
HOLLYWOOD, CA 90038

Mr. Penn:

First of all, we want to say we are big fans. You are an unbelievable actor. You were awesome in *State of Grace* and truly funny in *Fast Times at Ridgemont High*, and women loved you as the retarded guy in that movie with the little blonde girl, who is also very good but quite frankly we are getting a little sick of. Also, congratulations on winning an Oscar. We didn't catch that movie or many of your movies recently because we don't much go in for that arthouse shit…but still, an Oscar…that's great.

We did try to contact you personally, but numerous efforts to do so were rebuffed by your representatives. We understand you are a very busy and private man and that your security people are just doing their jobs. Although to be frank, the level of manhandling we encountered had us questioning the professionalism of some of your detail. We don't believe real ex-Mossad would be so quick to anger, and being asthmatic, many of us did not fare well during the macing.

Anyway, we are writing because it is an election year and judging from public comments you have made, it is pretty clear you have strong opinions about who should win. We are respectfully requesting that those opinions and the opinions of the many other talented actors you "lunch" with are kept to yourselves. This is not to say we aren't interested in you, Mr. Penn. We are very interested. If you are acting in a movie or looking to beat up a photographer or to plow your car through a store window in a drunken rage…please do. By all means, get busted trying to get a gun through airport security. Your bad boy antics and sullen, mischievous ways delight and beguile us. It is your earnest interest in our well-being we are not so crazy about.

It's not that we don't think you are smart or well-informed. It's that somehow your public chastising of our political leadership is, even when dead-on target, really fucking irksome. We realize our reaction is based on an emotional response and not an intellectual one. It is the feeling that somehow you believe your standing as an artiste allows you to understand issues on a deeper level than the less-enlightened, when in truth your sober analysis, however correct, elicits a reflexive feeling of wanting to yell "Shut the fuck up, finish your Cobb Salad and get back to the set – Terence Malick says it's Magic Hour."

In conclusion, obviously we cannot force silence upon you. Perhaps you could express your opinions through the medium of acting, in which you are of unparalleled skill, and not on Larry King, where you seem like kind of a douche.

Sincerely,

AMERICA
(The Book)

P.S. We have a screenplay we would be honored if you would read. You would be perfect for the part of "Tyler." Joan Allen is attached.